They liked it:

Editorial Reviews:

★★★★★ **ReadersFavorites.com:**
...Roxanne Jones did an excellent job bringing Sybil's story to life. I felt as if I knew her personally. She also described the Guardian Angels in such a way that I could see them in my mind's eye, Sybil was a remarkable woman and *this is a remarkable* book.

★★★★★ **IndieReader.com**
...The blending of the two voices makes for a powerful, moving and suspenseful novel.

★★★★★ **AllBookReviews.com**
I recommend "While I Was Learning to Become God" to anyone wanting to delve deeper into harnessing their spiritual power or to anyone wanting an entertaining read.

★★★★★ **Simple Self Publishing**
After reading "While I Was Waiting for God" and watching the book trailer, I was embraced in the calmness and peace surrounding the story. This is a book that readers will either love and take to heart or misunderstand and put aside.

Reader Reviews:

★★★★★ Maya, Sweden:
..."While I was leaning to become God", is a magic book filled with positive energy that has helped me to feel great and grateful and take major decisions in my life. If you want an example of how to start your own transformation, this book is the one for you!. Thank you!

★★★★★ Alvaro Posada, FL:
...This is the type of book I would recommend to men and women that are looking for examples of true change...

★★★★★ Nicole, South Africa:
...Ascending is finding our Sovereignty and Roxana is pointing it with her own Story... Thank you Roxana for being such a messenger to all of us, to all the women who are holding this divine feminine power...

Find more reviews and your Book Club Guide on
www.roxanajones.com

Roxana Jones

Roxana Jones has been writing all of her life but it wasn't until 2009, when she surrendered to life's will, and became a full-time writer. Since then, she is a traveler whose books are dedicated to communicate the transformational experiences she keeps creating as a result of the new heart and mind she carries within. Roxana lives in New Orleans and Sedona and shares her life with her partner, two daughters, family and friends.

Follow her on www.roxanajones.com

WHILE I WAS LEARNING TO BECOME GOD

Roxana Jones

This book was originally written in Spanish. Jimmy Weiskopf has translated it into English.
Cover illustration by Diana Prata Amaral.

Published by Tapuat Publishing
A division of Simplyfly llc.
7950 NW 53rd Street
Suite 215
Miami, Florida 33166
USA

Visit us at http://tapuat.com

Order online our books or by phone at +1 (305) 507-8864

Printed in the United States of America

ISBN: 978-1-937296-19-3

Published date: 06/15/2011

To my daughters, Luna and Sol, who, from an unsought distance, continued to illuminate my days and nights, like invisibly twinkling stars.

Jesus answered them:
Is it not written in your Law: I have said you are gods?

John 10:34

A THANK-YOU NOTE

Night after night, day after day, for a few months, the woman who acted as my scribe would patiently sit next to me and listen to what I had to say. We began with notebooks; she did not take me seriously at first when I asked her to give shape to my story. When she began to bring her laptop, I breathed a sigh of relief; she had become intrigued by my tale. She then brought a tape recorder to speed up the process, sensing that I was approaching my end and she might not gather all the details. What a relationship she and I were able to live; no one has better understood me. Her mind stayed lucid while mine slowly lost its strength as it gave way to the reality of the heart. Thanks to you, my unconditional friend, I now rest in peace with the certainty that my life had the most perfect purpose. I rest in God like the open book I always wished to be.

Sybil Vaughan
1966–2009

Hidalgo Street, March 2009

That year, it was as though winter had decided to be shorter and the sun to change its warmth. One breathed a new beginning, an early spring. The flowers gaily began to show their buds, even though my heart had not got over its loss.

When I arrived that morning, she was not there. I opened the door with the keys she had given me months before. The first thing I did when I came in was to call out her name several times. I sought her in every corner, wishing that she were only playing hide-and-seek and would magically appear behind one of the pieces of furniture in that very beautiful space she called her home. As soon as I entered the bedroom where she and I had shared so many moments, I began to realize that I was waiting in vain. It was there, in that room where we had so lovingly created every page of the story to be published, her true story. She had lingered in this plane only enough for me to know all the details that would allow me to fulfill my promise to write her book once she was no longer with us.

I felt a profound abyss when I saw her immaculately made bed, with its marble-white duvet and decorative pillows. The still-fresh roses perfumed the air and the rays of the sun filtered through the window, although the lamp on the night table was still on.

It was if she had left during the night.

I had to sit in the same armchair where I used to sit to hear her stories as I typed and recorded the raw, unedited material. My mind began to summon memories from the recent past, all the roars of laughter and all the tears that had made us so close. I was there now, breathing deeply through my ears as I tried to hear her sweet voice, tried to bring back her presence to my reality again.

CONTENTS

THE FOUR ELEMENTS OF LIFE

THE RED OF THE BURNING FIRE

It was a time of great transformations. Sybil had decided to be born in one of the most turbulent epochs of recent history, the height of the Vietnam War. The hippies and LSD were responsible for showing, for the first time, that one *could* live on love and peace. And despite excess and addiction, they opened the human mind to the possibility of other realities and other dimensions that none of the wars and their victims had allowed us to imagine.

I came into this world in the midst of daydream and tragedy, pleasure, and pain. Mankind landed on the moon, or at least I'd like to think that it did and it wasn't staged in some studio in Las Vegas! Kennedy and Martin Luther King were assassinated, the Beatles were the only ones teenagers wanted to listen to, and Woodstock left its mark on the hearts of a generation that longed for the change which had not yet taken over the world. Doubtless, there were lots of Supermen and Wonder Women but I don't know in what attics they were hiding. I cannot speak much of those days; I was in diapers, a baby whose fontanel had just closed as its brain was switched on. But I picked up from them the yearnings of those who came before me, the yearnings to establish a new order despised and misunderstood by those who still do not realize that they are asleep.

She was three when, suddenly, she fell gravely ill from an acute pyelonephritis which left her life hanging by a thread. From a tender age, Sybil confronted the duality of the world with its two extremes. Such a fragile mind, trying to own so many vivid details. When she tries to recall that time, perhaps she remembers more of the "other side" than this one. In those early years, her dreams were connected to an ethereal world where she lived through a pitched battle, between the forces of evil that only wished to annihilate her and the forces of light which revived her and kept her heart beating on nights from which it seemed she would never awaken. One should give credit to the nightmares children have. She would feel life and death at the same time, but life, which she so passionately wanted to live, was stronger. Forced to fight against the dark knights, little by little, her fears led her to build a nearly impenetrable armor; her timidity was so apparent that her mother, Cassandra, feared that she might be a deaf-mute, since she refused to utter a word. While all this was happening, she felt very weak; she was not a hardy girl and looked, for a long time, like an Ethiopian child suffering from famine. Her head was much too large for her body and her ribs stuck out of her skin. She paid little attention to food but did not care; the light from the other side nourished her deep inside. At that age, she could not defend herself and did not even understand the fight she had been thrust into. She only knew that her angel— that beautiful, enormous angel with cobalt-blue eyes and shining golden hair—was always by her side and he protected her.

He was like my other dad or mom, or the two in one. The love of that angel reached beyond all the limits of the universe. With a single word of his, I felt that my body was completely illumined and my human nature had vanished; that angel was the essence of pure love and at the same time the essence of the security all of us look for. My angel was the light leaping along behind me, so that he wouldn't lose sight of me and would be able to save me from the shadows.

Her grandmother, Ofelia, made her say her bedtime prayers every night before going to sleep. In addition to the Lord's Prayer and Hail Mary, she also taught her the Prayer to the Guardian Angel. Thus, the angel remained nameless until she became an adult; he was simply her guardian angel, who was always there when she needed him. Why give him a name if he came unbidden? The secret was to think of him, to keep him in her mind, and he would immediately respond. Like everything in a child's world, it was easy and simple.

Her little piece of heaven was the island of San Andrés, where she spent the first thirteen years of her life. Her father, Dylan, a mild, bohemian Welshman with glassy blue eyes, had arrived in Colombia at the age of twenty-four to work for an oil company. Crossing seas and continents, he bravely followed the promptings of a heart which told him how to make his dreams come true. He met Cassandra, Sybil's mother, in Cartagena and they lived there for several years after they married, during which they had three children, Betrys, Glyn, and Sybil. Another two were meant to embark on the Welshman's adventure, but they were stillborn, one three years before Sybil was born and the other, three years after. Her mother still remembers them with nostalgia but she wonders what that period of her life would have been like if they had lived. They were poor enough with the three who survived.

I was born in Cartagena, but from the age of six months, the landscape of San Andrés lulled me to sleep and colored my essence in this lifetime. My mother, on the maternal side, was a descendant of the Morgans and Powells, old San Andrés families who had emigrated from Jamaica to the archipelago in the nineteenth century. My maternal grandfather, Judge Eladio Cruz, was Colombian and had come there from Santander. My grandmother, Ofelia, was widowed at the age of nineteen, when my mother was a babe in arms.

In the Old World, her paternal grandmother, Anwen, had also been widowed young, at the age of twenty-two. Dylan only lived with his biological father when he was a young child. It is curious how both of Sybil's parents lost their fathers like that and were both an only child. She never had any uncles or aunts, although her close cousins soon took on that role. Ofelia never remarried and always lived with Sybil's family. Dylan generously welcomed her to his home; it wasn't a problem since she was his wife's mother. That was not the case with Anwen. She met Wyn a few years after she was widowed and married him. Dylan quickly accepted him as his stepfather. They both lived in Llandeilo, a charming little Welsh village, until they died of old age.

Wyn was like my real grandfather, the one who died I only knew from photos. We human beings earn our roles in life and the love of those who come after us, without any need for DNA proofs. There was so much kindness in the heart of that dear old man that today, years after he died, I still bear in my heart the way his eyes glistened when he looked at me and the gentleness of his trembling, spotted hands, when they stroked my tiny ones.

Sybil was not even one when, in 1967, her father quit his job in the oil business and decided to leap into the void. He took the next step in making his golden dream come true: to build in San Andrés a hotel for foreign tourists interested in scuba-diving and fishing. Starting in South Wales, he had become an assistant professor at Toronto University in Canada, and a maintenance supervisor of a refinery on the Atlantic Coast of Colombia. Now, he was an independent businessman on a tiny speck of land in a hidden corner of the Caribbean, where the magical legacy of pirates and corsairs was still alive. If he hadn't emigrated, he would simply have been a miner, as all of his school friends were, and his father before them. But Dylan was always a visionary, running his personal movie in his mind, down to the last scene. Whether the scenes were good or bad, he would act out all of them, no more, no less.

That is where my talent as a dreamer and adventurer comes from, from my father, who gave everything up one day and set out to build a life designed by him and not by society. He wanted to live in a place that would offer him the possibility of creating an unprecedented existence. He was full of illusions and my mother followed him with her litter. It was her island in the end and she believed in his vision.

***

"Doctor Barreneche, please give me your honest opinion and don't hold anything back."

"I must be frank with you, Cassandra. Your daughter's condition is very delicate just now and the amoxicillin we are treating her with isn't producing the expected results. We haven't been able to eliminate the infection, and what worries us is the possibility of permanent kidney damage."

"Sybil is very weak, Doctor, and doesn't gain weight because she hardly eats anything. I lay awake at night wondering whether she is going to recover. My maternal instinct tells me I should take her off all those antibiotics. In short, she is not getting better and all I see is that she's fading away."

In another room, little Sybil listened to the distant sound of the conversation between her mother and the urologist. She was shivering with cold. They had made her lie down naked on a kind of stainless steel stretcher, on top of some very thick, starched blankets with a checkered pattern in pastels. While the nurses distracted her with their silly talk as they inserted the probe which had frightened and hurt her so much on previous occasions, she turned her head around to scrutinize a giant Pepsi bottle cap hanging on the wall, which was painted in that shiny green you find only in hospitals. It was the kind of cap they don't make any more, for those single-serving-size glass bottles of soft drinks that would be recycled after use. It was a symbol of a lost time and mentality that was slowly dying because capitalism had come up with the idea of cheaper materials like aluminum and plastic and began to ruin the planet. That horrible decoration was the only way she could avoid looking at the faces of the nurses who manhandled her. It was her only hope to shut out what she did not want to feel. It was so traumatic that any description of what she felt would sound more like rape than the routine medical treatment it was.

Her mother left Barreneche's office, disillusioned with what he had just told her. The sight of Sybil lying down on that gurney, clearly suffering, brought her helplessness to a head. The nurses had to shoo her out, but Cassandra had already had enough; it would be the third and last time Sybil would travel to that children's hospital in Medellín. Her mother called Dylan in San Andrés and persuaded him to stop the treatment. She would return to San Andrés without having achieved anything. It was a difficult decision; in those days the health service there was basic, almost non-existent. The only hospital was a primitive health center.

It seemed, on the face of it, that I was adrift, with an illness I wasn't able to fight back, but my mother acted with certainty and by remote control. Subconsciously, she was being guided by my angel and though her rejection of conventional medicine looked crazy, it turned out to be the definitive cure for my disease. In those days, an American doctor had arrived to the island at the invitation of Doctor Alberto Elizondo, a personal friend of my parents. It was the most perfect synchronicity. Without knowing anything about my condition, Doctor Elizondo took him to visit the hotel project. My father had started construction on a lot facing the sea, the same lot my mother had inherited from her mother's family, the one where my father had already put up three pre-fabricated houses: the little house, the big house, and the round house. One of them was for our family; we lived in the "big house" at that time. The other two were rented out, for long periods, to tourists. We lived off that money. My mother took advantage of the visit to tell the two doctors what Doctor Barreneche had told her in Medellín. The

American doctor's prescription was as simple as it was startling.

> "The water of green coconuts, Cassandra. The more cups she can drink a day, the better, and don't tell me now it's going to be difficult to find the remedy on this island!"

The physician's irony set off a round of laughter. From there on, Sybil drank and drank so much green coconut water that her veins must have turned into transparent tubes flowing with the milky, miraculous liquid. Her disease subsided and in a matter of months, she began to recover her appetite and life force. As ill as she had been during those years and despite the trauma it caused to one so young, the memories that most linger are those of a happy girl, full of life. In those surroundings, it was as if the whole world had been made for her and her alone: the sky, the moon, and the stars. For her, they were as reachable as the transparent green of her eyes. She could dream without endings if she wanted to. There was no way for her to be unhappy.

What a special childhood I had. Life didn't shower my parents with prosperity. I always saw them suffering from their fear of poverty. Although San Andrés was a poor, backward island then, just taking the first steps toward its later – and corrupt – socioeconomic development, I felt rich and fulfilled. My world was perfect. I didn't feel sick when I was ill and I didn't experience the hardships that kept my parents awake, night after night. From the time I was a girl, I had a knack for choosing what I wanted to believe in and how I wanted to feel. I always chose the full half of the glass and forgot about the empty half, if indeed it existed!

There is no doubt that her resilience was already emerging as a key feature of her character, one that would later save her in moments when she completely lost her faith. Her innocence kept her from seeing danger or surrendering in the midst of the war without truce she found herself in. The forces of evil may disturb even the holiest saint. The illness they sent her had not been able to destroy her, so they tried again—and this time, they used the male figure she would most need for her future balance and stability.

On one of those crisp, sunny mornings typical of that island, Dylan left the big house in his Ray-Ban sunglasses and gringo tourist sombrero. He was about to set off in the white Chevrolet pickup truck that had recently been shipped from Miami. He was heading for Fortunato Bailey's building materials warehouse downtown, to buy lumber and cement. There was no way he could have seen Sybil, who was in the most unlikely spot of all. He crossed in front of the truck, opened the door on the driver's side, got in, and started to go at once. To do that, he had to back up, since there was a paved surface about eight inches high in front of him and the road was behind. In her innocence, she had decided to crouch behind one of the truck's back tires to play with the stones on the ground with the Raggedy Ann doll that Dylan had brought back from the trip to the United States when he bought the prefabricated houses. Just when she was on the point of being accidentally killed by the father who loved her so much, Acario—the worker from Cartagena who helped Dylan with all his chores and was then watering the garden—happened to see her. He threw down the hose in a split second and ran toward them like a man possessed, screaming as though his throat was red hot while he tried to make himself heard.

"Don *Dila,* don *Dila,* the kid, the kid!"

Since the engine was on, Dylan could not hear him but he did see him running toward him. The look on Acario's face was enough to freeze his hands and feet. As though in slow motion, with a presentiment of the tragedy he had been about to cause, he climbed down from the truck, and along with his right hand man, bent down to look, his eyes now full of tears at the sight of her. She was sitting behind the tire, watching him with her enormous eyes and brightest smile, wrapped up in herself as always. A short time before, an unknown foreign doctor had appeared out of nowhere with no other purpose than to save her life with a remedy that was both simple and unbelievable. Now, a humble workingman had played the same role. Her nameless guardian angel turned them into great heroes and defeated death's second pitiless attempt to leave her bloody and dying.

She would have preferred to be bound to her angel forever. He had led her safely through life while the two of them lived the most innocent idyll of unconditional love. In the mornings, they both sat in a rocking chair on the terrace of the house, watching for endless hours, the flirtatious play of the sunrays on the waves of the sea and the seagulls diving into the water in search of food. Seated on his lap while they rocked, that strong warrior angel showed her the beautiful dance of nature in action, so that she would guard it in her heart forever. The time to shed her innocence had arrived; she was to study at the school the nuns ran and begin to learn the survival tactics that would let her defend herself in all the wars to come. While she would no longer see her angel as she saw him now, it would only be in appearance that she would fight them on her own.

How much the Western World has changed, including the wrongly named third world! I began my forced indoctrination at the age of five, at the kindergarten of La Anunciación. Nowadays, children start going to nursery school without even knowing how to say mommy or daddy. Such children cannot see their angels, but even though they do not see them, I am sure they have them as I had mine. All thanks to a social system intentionally designed to completely wipe out the space and time we all need to develop our emotional bonds with the other side. Sending a child straight from the mother's womb to a school that kills its spiritual essence? How shameful a society that blinds those who come with the most beautiful vision!

Outbursts of laughter full of a nostalgic and infectious helplessness. Who would have thought school would be like that? Her angel believed she was in good hands and that the nuns would take charge of conserving that inner world full of light which both of them had made such an effort to keep safe and sound after so many battles. But it was not to be; the Catholicism practiced by her teachers, her mother, and her grandmother would transform the secret world to which Sybil had access. With the passage of time, God would become to her an old man in a white beard who punished, one to whom she would have to render accounts in order to go to heaven. More rendering of accounts? She was already having a hard time keeping up with the guilt her mother unconsciously instilled in her, for no other reason than "I say so!" She had been sentenced. She was very good at learning the sense of guilt which had already begun to exude from all her pores, though she was not guilty of anything.

She remembers her first day at school as though it were yesterday. Milena was the name of her kindergarten teacher. Sybil cried all the time because she did not find her angel when she thought about him; as hard as she tried, she could not connect herself with him again. Milena did not have the patience to be a teacher of shy and sensitive children. Seeing that Sybil was inconsolable, she became desperate and took her to a small room next to the classroom and struck the palms of her hands with a wooden ruler to silence her. It was from Milena she heard for the first time that she was a spoiled and badly brought up girl, and she quickly learned what it meant to stifle your feelings and shut up so that you wouldn't be beaten anymore.

I can still hear the sound of that ruler, feel the wood scorching my skin. That was my punishment for bad behavior. "Not behaving myself" meant silently whimpering because I missed being happy. Happiness had been my choice and it was no longer open to me in my new surroundings. I was beginning to understand the bittersweet, contradictory world into which I had chosen to be born and study the lessons of life. My timidity and introversion grew when the classmates of my sister Betrys, who also studied at the nuns' school, said hello to me in the breaks in order to take in the details of my eyes and lashes, and that wasn't only once in a while. It was horrible! The more I avoided it, the more it happened. They looked at me with amazement and I didn't understand why they found what they saw so strange, when it was so normal for me. My angel had taught me I would transmit light with my eyes when I was older but all I felt now was that they just wanted something to gossip about and did not have good intentions.

> "Open your eyes wide so we can see them better."
>
> "It's a miracle they didn't give you the evil eye!"
>
> "My, what long lashes you have for a little girl. Let me touch them to make sure they're not false!"

They were in an uproar, shouting while she bent her head down and closed her eyes. She was beginning to learn from the other little ladies what it felt like when people did not speak from the heart but from envy. Now that she would be without her angel, learning to feel what others were like inside became indispensable, if she were to play the game to its end.

Everyone sees the world through his or her own filters. Our filters are what let us interpret what we observe. My filters did not only belong to this life, they were the sum of many others when I had to struggle against human wickedness in all its forms, insofar as I had died many times before, to the point of having been burned at the stake and stoned to death by my executioners, to be later reborn out of a fervent desire to continue evolving. That is why I needed those who were willing to play such drama-filled games with me as I kept to the path leading back to the light.

As her socialization turned into an ongoing and irreversible process during her childhood and puberty, her world in San Luis—the native town on the south side of the island where her father was building his hotel—was the perfect setting and driveshaft for her mental well-being. She soon adapted completely to her school, where she was always one of the best students. For her, learning to subject oneself to the rules of the game of life was never a problem. Naturally, her favorite subjects were the sciences that would answer the questions of a restless little mind, hungry for knowledge. She wanted to know everything about the workings of this world, the materialized world different to the one she used to visit in her imagination and which was now beginning to look like a distant mirage.

Since she was like an enormous sponge absorbing such knowledge during the day, she needed a refuge where she could be alone and reconnect herself with her angel, whom she only saw from time to time at night. The natural setting she was growing up in was unspoiled and exuberant, but she also needed privacy and solitude, a hidden corner where she could return to her roots and be the girl no one understood she was. She found that place when Dylan leased the big house to the Persian prince, Sadruddin Aga Khan, who was visiting the island for a few weeks in his role of high commissioner of the United Nations, and the family moved to the little house. She had been sharing a room with her sister Betrys even since they had arrived from Cartagena and the visit of that distinguished guest, perhaps the nearest thing to a real king ever seen on the island, would at last give her the privacy which her inborn independence needed.

My new bedroom didn't have any windows and was located in a pretty strange place, the middle of the house. It was originally going to be the kitchen, but then the house was enlarged and the kitchen was placed somewhere else. My bedroom was so small that my bed and I hardly fit into it. My father had built me a mini single bed only twelve inches high. For a night table, I used a little plastic table with a mushroom-shaped lamp, which shed a warm and soothing light over the whole room. Right at the foot of the bed, on top of a small wooden bench, I put a rotary fan, which kept off the mosquitoes and cooled me better than air conditioning. My sheets were sky blue, like the walls, and had on them, in indigo, the outline of a mountainous sea coast, a landscape which inspired me to dream and fly.

From her girlhood, she began to display a fascination for decoration and interior design. She'd speak of her bedroom as though Vera Wang and Giorgio Armani were alive in her. Her creativity was budding at the same time that she was beginning to leaf through her father's books on anthropology and ancient history, without understanding them. She was fascinated by the pyramids and all those mysterious and vanished cultures she hadn't yet deciphered. The whole of that past was so familiar to her, and yet—at the same time—so alien.

I would play on my own for hours on end. I kept my dolls on a shelf my father built there for me. It was too high to reach without standing on a chair, but there was simply no other place for it. When the time came to play, I took down everything I kept on that shelf and put it on my bed. It was like waving a magic wand; all at once, my dolls would come to life and I would feel like a new version of Alice in Wonderland. *My life with those dolls was as real as the one I lived at home or at school; it was clearly a parallel reality.*

One can be happy with so little. The hours she spent in that tiny space were enchanted ones. No matter what might happen outside of it, good or bad, there Sybil was able to regain her balance and recharge her batteries night after night. She had only to close the door, drape a kerchief over the lampshade, turn the fan on to its highest speed, and she would shut herself off from this reality and be transported to the world of the wizards where she felt she was the luckiest creature of all. Nearly always, these nocturnal astral voyages transported her to two very specific places on the planet. She did not know why, but she would invariably head toward them without being able to control it. One was the Indian Ocean, where she'd find herself sitting in the bow of a gigantic and luxurious white sailboat with dark blue sails and a captain she did not know. The other was a heavenly oasis in the middle of the Sahara which she'd reach skillfully riding an enormous camel who did seem to know her very well. She experienced those adventures in an intense and vivid way. The only silent witness to them was her angel; no one else knew the secret of her other, hidden worlds. She would get up at dawn, go to school and return, for another day, to being the shy girl with big green eyes everyone knew.

***

"Auritaaa!"

"Whaaat?"

"Come and plaaay!"

"I'm comiiing!"

Her house and Aura's were only separated by a six-foot-long patch of dense weeds and native palms, but they always liked to shout out those four lines—no more, no less—so that the whole neighborhood heard the ritual when they were about to play together. Aura, her only friend at that time, was the daughter of Heriberto and Noelia, who had moved to the island from Medellín. They were *paisas,* as the islanders called them. They came to seek a better life, attracted by the same seductive and intoxicating magic that had lured Dylan and all the other outsiders to the island. Aura's family was very poor, but that never got in the way of her love for her friend. That fact pointed to the contrast between them and made her grateful for what she and her family had. The few times she entered their modest house, her heart shrank. She could not help noticing its untidiness and dirty smell, understandable when a family of four lived in a space of four hundred square feet.

My first friend had appeared in my life because she needed me and I needed her. As the two of us grew up, we would teach each other tacit and explicit lessons about life. She taught me about self-interested love and I taught her about unconditional love. I don't think I was a good teacher for her, but she did teach me every detail of her lesson. I didn't have much in common with my siblings at that time, since they were much older; Betrys by eight years and Glyn, by five.

All that was lacking was for Sybil's parents to adopt Aura. They went to school together, played, and swam in the sea together when school let out. Both ate in Sybil's house and— most importantly, before it is forgotten—fought the whole blessed day!

As friends, our love was never two-sided. I accepted the fact that she used me, because she provided the company I didn't get from my siblings. When she felt like it, it was as if she was able to rip my guts out; she was a better warrior than I was. We were both five years old but the material limitations on her life had already marked her as a survivor and opportunist far too skillful for me, a girl who was barely beginning to recover from death's unsuccessful assaults, not long before.

It was the beginning of her emotional relationships with people other than the family she'd been born into. Aura was the first person who hurt her. From her, she would learn about bitterness and frustration, about the failure of some human beings to see that hate is only an inch from love, and that we have in us the power to join them or keep them apart.

***

During the whole of her childhood, her parents had gone through tight spells; the money they had saved and the little they earned went to building the hotel. She would soon be six and her grandparents in Wales had not yet met her. When her father had been working for the oil company in Cartagena, the family spent every summer in Wales with her grandparents, but Sybil had not yet been born and she had to live through different times.

It was as though just because I was the youngest, the littlest, I had to be the least favored. Giving my elder siblings a good education in life was the priority. I still remember my mother droning on about how, "I'm saving to get such and such a thing for Glyn" or "We've got to pay for this or that for Betrys." In the sharing out of the little there was, it seemed that what I got was proportional to my size.

But from the time she was a little girl, she chose to dream about the end of the rainbow, where she would finally find her pot full of gold coins—and she always believed that the one who laughed last, laughed best. So, funnily enough, on this occasion, they thought of her for once. That year, Dylan wanted to send her to Wales with Cassandra so that his Welsh family could get to know his latest offspring, the one who would most closely resemble him as time passed and life shaped Sybil's personality. In contrast with the traumatic trips she had to make to Medellín because of her kidney condition, this time fate was beginning to show her that she was right to stick to her belief in the end of the rainbow. She was going to visit Europe for the first time! She and Cassandra set out in a Constellation belonging to the old Aérocondor airline. Immersed in her new adventure, she did not even take in the thunderous roar of its engines. Despite her shyness, she felt calm because her mother sat beside her and her angel had also reappeared, as if the occasion were so important it merited his presence. She clearly saw him flying above them, covering the plane with his enormous wings, which had no feathers but were full of light. She had to go to the toilet several times, but only to put into her little handbag some of the free soaps and creams which the airlines provided for passengers at that time. She was fascinated by the tiny bottles they came in. While she filled in the coloring book the stewardess had just given her, she would pause to delight in the blue she visualized in the sky behind the white clouds in the form of angels who approached the little window of the plane to greet her. This was her thing—to travel and fly as her angel had taught her on those imaginary nocturnal flights where Africa was just around the corner.

Their first stop was Miami. That was the only route to London. In the airport, the immigration official who looked at their passports at once fastened on Cassandra. A dark-haired Latina with a strong accent and a little girl as her traveling companion met all the conditions of a suspicious person or a drug smuggler wanting to experience the American illegal dream. Although they were in transit, only spending a night there, and Cassandra was a British citizen by virtue of being married to Dylan, they were both taken to one of those famous rooms in American airports where they were questioned and examined for several hours. Since she was so young, she did not understand what the word *humiliation* meant yet, but on seeing her mother standing in her underwear and answering so many questions, she quickly learnt the concept, without the aid of a dictionary. Even so, that sight did not spoil the party. She had inhaled the air of American freedom as soon as she descended the stairs of the plane. It smelled of the new and she would long for and dream of it from then on.

After that unpleasant and unexpected greeting, we must have been exhausted. All I remember is that we left San Andrés in the morning and it was already very late at night. Our hotel, the Columbus, was located in downtown Miami. I loved it the moment I entered. It's no longer there; the agents of capitalism tore it down to make way for four spanking new skyscrapers. When I went into the bathroom, the first thing I saw was the gleaming porcelain bathtub and a bunch of white, snuggly towels hanging there. I had to have a bath at once. I had never used a tub before; I felt like a Hollywood star. My house in San Andrés did not have towels like that, so perfect, and the bathroom I shared with my brother, sister and grandmother had a shower where there was just about enough room to stand, if I didn't move around. The duvet and curtains of that luxurious room never escaped my memory. The fabric had flowers in autumnal colors and the sheets on the bed were as white as the towels. It was as if I were the first to use them. Now I understood why my father wanted to have a hotel and if it would be like this one in which I was a guest for the first time, we were sure to be millionaires as soon as it was finished!

They were going to continue on to London the following day, but that night when she slept in Miami she confided her feelings to her angel, with conviction.

"I'm going to live here when I grow up."

Without realizing it, she forever fell in love with Miami at the age of five. She fell in love with a way of life which, for the first time, she had seen as possible in another part of the world. Up to then, her little patch of land in the middle of the enormous ocean had been everything to her. She had had no other place to compare it with. What her tender eyes now witnessed made her understand the deprivations that surrounded her in a life borrowed from her parents that she would soon want to start changing. She felt that she was happy on her island, but how could she continue to be so in a place where there were so few opportunities for creating and materializing? She marveled at all of the conveniences she was now experiencing for the first time: hot water, television, air conditioning, and even electric light all day long! On the island, there were power cuts that lasted up to ten or twelve hours on end. She was now in a diametrically opposite reality, with the Mickey Mouse film that made her fall asleep as she lay between the duvet and the sheets of starched cotton. For a few seconds, she left behind the buzzing of the mosquitoes which murmured into her ear at nights on the island. In her inner being, she understood that her happiness was innate but, caught between nostalgia and joy, she had a presentiment that this was her introduction to the world that would break her connection with her essence and truth. Even so, she was willing to drench herself in it. On the evening of the following day, she took another jet from the new to the old continent. This time, it was a jumbo belonging to Pan American, an airline that later became ancient history, just like the one which had brought her to Miami. She could not believe how big this plane was. It had stairs and so many seats that her mother had to accompany her every time she went to the toilet, lest she got lost.

The two of them celebrated her sixth birthday in London. Cassandra had a surprise: an aqua show. It was the biggest pool she had ever seen and the crowd there might have been bigger than the whole population of her island. The seals, whales, and dolphins were the ones celebrating with her. She watched in amazement, unable to move for excitement; those animals were dancing, singing, and even applauding! Open-mouthed for who knows how long, it was the first time she was able to enter into a telepathic communication with a dolphin. Her mother did not notice it, but without speaking a word, Sybil concentrated on talking to one during the show. That was the start of her fascination with them. With all the seriousness of a child, she wanted to take her new friend away to San Andrés, put him a pool of salt water where she could look after him, and have him as a pet. Her father could surely build one; to her inexperienced mind, it was that easy. The next thing she remembers, after putting it to Cassandra, was that the show had ended and they were in the gift shop of the theater, buying an inflatable dolphin packed in a plastic bag that read "Made in Taiwan" on the back. She would have to make do with it, and without a further word, her dolphin was named Flipper (so much for originality) and returned to the island with her, where he became a floating toy when she and Aura swam in the sea in front of her house.

They took the train from London to Swansea, where Wyn picked them up in the small, cream-colored Studebaker given to him by Dylan in boom times. The train was like the ones she had seen in the movies at the Majestic Theater in San Andrés, but the steam and the whistle were real. They spent too long a time in Wales. Then, in the 1970s, the British summers were still very cold. Sybil didn't like wearing overcoats and staying indoors. As soon as they arrived at that little village where her father had been born and grown up, she began to miss her little world and above all, Aura, her only friend. Used to walking barefoot in the dust, her feet were now covered in wool socks and buckled shoes bought at Marks & Spencer. Every day, she would ask her mother how long it would be before they went back and cross off the remaining days with a pencil on a piece of paper she kept under her pillow. Miami had enchanted her, but she still did not feel the pull of her Welsh blood nor understood why she was not fascinated by the old European energy. During that month, Cassandra took her to all the homes of the close relatives of her father who were dying to meet her and almost always, at tea-time, 4:00 PM. In addition to the sickly sweet mince pies, her great aunts prepared some smoked salmon sandwiches with homemade butter and whole-wheat bread straight from the oven that she was crazy about. Every one of Dylan's cousins whom she met would give her a fifty-pence or pound coin; it was the custom there. Saving all of this money, she was able to buy a Wendy doll at the end of the trip, her first life-size one that wet its diapers when she gave it a bottle. Her Wendy was a modest example of the way the outer world was already influencing her; it was the moment when her maternal instincts began to stir, something, in short, that she had picked up from her own mother over the years. She was a different girl when she returned to her beloved tropics. Now she was aware of hitherto-unimaginable realities which stretched her mind beyond its previous limits.

***

On a hot Thursday afternoon in 1974, life forced Sybil out of anonymity. Avianca flight number 226 from Bogotá landed at the recently-opened San Andrés airport with Cassandra and her official retinue. An official retinue? Yes, exactly that, since the President of Colombia, Terencio Méndez Tobón, had named Cassandra Cruz de Vaughan the first woman intendant in the whole history of the island. Her mother, that native-born matron, homemaker, and administrator of the hotel of her father's dreams, was now going to run the island where she had grown up. Many people were astonished that such a mistake could have occurred. What was the President of the Republic thinking? A woman in power when the government was still the exclusive domain of men? And to make it worse: a housewife! One with a fighting spirit, to be sure, but with no academic qualifications or political experience. No sir, it was not a mistake; President Méndez had promised to make a difference and *different* was what the islanders got.

My mother always had her own dreams, and though she locked them away in some subconscious vault, they were as important as those of my father. She had always wanted to help the people of that scrap of land in the middle of the ocean where she had been born. It is true that she was as surprised as her newly born enemies, because she never imagined her wish would be so powerful that she would wind up seated at the intendant's desk. It was a revolutionary event, not only for the island but the whole country, because of the thirty or so departments and intendancies Colombia was divided into at that time, only two were governed by women and one of them was San Andrés! There is no doubt that President Méndez Tobón, may he rest in peace, was a visionary. Perhaps his ideas would have found a much wider acceptance in a Colombia that was more modern and liberated than the one he had inherited from his predecessor. We are now in a new century and he is dead, but meanwhile, the men of the country where I was born still think that we women aren't fit for political power – although they know deep in their hearts that it is our inner power which empowers theirs. When I look in her albums at the photos of that time, I see so many favor-seekers who slandered her from start to finish; hypocrites with phony smiles, backstabbers, wolves dressed as sheep. The welcome my mother got from the public that day was worthy of a famous pop star or soccer hero.

The crowd was such that there wasn't an inch of room at the airport. As soon as Sybil's mother got off the plane, everyone wanted to have their picture taken with her. Then there was champagne and a big speech. Cassandra never thought of herself as pretty, but she shone that night; she looked powerful and sure of herself. The woman who had recently been sworn in at the San Carlos presidential palace in Bogotá arrived motivated and full of hope. By her side, Dylan, proud and moved, with his tear-filled eyes and silver hair still wet from a quick shower, wore a white, long-sleeved, impeccably starched *guayabera,* a kind of dress shirt they wear in the heat of the Caribbean. His attire was what emphasized the formality of the occasion for Sybil, since her father was almost always seen in faded trousers and a tee-shirt sweaty with work. After a formal reception, they traveled to San Luis in the intendant's official car, a new Cadillac convertible, first passing along several streets in the town center so that everyone could greet the person who would be governing them for the next two years.

We crawled along. Marcelino, my closest cousin, three years younger than myself, Aurita, and I sat on the car's trunk the whole way, as though on a float at the carnival. Unused to their sudden and unexpected fame, my parents waved to the people from the back seat, while Clarke drove. Clarke was an affectionate islander who acted as my mother's driver. He took better care of me than the bodyguard who was superfluous in such a safe community.

Everything about her mother's new role turned out to be a tremendous problem for shy Sybil. The girls at the nuns' school no longer looked at her because of her eyes but as the daughter of the Intendant. She did not know how to avoid all this attention, but fortunately, she did know that she could count on Aura, who did not leave her alone for a second now that she had become important. Her hypocritical friend desperately wanted the reflected glory.

While Colombia was being torn apart by political violence (too complex to go into here), the peacefulness of San Andrés remained a well-guarded secret. There were no strangers there; everyone knew everyone else and the island was so small that anyone who thought of breaking the law had no place to hide. In the little jail on La Loma, the only hill of any size there, most of the cells remained permanently empty. True, there was a marked social difference between the natives and the immigrants, because the former had not yet completely accepted the latter, but the two groups lived in harmony. It was so safe that the only thefts that occurred at the hotel were of its coconuts. This, which happened daily, was the work of Dylan's number one headache, who lived on a dark patch of scrubland near the hotel. Hard as it may be to believe, the thief who kept him from sleeping was a woman! Felicity wasn't just any old woman, however. She was about six feet tall, weighed 220 pounds, and was also one-eyed, blubber-lipped, and only had a few teeth in her lower jaw.

I can still hear my father cursing at night, when we were having supper, as he was frustrated because he'd caught her in the act again. Nightly, he would threaten to get a machete or even call the police, and nightly, he would learn that Felicity wasn't at all frightened of him. The bad guy always knows the good guy is harmless. Besides, she and her children – each by a different and nameless father – lived off the sale of those coconuts. When it was a matter of hunger, no one could scare her away. She had to dredge up the money for the pigtail stew or the rundown soup made of freshly-caught barracuda that would feed her family for a couple of days.

***

The first thing her eyes fixed on when she woke up in the morning was that sea of seven colors, which seemed to merge into the blue sky on the horizon. In the distance, as though they had been set down on that imaginary line, she would peer at two small islets where the tourists went by launch to snorkel or sunbathe. In those days, no one worried about ultraviolet rays, PABA sun creams, the ozone layer, or global warming. The coconut oil sold on the beaches was considered to be the best suntan lotion, although in fact it was only good for frying fish in a pan. When it rained—and it rained a lot on that tropical island—her soul grew sad. The sea and the sky were like two twins dressed in mourning and in the blink of an eye, the clarity of the sun would give way to a grey darkness which turned happiness into melancholy. She didn't feel like laughing anymore and would enclose herself in her little room and flee to her other worlds.

The sun, gleaming on the little waves that reached the shore with the breeze, was what made me feel alive. Whole hours would pass while I watched the glints of light, baffled by the prismatic effect of the water. All my eyes could do was to reflect that perfection and shine. When night fell over the scene, there was a new actress, the moon, who robbed the show. When it was completely full, it would appear over the outline of the little islets, slowly rising as it reflected its faint and comforting light, golden threads dancing on the sea. To witness that made my heart burst with joy.

Dylan built a jetty in front of the hotel, thinking of the launches and boats that would dock there in the future, when the hotel was up and running. That place belonged to Sybil. She spent hours at a time there, meditating on the dual world of joy and sadness, and learning to balance the two inside herself. She was in a waking dream at such times as she stared at the infinite and heard the stars whisper their love into her ears. From them, she learned that one did not have to be visible all the time to make one's influence felt and leave one's mark. During the day, they taught her to believe in the invisible, in what her physical eyes would never be able to see. That pier was another refuge, like her room. These were the two spaces in her world where she could be entirely genuine, free from the external influence of her mother, sacred places where she never had to ask permission to be herself. It wasn't Cassandra's fault; for reasons of love, she was training her daughter to be accepted and approved by the world which she, because of her filters, saw as the only one; the same filters which she had inherited from her own mother. Like Ofelia before her, she did not know any better. That world her mother imposed on her did not allow Sybil to spread her wings in this life, though she had the capacity for it. It was a sickly, over-protective love that gradually made her wings waste away. To her, it was clear that while the other boys and girls of her age went about carefree, playing and exploring life in that haven of peace, her mother never let her out of her sight—controlling everything she did.

Despite all that, her special sensibility found its own course. Sybil continued to grow at the rhythm of nature, turning into a pretty and gentle young lady despite being dominated by a mother who wanted her to remain a little girl, wearing a frock that was beginning to feel uncomfortably tight. Sitting alone on her jetty, sensing the mystery and enchantment of the moon, she learned what it was to feel love. The barracudas and mermaids would be the only ones to hear the sweet cry of her heart when she fell in love for the first time.

***

I haven't the slightest doubt that I was born in love with life and the little man my DNA had programmed to be my first love. I still don't know how a girl could have come up with such strong feelings at the age of nine. I first saw him one day in December at the home of the Pérez family, when Octavio, Aurita's brother, took him on a visit to our neighborhood. San Luis was a native community and the Pérezes, along with Aurita's parents, the Peláezes, were among the few families of paisas who lived on its surroundings. I was always indifferent to racial differences. I liked to be friendly with all sides. If a person was at one extreme or the other or in the middle, it was the same for me. Since my mother was a native and my father a foreigner, I thought of myself as a strange hybrid, so that everyone was the same for me. There was no separation at that time. That small and picturesque settlement was incredibly heterogeneous, a typical example of how special the society of San Andrés was. There, in an atmosphere of mutual respect, the blacks lived alongside the whites, the poor with the rich, the liberals with the conservatives, the Protestants with the Catholics, the adults with the kids.

By reason of one of those inexplicable synchronicities that happen in life, more as causalities than accidents, Sybil had arrived at the home of the Pérezes on her skateboard. She had gone there without Cassandra's permission and felt that disobeying her mother was the biggest sin. Even so, she could not resist the urge to break the rules; her heart forced her to be there at that exact moment.

I arrived there, barefoot – the way I liked to ride that metallic blue skateboard with phosphorescent-orange tires – somewhat dirty and in a mess, my hair tangled behind my ears. I was in that little light-green dress that was like my uniform by then, since I wore it all the time. I still recall the vibration I felt deep in my heart when Santiago looked into my eyes for the first time. I instantly melted. He didn't say a word, nor did I; it seemed as though both of us had forgotten how to talk. We looked at each other and our timid smiles met. That was sufficient for my heart to recognize him. It was he, the man who came into this life to teach me how sorrowful passionate love could be.

She was such a little girl that she still didn't know how to handle feelings so real. Her feelings for him were so strong, yet, not feeling worthy enough she could not believe his were the same, nor that she deserved his love. She was in love with an impossibility. How could he be in love with her if the only thing they had shared was a single smiling gaze?

> "The two of you were born to share your love in this lifetime and so it will be my girl, you will see, you will leave your mark on him and he on you, you will experience it."

The words of her angel, who hardly spoke to her anymore, were clear, although she chose to doubt them and believe more in her ego, which was beginning to impose its law and further lowered her self-esteem. Santiago had been raised on the island, because his mother, a beautiful *paisa* with a bohemian temperament and a star model in the glamorous world of fashion which was just reaching Colombia, had been bewitched by the licentious life of the island. Clara Luz lived there with her son until his father—her lover, a rich businessman from Bogotá—decided that the time had come to give some polish to his illegitimate child before the island turned him into a crude peasant. A short while after Sybil realized she had fallen in love for the first time, Clara Luz and Santiago moved to Miami, the very city she had chosen to live in when she was grown up, that one time she left the island. What a coincidence. By the time she managed to muffle her stubborn ego sufficiently to acknowledge that her feelings for him were true and dared to seek him out to tell him what she felt, Santiago had already left the island and was not going to return till the following year, on his summer vacations. Sybil would have to wait a whole year, but she did not waste her time while she waited. She dreamed of his kisses and embraces every night. God, how corny that sounds! She was only a child, not even eleven, and since television had not reached the island yet, there was no apparent way she could have imagined what it would be like to hug and kiss a man. Could it be that love was something so innate and essential that she did not have to learn about it because she already knew? It was as though her body was made of love, and not just any love, but the most passionate and alive kind. She would close her eyes while she embraced the pillow, which magically transported her into Santiago's arms and they would smile at each other again.

That whole year of eternal waiting finally passed and that evening, in front of the house of Aurita and Octavio, life offered my greatest opportunity. There were ten us, in a circle, playing spin the bottle. Someone made the glass bottle spin in the centre of the circle on the tamped earth and when it stopped, it clearly pointed to Santiago and myself. The penalty was for both of us. With a mocking, malicious smile, Edgar, one of the Peréz boys, shouted to Santiago.

"Kiss her on the mouth!"

Everyone laughed and agreed with the penalty. Without yet understanding that the power of wishing had turned my dream into a reality and the universe had become my Aladdin's lamp, I was already dead scared and beyond myself with nerves. With a mad longing, I had already imagined kissing Santiago, and although this was only a modest sample, the kiss came true. My face turned so red, I felt that the blood in my cheeks was burning. Even my fingernails trembled, I think. I was so nervous, my lips forgot how to smile; my facial muscles weren't up to it. Everyone was looking at me. My vulnerability was obvious to all my friends, and there wasn't one instant when I was in control. Anything might have happened when all of a sudden that youngster of fourteen stood up, in a very decisive way, turned to me, and took hold of my face as though it were a fragile and costly piece of porcelain. He closed his eyes and bequeathed me one of those kisses you only hear about in fairy stories about princes and damsels. It was my first kiss, the most tender kiss I could imagine. For the first time, I felt protected and loved by a man. There was no way I could forget the image that had just been graven on my memory. In his innocent way, Santiago stamped a love on me which would stay latent until the moment came to reactivate it in order to finish the story.

Betrys accidentally found out what had happened, on one of those nights, so common there, when there was no electricity and the sticky heat kept everyone from sleeping. Sybil and her big sister were complete opposites; Betrys was outgoing and blunt. She was telling her about her new boyfriend, a guitarist who studied at the boy's school in front of that of the nuns. Now, she wanted to become a famous singer and go on a world tour with him. After listening to her sister's ambitious plans, hers seemed so insignificant that she plucked up the courage to confide her own secret, down to Santiago's name. With the bubbly personality she had, Betrys could not keep it to herself. At breakfast the next day, before she went to school, she told the whole family.

I felt betrayed and from then on, felt very ashamed when anyone brought up the subject. I did not understand why they laughed at my love. I thought they were laughing at me because I didn't deserve to be loved and nobody told me it was a mistake to think like that. My sister even invented a funny song, singing it over and over again so that I never forgot it: "Santi-Santi, Cuchi-Cuchi, Ala-Ala, Bugalú."

She sang it every time she wanted to tease her, so long as Dylan was not nearby to defend her from the thoughtless cruelty of her big sister. Revealing the secret had a harsh effect on her, because, being so insecure, she was afraid that her brother Glyn would tell the story to his close friend, Octavio, who would then pass it on to Santiago. He would make fun of her like all the others.

> "What a presumptuous little girl, with such high expectations. I give her a kiss in a silly kid's game and she has to fall in love with me!"

He was sure to think of her like that, but that was only her version, since there was no way she could know what Santiago really thought about it. Sybil grew up without having guides who might have helped her to strengthen her self-esteem. There was no one and nothing around to make her feel that she deserved all the love life had in store for her. Her ego continued to crush her illusions and her ability to understand that she was the creator of her external reality still remained dormant.

She saw Santiago for the last time on that morning when she and Aura, without telling Cassandra, decided to see him off at the airport. His vacations were over and he was returning to Miami on the same Aerocóndor flight she herself had taken, some years before, to visit her grandparents in Wales, only now the plane was an ultra-modern turbine jet. They caught the bus on the road in front of the hotel and had to run two blocks to reach the airport in time. Sweaty and agitated, they climbed to the terrace on the second floor, where they managed to see him before he got onto the plane. The boarding announcement had already been made, and they were not sure whether they had got there in time, so they were excited when they caught a distant sight of him, walking along the runway to the plane's stairway, and they shouted as hard as they could.

"Santii!"

He stopped, turned around, and saw their lifted arms and waving hands frantically saying farewell. His only response was to smile, bring his hand to his mouth, and blow a kiss, staring at them for a few final seconds. All in all and despite her injured self-esteem, she felt that he only had eyes for her and the wind-borne kiss sealed an agreement between them. It was if his gaze had sent a telepathic message, telling her that someday they would meet again. Without knowing how or why, she once more felt loved. That seemed to be the end of her innocent love story; an image of a male figure with jet-black hair in a military crew cut and the deep gaze of his black eyes. She would hold onto it till the end, a loose strand still to be tied.

***

After that loss, she could not restrain a growing feeling that something was missing in her life, that there was an urgent need to fill the gap. Still a student at the nuns' school, the older she got, the more she realized that that fleeting childhood visit to the United States and Europe had left a deep mark on her. Its pull was so strong that by the age of fourteen, she was already sure that her next step would be to leave the island for destinations still unknown. At that time, there were no personal computers, much less the Internet. There was only black-and-white television, which was rarely seen because of the power cuts (and was not very interesting anyway). It was canned, broadcasting programs that had been taped some seasons before and were repeated several times each week. The life she lived was boring and uninspiring, as if she needed a sufficient store of such disappointment to fuel her wish to emigrate. Her father's books, full of photos of magical places like ancient Egypt, Greece, Mesopotamia, Assyria and the like, plus the *Encyclopedia Britannica* which he had brought back from one of his trips to help his three children do their homework, were her true sources of inspiration. They helped her to understand how much was going on in the world beyond the island, so far from her sight. That great beyond was the next thing she set herself to discover. Her life was always full of contradictions. While her father encouraged her to study, learn, and sharpen her curiosity, her over-protective mother acted like a brake that stopped her from going forward. She had slowly been losing the happiness innate to her soul. Her spark was being snuffed. She no longer found her childhood joys and didn't know how to recover them. She felt cut off from that spiritual world to which she had once belonged.

Having lost Santiago was no help. So many unsaid words remained in my heart along with so many unrealized dreams. Insecure as I was, my mind interpreted that silence between us when things didn't work out, as rejection and scorn. Not knowing where I was heading for, I felt completely abandoned inside. I had stopped being a girl. The rhythm of my life was beginning to change and I didn't know how to flow with it. It was the start of a very confusing stage. It was like having put on glasses with dirty lenses, smeared with grease, and then finding, once I cleaned them, that they were even dirtier!

***

Many things around her had changed. Aura, her inseparable friend, had moved from her rented house in San Luis at last. Her parents had done well and built a comfortable house in another neighborhood on the north of the island, near the airport. With the move, there arose an unbridgeable gap between them, different realities which prevented them from finding anything in common again. But another friend soon filled Aura's place. Maya had arrived from Medellín and moved with her family to a house on Rocky Cay, very close to the hotel. Jacinto, one of the Pérez boys, introduced them and from the start, their hearts connected. They shared a liking for racing bikes and skateboards, and the favorite books of the two budding philosophers with an insatiable thirst for knowledge were *Jonathan Livingston Seagull, Illusions,* and *The Prophet.* A while later, Azalea would join them to form a trio, her father, Joaquín Gallego, a taxi-driver from the island, was building his house on a lot he had bought near the hotel. They had just moved in, and Azalea was only a year younger than Maya and Sybil. The three were to spend many idle hours together, seated on the jetty in front of the hotel, while they dreamed about their future selves. They liked each other just as they were. It did not matter who they were or where they had come from, nothing was expected in return.

When I finally attained a perspective on us, I understood what Aurita had meant in my life. She and I never had a decisive fight. Our time together simply reached its expiration date and the moment came when it wore out and had to be thrown into the garbage bin because it was no longer of use. It was very strange; despite living on such a small island and studying at the same school, we never ran into each other again.

Another big change became evident. Sybil had become a rebel without a cause. It was not due to obstinacy but her need to leap up to the next step. She was an intelligent and persistent young lady who stuck to her plan of leaving the island, so she continued to be one of the school's best students and won prizes for it at the end of each year. Her strong sense of responsibility was her way of proving to her mother that she was ready to fly on her own, ready for her parents to give her the chance to show them she could. Having no other way to justify herself, Cassandra had to accept. She fell in with Sybil's idea of sending her to live for a year in Medellín, at the home of her cousin Cordelia.

It was a very critical time for my parents; 70 percent of the hotel, as originally planned, was already built and the business was not bringing the results they had wagered on for so many years. They owed an enormous amount to the banks that had lent them the money for it and my siblings were already studying at university in the United States. Turning them into professionals was the priority.

Somewhere along the way, Dylan gave up; he felt that his hotel had failed. One of her tenderest memories was seeing him in the garden with the lawn mower, his turned-brim straw hat shading his red, sweating face. She also remembered the enormous pitcher of iced shandy that would give way to all the whiskey he drank when he finished work in the evening to forget, for a while, what was so painful to accept. He had built a work of art. Every detail of that hotel had been created with so much love it was impossible to grasp why the story did not have a happy ending. In addition to being an engineer and architect, Dylan was a plumber, electrician, and decorator. He even acted as bellhop and redcap for the guests who arrived in those charter flights that reached the island in the wee hours of the morning during the high season. In short, the hotel was him and he was the hotel. For her part, Cassandra had already finished her term at the intendancy. It could not be said that she came out unscathed, considering the criticisms of her political enemies, who blamed her for worsening the ills which afflicted the island. She would never erase the bitter disappointment this left in her. In the midst of all these unwarranted accusations of corruption, it was ironic to see her desperately seeking a buyer for the hotel to solve the financial problems of the whole family. For Sybil, it was always clear that her father was the dreamer and artist of the family, while her mother was the realist, especially when it came to planning the budget.

I will never forget the car my parents drove at that time. It was an old, sky-blue Chevrolet Impala station wagon whose bodywork was so rusty from the salty air that I didn't know what to say to my classmates when they asked me when we were going to buy a new car. At that time, thinking about what people would say affected me so much it made my life miserable. The station wagon met its end one day, when the brakes went and my mother crashed into a coconut tree on a plot of wild land along the road on her way to the hotel. Nothing happened to her but I never saw her so furious. She reached the hotel after walking barefoot for several miles, high heels in hand, looked for my father and, amidst insults, told him it was all his fault. It was a total write-off. They took the station wagon from that scrubland directly to the town dump. In that period, when there was no environmental awareness at all, the waste which arrived there wound up being tossed into the sea.

Everything around her was very discouraging. It was hard to hold on to her optimism when the whole reality around her felt alien. It was very distressing to hear her parents arguing in that dead-end street they had put themselves into. Sybil longed to immerse herself again in the peace and silence of her childhood, which were now gone. Her days were increasingly filled with problems she had not asked for. She had to leave. She could not put up with the same old things anymore.

If my mother hadn't decided to send me away, I think I would have been yet another of those teenage girls who run away from home all the time. I was desperate. I was leading my life in an atmosphere so dense I now understood why I wasn't able to hear my angel anymore. There was so much noise and garbage in my head! My angel had not gone; it was simply that with my mind so polluted I was no longer aware of him. He spoke to me and I couldn't hear him. I felt my parents' failure as though it were my own; the misfortunes of others were contagious.

But the plan came to fruition at last; she was to live for a year in the house of her mother's cousin. It turned out to be a resounding triumph for her. Maxine, Cordelia's daughter, was three years older. She looked like Olivia Newton John, who had become her favorite actress at the time after seeing her alongside John Travolta in *Grease* at least a thousand times. God willing, the move would help her. She was sad about what was happening to her; interacting with the external reality had worn away all the magic of her inner one. She had turned into a little lady, and without knowing how it occurred, the little lady had become a caterpillar like any other. The countdown had started. Could that young caterpillar someday transform herself into the beautiful butterfly she was meant to be?

THE ORANGE OF THE BITTERSWEET CITRIC

For hours on end, Sybil would rake over what she had lived through, trying to find the roots of her feelings in the infinite ocean of the subconscious. She grew up feeling that she was not important. It wasn't that her parents did not love her, because they always gave her all their love. It was simply that her dreams never seemed sufficiently interesting for them to encourage and support her inner life.

> "I'd like you to marry a nice man, a millionaire who'll give you everything you want and make you happy."

That is what she usually heard from Cassandra, as if the only way she could be happy were to have a man in her life. When she was a little girl, her angel had taught her about independence, but her mother had fixed ideas and only spoke to her about depending on someone. It was not her fault; she was just another victim of the society of her time and place. She herself had been the woman who depended on Dylan and she could not teach her daughter anything different.

My dream wasn't to get married. I wanted to play electric guitar in an all-girl band and so I spent two years studying the guitar. I wanted to be a painter and so I spent my spare time doing oil paintings of the landscape where I had grown up. I wanted to be a writer and so I kept a notebook in my bag where I wrote down what I felt every day. But despite preparing myself for those dreams, there was no way I could reach them, because none of it had any value in the eyes of my mother. They were the silly fantasies of her youngest daughter. The "dreamiest of my three children" was how she described me to her friends. She was going to make sure that my creative passions would only be the hobbies of a married lady once the marvelous millionaire turned up, the one she had long had in mind as a suitable husband for me.

She gradually kept losing her self-esteem. Though a number of people told her that she was the best student, with the prettiest eyes and most radiant smile, "the slender, good-looking one", and so forth, there was no way that Sybil could believe in things her mind had not absorbed. The manner in which she perceived herself left much to desire. She was not able to recognize her worth, because no one had taught her how to do it. Her father gave her his unconditional love and that eased her soul, but it was always a silent encouragement; he was a man of few words. Her mother wished the best for her, but from the standpoint of her own experience, never paid much attention to her daughter's innate creativity, so that its power waned because they did not teach her how to feel it. Little by little, it disappeared, that power which her angel had fought so hard to bequeath to her. There came a day when she no longer felt able to follow the teachings of that angel. The world clearly had no place for angels or at least she did not see them anymore. One day like any other, she admitted defeat and decided to start fitting herself into the mold they had prepared her for, even though it did not respond to the promptings of her heart.

The Medellín stage of her life only served to strip away more layers of her self-esteem. She continued to live in this world, where others had the leading role while she remained invisible. She worshipped her cousin Maxine, simply because she considered her to be perfect. She wanted to be like her; she was the center of her world. Maxine had successfully begun her modeling career and everyone in her family was happy about the prospect of her becoming popular and famous. Cordelia, a woman who was still beautiful despite being overweight, fully supported and encouraged her daughter. She was reliving youthful dreams which had been cut short. She had wanted to be a beauty queen, but dropped that to marry Maxine's father. This complicitous relationship between mother and daughter would be useful to Sybil when she compared Cordelia with her mother and herself with Maxine. How different their values were! Confused, she asked herself whether some were better than others. She felt at ease with her new family, and grateful every day about having achieved her goal thanks to their helping hand to escape from her labyrinth. While her mother paid Cordelia a monthly sum to cover her living expenses, no one could put a price on the new air she was able to breathe. Although it harmed her self-esteem, she had peace at a time when her parents were still trying to break out of the vicious and addictive circle in which they both lived. Despite being what she had wished for, the year she spent in Medellín was an encounter with loneliness.

From one day to the next, her cousin had turned into a butterfly and was no longer interested in the caterpillar who shared her room, almost like her shadow. Parties, fashion shows, photo shoots, and people who were "in" did not fit in with the cousin who lived in her home as a refugee. Ironically, what saved her were the school vacations, when she would return to the island she had wanted to flee from. It is often said that you do not know what you have until you lose it. There, she had left behind her best friends, the ones of her own age, provincial girls. Maya and Azalea gave her an injection of their pure essence. They were the lifebelt that enabled her to keep afloat in the waters of an inconsiderate world.

When she returned, she used to think of Santiago. It was as though a tiny piece of that love had remained there so that she would never forget the unforgettable. They never met up but he continued to visit the island, accompanied by his girlfriend. To see them at a distance, without his being aware of her presence, acted as a further confirmation that her ego had always been right; she did not deserve that love and that her angel had been a liar who fed her illusions, though who knows why! One thing was clear: she had to forget those angelical voices once and for all. She was too grown up to keep believing in silly things like that. The fever of the 1980s was about to begin. Those years would be full of magic and innocent craziness. Sybil was already friendly with a lot of boys and girls who lived on the north of the island, where the action was—parties and fun. Maxine and two other cousins who lived in Santa Marta, Miranda and Serena, stayed on the island with her for a few weeks during the summer and Christmas holidays. Miraculously, her parents still just about managed to keep their ship afloat, steering against wind and tide, so luckily, there was always a room at the hotel for her and her cousins to stay in. The house was too small for so many rowdy teenage girls who were full of irrepressibly high spirits.

By then, we were all pretty grown-up but my mother still insisted on over-protecting me. My cousins were allowed to go to parties on their own, but not me. How was such unfairness possible? We were supposed to be spending the vacations together, without my being excluded from anything. My rebellious streak flared up. It was clear I would find a way to defy my mother.

She had a brilliant idea. That night, the four cousins decided to put Sybil's plan into action. Since she was the oldest, Maxine could come and go as she liked. Damián, her boyfriend, had arrived around 8:30 PM to take her to one of the parties at Leonidas' house, which were the best. San Luis was so far from the other districts there it was like an island in the middle of another one. While Maxine and Damián were on their way to Leonidas' place, Sybil, Miranda, and Serena, already in pajamas, said goodnight to Cassandra and Dylan, who were talking on the terrace of the house. As it happened every night, they spent a few minutes telling them about the day's happenings—their outing to the beach and window shopping trip downtown—and then, each holding her glass of water, they wished them goodnight and went to their room in the hotel to sleep. As soon as they closed the door of room 11 on the first floor, they began to change out of their pajamas at lightning speed. It was already 9:30 PM and they were going to be picked up at 10:00. Maxine had arranged for someone to drive them to the party. To avoid suspicions, they had to dress and put on a little makeup in the dark, and quickly leave by the back part of the hotel, so that Isidoro, the old and sleepy watchman, would not catch them red-handed. While they were going along the path through the bushes that took them to the pick-up point on the main road, Sybil felt like a character in one of the adventure stories of her favorite writer, Enid Blyton. She did not doubt that the crazy idea which had occurred to her and was now being put into action with her cousins was the result of years of reading and rereading the feats of the five characters which that author had created for the sole delight of her most faithful reader.

We covered our mouths with one hand so that our mischievous howls of laughter wouldn't be heard now that we were in action. From a distance, my parents' voices could be heard. They were still sitting on the terrace while we walked through the vague darkness, exhilarated, holding the shoes we were going to dance in so the heels wouldn't be damaged. That night, it was Nemo's turn to collect us, a friend from the island who had tapes of the best music in his car. Kool & the Gang, and Earth, Wind & Fire were the sensations then, American bands who made me fly without the need of drugs or sex. Maxine had instructed Nemo beforehand to slow the car down once he got close to the pick-up point and switch the lights on and off a few times. When the signal was given, we rushed out of the bushes, our hearts beating like mad, and immediately jumped into the car, where we finally were able to laugh out loud.

Meanwhile, back in their room, pillows had been stuffed under the sheets in the shape of their bodies, in case Cassandra decided to enter and make sure that everything was under control in its dimly lit interior.

Our feat caused a sensation; everyone was talking about it at the party. It was a spice that made everything taste better. I didn't ask for permission to go out anymore. I didn't need to. I had been looking for my freedom in the wrong place, my mother's mind, when it had always been waiting for me in my own heart. I had defeated her suffocating rigidity. I had made my own reality more flexible, opening it up to make my own choices and take care of myself. What a critical moment of liberation that was! At first sight, it seemed to be a matter of licentiousness, not freedom, but it all resulted from my innocence. The magical formula did not include sex or drugs. At that time, in San Andrés, you could still go crazy like that without harming yourself and everyone became my accomplice, because they could see how ingenuous it was. The housekeepers at the hotel, the parents of my friends who held the parties, the owners of the two or three discotheques in vogue, they all knew my mother, but they seemed willing to make a tacit agreement with me. They only smiled and kept my secret.

Who knows how many times they escaped. Each night had its own mark and at least one story to tell. Following her urge to write about everything she experienced, she kept a diary where she gave a blow-by-blow account of each and every one of those exciting nights. Maxine bawled her out for it several times, reminding her what might happen if her confessions fell into the hands of Cassandra. And, as if knowing how to read the future, Maxine spoke like a fortune-teller with her crystal ball; one day the diary would vanish without a trace. A few months later, when Leticia—her favorite housekeeper and accomplice at the hotel—managed to ring her in Medellín. She soon learned that a few minutes after she had gone to the airport for the return flight, her confidant had come across the diary among the sheets she had thrown in with the dirty laundry, and to prevent a world-shaking disaster, decided to burn it. At last, she could breathe freely again after so many sleepless nights expecting the worst; at times, she thought

Cassandra had already found it and wondered why she was so silent and calm. After the anguish of that uncertainty, her wish to become a writer all but disappeared. Maxine was right, she thought then. The chance that her adventures might become public knowledge wasn't worth the risk; they were private property.

***

Medellín awakened the nomadic spirit of a girl who never wanted to stop roaming from then on. The situation at the hotel was fast approaching its expected end and Cassandra was making preparations to transfer her frail and wretched nest to Bogotá. While they were going ahead, Sybil had to move to her godfather's house in the capital ahead of her parents, in time for the beginning of the next school year. In this second stage, she no longer knew if this business of remaining a refugee fit in with her goals. For the moment, she only understood that life had granted her the wish to leave her island by quitting her of a home of her own. Without being aware of it, she was forced to experience the everyday reality of the uprooted. It was her first lesson in material detachment and would be very useful later on. Moving to that enormous city was the next step; the world would doubtless continue to enlarge itself as she continued to experience more and more. Her longing to expand her inner world meant that her outer one would follow the same pace. Her environment grew bigger and bigger, both in size and the possibilities it awakened in her restless mind. Bogotá had more inhabitants, more contamination, and more violence; what better laboratory for an innocent student of life who had to keep toughening her delicate skin, which still exuded the salty sweat of a tropical island?

I kept to my path as a wanderer. I learned to observe happiness, without really possessing much of my own. Despite having a family, the concept was distant and remote. At that stage, I felt what the millions of orphans in the world must feel. I cried all the time in a small bathroom, which was the only place where I could lock myself in without causing notice. At times, there was no room in my heart for all those unknown emotions which welled up in me, like the rainwater which leaks through an old, moldy roof full of holes. I couldn't control them. My transparent, expressive eyes sometimes drowned in sadness. I often asked myself what I had done to deserve this role of a tiny and insignificant human being. It seemed that there wasn't the slightest bit of love set aside for me in this dimension, not even in its most miserable corner. When I woke up, I would lie there for a few minutes, spread out on a strange bed and look through the window, with the half-open curtains of virgin wool. I watched that dark, cold dawn approach to show me the dreary scene outside, the one that was supposed to inspire me then and in some way fill me with hope.

She did not only worry about her own life; the change in her parents' lives intensified her sadness. For them, it was the end of everything and the beginning of whatever fate had in store. She was full of uncertainty, a lonely adolescent girl who felt empty without anything being able to give her a bit of happiness. She had already started at her new high school on the outskirts of the city. The school bus picked up her at 5:30 in the morning for a two-and-a-half hour journey. At times, the ride was even longer, depending on the absurd traffic, jammed at times by junk men's carts which moved at the pace of a tired, old mule.

None of this was living up to my dreams. For me, it was ironic how, when I actually lived the life I'd previously imagined, it did not meet many of my expectations. I still did not know how to express my wishes. It was as though the recipe lacked a few key ingredients and I only became aware of it after tasting the dish, when it was already cooked and too late to correct things.

Seated on that bus, looking through the half-open window, back and forth, day after day, for the next three years, she would witness the narrow, unjust world that passed by, a manifestation of the collective unconscious. That beautiful country in which she had been born displayed its spirit, devastated by violence and indifference. The upheaval was felt on every corner and every face she saw wandering along the dusty sidewalks eaten away by rottenness and corruption. The nuns at her provincial school had not taught her about this world that she now watched, live and direct. She felt cheated and resentful. They had not taught her the truth about her country's social problems, about the children who learned to survive on the streets long before they could speak and walk. Kids were happy to be given a few coins by one generous pedestrian or another. Their faces, dirtied by soot and snot, framed lost, sightless eyes. Their cheeks were red from so much cold and their stiff, greasy hair was nauseating. All this made Sybil's heart want to burst with helplessness and frustration.

But my own life wasn't much better. Those children and I had something in common; the world in which we lived was lacking in love and understanding. I don't know whether it was my subconscious wish to express my solidarity with them that decided me to endure the same hunger. All I know is that, in my new city, I learned for the first time what it meant to fill your empty belly with air instead of food. My poor mother; if she had known what her super-protected daughter went through when she returned from school around 4:00 in the afternoon to find that that there wasn't so much as a leftover crumb of lunch for me in my godfather's house! I'd buy some junk food in the school cafeteria to take with me, so that I'd survive till the evening meal, but the splitting headaches I had in those days were surely the result of my bad eating habits. No one cared or asked whether I had eaten or not. For the next six months, I got by on packets of potato chips and corn crisps full of preservatives.

From the moment she left her enchanted island, she had come across nothing other than small instances of the taste of hell on earth. She couldn't understand why she could no longer be inspired by the starry sky above her. It was supposedly the same everywhere, though it was now covered by storm clouds or smog. Paradise had been left behind, the one she had had to lose in order to appreciate and find meaning in everything which was now only an illusion. Her mind had finally been presented with the contrast between the past and the present. Now she was able to compare. This stage represented the cutting of the umbilical cord which had connected her with the true world. The denseness of that city helped her to fully blind herself and begin to live in the same hypnotic state of those who now surrounded her. It was difficult to swim against the current at such a tender age. She did not have enough strength. It was a matter of learning to survive. Like the streets kids who made such a strong impression on her, she would only survive by going with the flow.

So I began to depend on the God that the nuns had injected into my veins like serum. With that bearded old man at least, I could unburden myself on a bench in some empty neighborhood church, and ask him what I could not ask of anyone else.

She never made any real friends in her new high school. Her classmates had studied together since they were kids, and she never felt that she fit in. They never understood the very different world in which she had grown up, and she did not know how to explain it to them. She felt like the ugly duckling and regarded the fact that she was different from them as a defect, not a virtue. Her memories were all that kept her imagination alive, that and her talent for smiling. She had put the suitcase in which she brought her things from Medellín in a corner of the bedroom she now shared with one of her godfather's daughters. Everything that mattered to her now was there: her school uniforms, her pajamas, her two weekend outfits, and a little red box with the photos that kept her from losing her way. They had been taken during her last vacation on the island. With a premonition that her father's dream was near its end, she had captured all its scenes on her small hand camera. She wanted to fix them forever, to keep her heart beating. Photos of different aspects of the landscape, of the sun and moon, of that sea and sky which only seemed like a trick now, deceiving her mind into believing that what never was had been lived.

Those pictures kept my ability to create fantastic realities in an embryonic state, my ability to be happy, though I wasn't now. They were like switches that activated certain chemicals in my brain which showed me the way to go forward. And so, I kept walking a little more. The hotel was finally sold, and I didn't know whether to feel relieved or depressed about it. I knew that it would mean the start of a new stage for my family, but I also knew that the whole of a brief past which helped me so much to hold onto a sense of belonging was buried there. My parents arrived in Bogotá, and after a couple of decades out of the job market, my father went back to work. It was a middling, ill-paid position in the oil industry, the same one that had brought him to

Cartagena as a daring young adventurer from Wales. It was clear that he was starting from zero again. The money from the hotel only covered their debts, with nothing left over. He still had three children to raise. My siblings hadn't finished university yet and I had two years to go before getting my high school diploma.

They rented a small, minimally furnished apartment near the Campín stadium, with no spare room and quite a few deficiencies. There was not even a bed for Sybil, who had to sleep on the couch in the living room, while the small, round dining-room table became the desk where she did her homework. How unpleasant those memories are! Her nights on that sofa where she could not even turn over became a spell in a madhouse when she caught chicken pox. In her desperation, she could not stop scratching the sores, so they left permanent scars. She had got her family back but still felt homeless, her soul stored in the suitcase that was still thrown into any old corner. Perhaps it was part of the plan to make her understand that the real home was inside oneself, the same lesson her angel had taught her and she—in her stubborn disbelief—had rejected. She would have to pay tears of blood to prepare herself, much later in life, for the path that would again lead her back to that elusive place.

***

I was so ashamed to show people the apartment where I lived that I never invited the few friends from San Andrés who studied in Bogotá to visit me there. I don't know what made me feel so bad about living under the modest roof my parents willingly provided me with. It wasn't as though they'd murdered someone. They hadn't done anything but struggle against wind and tide to get ahead and little by little, they achieved it. I don't know where those stupid complexes came from. I didn't ask for them, but I could not stop them from torturing my mind. When I compared myself with other kids, I felt inferior. I thought that all of them were better off and had more than me. I was infected the disease of the poor, the syndrome of thinking so much of external hardships that I forgot my inner wealth.

Her self-esteem kept going downhill, and the circumstances in which she lived did not help her much to break out of the vicious circle in which she was trapped. The part of the city where she lived was a depressing commercial area and her apartment was the penthouse of an old corner building of four stories which housed the neighborhood's most popular fried chicken place. The nights there were troubled by the noise and smells that penetrated the broken windows of the apartment, which did not keep out the cold and contamination even when they were closed. Having to get up for a shower at 5:00 in the morning did not help the situation. The electric heater was so small that the little stream of water did not even become lukewarm and did nothing against the cold air, which gave her goose bumps. She would have her breakfast and run down the stairs to the spot, two blocks away, where she would stand on the mean sidewalk of an unfriendly city to wait for the school bus. She was mugged more than once at that miserable bus stop. The fear and lack of confidence she emitted made her an easy prey for any skilled vagrant.

That day, I decided to put on the ring my grandmother Anwen had left me. She had died two years before, when my family was in one of its worst financial crises, and only my father could go to her burial. When he returned from Wales, he brought me that ring which she'd wanted me to have as a remembrance of her. Its value was more spiritual than material. Two street kids more alert than I grabbed me, one in front, the other behind, and shouted that they wanted the ring. While the one in front threatened to cut my face with the Gillette razor blade hidden in his palm, the one behind roughly pinned down my right forearm, showing me a knife that almost made me faint.

Her eyes fill with tears of disillusion whenever she remembers how the cowardly people passing by in slow motion watched the scene out of the corner of their eyes while they crossed to the other sidewalk, and the passengers in the buses who stared through the windows with a morbid curiosity. They not only stole her late grandmother's ring that day, they also stripped her of her dignity. She wet her pants and shoes out of fright, and drenched in shame, had to return to the apartment to shower and change her clothes. The old saying puts it well: God squeezes but does not strangle. Sybil's life could not have been worse. Everything stayed so dark that the only possibility was that there would soon be a little light at the end of the tunnel to restore her faith in the future.

At last, the disease of deprivation began to subside. Dylan soon did well and one day the opportunity which they needed so much arose. He was offered an important executive post at a multinational oil company that was beginning to operate in Colombia. It meant he would have to travel to remote places. The job was dangerous and risky, but the money would bring stability to the whole family and be more than enough for his three children to finish their education. After talking it over with Cassandra, Dylan quickly accepted the offer. The old penthouse that smelled of fried chicken was left behind, and they moved into a very pretty apartment in the Rosales district, which Dylan's company paid for. Sybil now had her own bedroom and toilet, and there were even two spare rooms where her siblings could stay when they visited them on their vacations. She was so excited she could hardly believe what her eyes saw now. The big picture windows looked out on a waterfall surrounded by pines and eucalyptuses. She could breathe pure air again and feel the peace which been missing from her heart for so long. Her prayers and supplications to the bearded God which the nuns had taught her to worship and fear had brought results. It was not long before the sharp tongues of her parents' so-called friends, who found no joy in the good fortune of others, sarcastically dubbed them "the Carringtons"—after the family in *Dynasty*, the American television series that was very popular at the time and depicted the life of oil millionaires in Denver.

Despite the envy of others, everything drastically changed from one day to the next. Suddenly, everything began to flow and we were all realizing the dreams we had set for ourselves. With his new responsibilities, my father was happy at work. My mother's mind was calm again, now that she no longer had any debts and everything was under control, the way she liked it. My brother and sister would soon finish their university courses and were beginning to work out their wedding plans. I was finishing my last year at high school, longing to graduate so that I'd be able to study anthropology in the United States. Yes, it was that science I was going to study, the one I'd pored over in my father's books when I was a girl. It would enable me to understand the vastness of the world. I was going to study all of its cultures, without missing the most remote one, and even better, dig up and discover the remote past which continued to intrigue me so much. I had a feeling that it was there I would find the answers to the endless questions in my heart. I wanted my diploma to say I was an explorer, but the universities did not give you a degree in that, so I picked the one subject which most resembled it.

Dylan, above all, continued to support her on all fronts. The resounding no she had gotten from her mother when she wanted to be a singer, guitarist, painter, or writer was now a thing of the past. She had finally found the external approval she had longed for so much, while she would be studying something that excited her. Dylan called himself a would-be anthropologist, so he would be very proud to see his daughter pick up what he had left off in his youth. *The precision with which life was taking care of things for me is scary,* Sybil thought. If her father had not gotten that new job at exactly the right moment, everything in her present life would have been different. It was as though, step by step, a benevolent invisible hand were presenting her with every tool that she needed—neither a minute too soon nor a minute too late but always at the right moment. With only a couple of months to go before she graduated from high school, the company gave her father a bonus that would cover the expenses of sending her to university. Thanks to her great ally, her father, her plans were turning into reality. How could she guess at the plans her mother was subconsciously laying down at the same time. Her mother had such high expectations for her daughter, even before she was born. Sybil still did not have a boyfriend, although she had fallen for one or another of her friends from San Andrés, without it turning into a serious relationship. The poverty and restrictions that had filled her recent past had made her more grown up than most girls of her age. They had not embittered her or made her into a pessimist, but she was too serious and determined to wait for a real boyfriend. Although she did not feel attractive, she was, both within and without. The mixture of races in her blood had produced a harmonious result, although vanity was not part of her makeup.

The night before, my parents had gone to a formal reception at the home of Domingo Obregón, an old friend of my father. The two men hadn't seen each other since the time they both lived in Cartagena, long before my parents moved to San Andrés, so it was a very special occasion. Sebastián, Domingo's eldest son, was at the party. He had just returned to the country after graduating from a prestigious university in the United States and was now running several of his father's companies. My mother didn't stop talking to me about this marvelous, good-looking young man she had met the night before, while I, indifferent to her story, sat at the breakfast table, stirring my hot chocolate, with my legs crossed and right foot playing with my slipper.

"How old is he?"

"Twenty-six, and I told him about you. I said I had a very pretty daughter with green eyes and tanned skin—and no boyfriend."

I felt completely exploited. My mother had no right to auction me off like that! But it was too late to undo things. At that moment, I was angry but kept quiet as I always did, out of respect for her. Maybe it was all right that she had punctured my girlish dreams, but wanting to pick a boyfriend for me when I was just short of majority age was going too far. For the love of God, how could she know what I wanted in a man! But, still, my mother had also told him that in one month, I would be going to Boston to study. I was pretty sure that this Sebastián guy wouldn't get very enthusiastic about the daughter of this indiscreet lady, not when she was practically on the plane. How wrong I was. My mother had played the role of Cupid too well. Three days after the reception at his father's house, Sebastián called to ask me to dinner that very night, and out of curiosity, I accepted without giving it any thought. As soon as I hung up, I realized I didn't even have anything to wear. I was seventeen and never went out at night. My mother was very strict about my going out on my own. Those nocturnal escapades on San Andrés had only been a small-town game. On this occasion, since it was with the son of Domingo Obregón, she was happy to give her permission. The next thing I remember, we were in a nearby store, buying the whole of the outfit I would wear that night. My God, why had I said yes? When I looked at myself in the mirror, I felt horrible. That very day, I had chosen to squeeze out my pimples, the roots of my hair weren't dyed and I hadn't painted my nails.

The trick she hit upon to bolster her ego was to remember that she would be leaving for Boston in a month. Sebastián would soon be a thing of the past and it would not matter how ugly she had been that night.

He picked her up in his black Porsche at the appointed time. She was still stunned by the quickness with which the day had unfolded. It was such a new experience. She knew nothing about etiquette or glamour and to top it off, had bought a skirt much too large for a beginner with no idea of fashion. When Sebastián politely opened the car door for her, beckoning her to sit down, she tried to pretend she was experienced, but her heel got caught in her skirt and she tripped. It must have been obvious to him that Sybil was only a diamond in the rough.

The night was really chaotic. After the clumsy incident with the skirt, my inner demons completely took hold of my brain, which made me feel even more insecure. We arrived at the French restaurant Sebastián had chosen. The menu was in French, so, ashamed to ask the waiter and reveal my ignorance, I ordered a filet mignon – me, who didn't eat meat! But that was nothing. Before serving the meat, the waiter asked me what I wanted to drink and the first thing that sprang to my mind was a Dubonnet, because I remembered the times when Fabricio, the barman of my father's hotel, had taught me about liqueurs. They didn't have Dubonnet, so I said I'd have the same as Sebastián, Black Label whiskey on the rocks. It was the first time I drank whiskey. Why the devil hadn't Fabricio ever warned me that you should drink that potent stuff with caution! After dinner, we went to a discotheque where we met up with two couples who were Sebastián's friends. Giza, it was called, the best in the city and my mouth was still agape.

Trying to keep up with her new, sophisticated friend, Sybil drank her fourth whiskey and began to feel sick. Sheer instinct enabled her to reach the ladies' room, where she had to lie down on the floor stained with piss in an effort to cope with her chronic low blood pressure (which, she was certain, was already below zero). She lay there, alongside the foul-smelling toilet, for nearly an hour or so it seemed to her. When she left the ladies' room, Sebastián was waiting at the bar with a worried look, but the others had already left, so it was a short night. She was so ashamed of herself by then that all she wanted to do was to get back to her bed and sleep off her drunkenness. Her head was full of all the mocking remarks she imagined Sebastián was silently uttering about her. He wouldn't call her again. The matter would not go any further.

My mother was right. Sebastián was an attractive man and lots of fun. My first impression hadn't been very favorable, because I saw him much older than he was. I was a little intimidated by his moustache and tweed blazer. What most attracted me was the simple fact that he was interested in me. Despite my mother's salesmanship, I felt flattered, important, perhaps for the first time, because such a man of the world had fixed his sights on me.

She suddenly realized that if it served for nothing else, the presence of this man in her life helped her to accept that she had been running away from love up to then for fear that the story of Santiago, her first love, might repeat itself. She had suffered so much from that unrequited love of a young girl she had decided—who knows how long ago—to shut all the doors and windows of her heart.

Despite that disastrous first night, I went out with Sebastián a few more times that Christmas before my trip to Boston. There was so much I didn't know, so much he could teach me. He wasn't outgoing but he made me laugh a lot, and I felt protected when I was with him. It was a feeling of safety I'd never had before. How good I felt next to him.

The feelings you have at seventeen are not the same as the ones at twenty-six, and much less so are a man's feelings the same as a woman's. Worried that she might be misinterpreting things, Sebastián had warned Sybil that they could only be friends. He was a bachelor, much sought after, with the world at his feet, the kind of man every woman desired. There was no way he would wait for her to grow up, arms crossed and without dating other women. In addition, he already knew how to adjust his emotional thermometer. Sebastián was not as much in love with her as she was in love with him, but she could no longer tell her heart to go backwards. If she were to fall in love, it had to be completely and this man seemed to be nothing short of perfect. Cassandra accompanied her to Boston, to help her settle into her new life as a university student in the country she had chosen to live in as a girl and was now before her, giving her a welcome. The harsh winter was no help and much less the inhospitable dormitory that smelled like a jail, where she spent her first term. Bogotá was cold, but snow never fell there. There was no need for all those layers of thick wool she had to wear to be able to walk across the campus without getting frozen. All the illusions she had built up for so many years were now within her reach, concrete at last: her course, the country, and all the other circumstances that would enable her to become independent and finally live life in her own way. But what was her way? God, what was happening to her? One may suppose that she must have been happy about all she had achieved, but she was not. The weeks passed and she soon had to admit to herself that she had left behind, down South, what now became her new priority. The subliminal programming she had received from her mother's collective unconscious now seemed much more powerful than anything else; she only thought about Sebastián. Without wanting to, she had fallen in love with the most marvelous man imaginable. Fine—only this time there wasn't even a need to imagine him; life had presented him on a silver platter!

She wanted to understand how her mind and her heart worked. None of this had been intentional; she wanted to understand how this whole change in her had become possible. Suddenly, all she saw was being married to that man, living in a beautiful house surrounded by trees and gardens, and raising a couple of little children. Her priorities had taken a radical 180-degree turn. The social aspirations others had for were now her new goal, while her studies and life in Boston receded into the background, without her knowing when or why. And it was not as though she had not tried hard. Eager to adapt, she rented a small studio for her second semester in Boston, where the living conditions were much better than those of the dormitory. But her heart remained in the south. Burger King, Baskin-Robbins, and the other novelties of gringo life exerted less of a pull on her than the idea of returning to Sebastián. When she finished her end-of-term finals in December, she packed her clothes and books and was soon aboard an American Airlines flight that would take her back to Bogotá for good. In the midst of this emotional whirlwind, she never stopped being disciplined and devoted to her studies. She had excellent grades. In her third semester, it was easy to transfer to one of Colombia's best universities. From the time she was a girl, she had an exceptionally organized mind. She knew what she wanted without being confused or indecisive about it. Once she set herself to something, she accomplished it, come what may. Her elder siblings still laughed when they remembered how, with notebook in hand to keep the accounts straight, she used to lend them money from her savings so that she could earn interest and buy something she craved. Too often for the young girl, her mother had refused to help, with the excuse that she did not have the money. She was persistent, focused, and stubborn. With her return to Bogotá, she would once more make use of those virtues disguised as defects.

Sebastián and I dated for three years, and though his womanizing led to fights, I was still madly in love with him. Quite simply, I didn't see any faults in him. How was I going to notice them if I didn't have another man to compare him to! He was my world and I admired him from top to bottom. Everything he did or said became law for me. He was nine years older than me and his influence on my personality was obvious. I adopted his values and principles. I wanted to please him in every way, I wanted to become his ideal woman. During those years, the diamond in the rough slowly polished itself until there came a day when he could see how I shone – and admit that he didn't have to look any further.

> "What am I waiting for, if everything I'm looking for is now in front of me? You meet all the conditions, Sybil. I've been so blind all these years since I met you. Let's get married!"

Sybil happily accepted Sebastián's proposal of marriage. There were no formal commitments. The wedding would be the following December. It was so unreal that she had to pinch herself. How was it possible that life continued to grant her all that she asked? Immature as she was, she did not realize she wasn't wishing well. Ignorant of the workings of the universal laws, she did not understand that she was continuing to create more of the same incomplete reality. It was like ordering a plate of spaghetti in your favorite Italian restaurant and being told by the waiter that you had to eat it without sauce. This time, with Sebastián, it would be different. His experience would help her to refine what she asked for, so that it would be served with cheese, sauce, and the rest. The dishes he ordered seemed to be perfect when put on the table. Her mother was as happy as she was and turned a deaf ear to Dylan's remarks. He was not in favor of the wedding; at the age of twenty-one, his daughter was not grown up enough to take such a step. He wanted her to know more of the world, now that he could do that for her. He did not agree but knew how determined Sybil was, so he only gave his consent on the condition that she would finish her course and graduate, despite being Señora Obregón.

To please my father, I agreed, but that diploma didn't mean the same to me anymore. Now that I was a woman in love, my head was spinning so fast! Only a couple of years before, I'd wanted to conquer the world with my anthropology degree. I wanted to undertake so many adventures with it. With my father's permission, I had already traveled to Yucatan on my own, with a team of American professors who were studying the world of Mayan archaeology. I also wanted to specialize in primates so that I'd be able to work for the Jane Goodall Institute in Africa. The evolution of man, from every angle, had been my passion. It was what kept me awake at night and made my heart race. Now I threw my passion into the garbage can for a man who provided me with a new surname that gave me the status of a married lady, fit to play house with flesh-and-blood dolls.

For a short period of time, Sybil Vaughan tried to compete with Sybil de Obregón, but it was already too late; the battle was lost. Sybil continued to attend her classes at the university, although the wedding preparations were what most absorbed her. A fairy tale that was becoming true, everyone would be content. Her outbursts of rebellion about feeling dominated by the establishment dimmed until they disappeared and what she really wanted now was to please everyone. She felt that this wedding would not only please herself but also her mother and even the nuns from the school she had gone to as a girl in San Andrés. Surely, the sisters would be proud of her for having obeyed everything they had taught her in the catechism and religion classes. When you lack love, your mind gets trapped in habits, creating unbelievable thoughts. You forget what's important because you only want to fit in, to please, to be accepted. Poor Sybil; she still did not understand that she would never be able to satisfy the insatiable expectations of others.

THE YELLOW OF THE BRILLIANT SUN

The church was the most beautiful any bride could have imagined. Its interior was surrounded by stained-glass windows of every color, so that the rays of the sun, as they filtered through, bathed Cinderella and her prince in an enchanting luminosity. Standing before the priest, in the midst of this magical dome, they seemed to be acting out the final scene of the Walt Disney movie. She designed her dress herself, following one she had seen in a French magazine. She did not want a train or a veil, one remnant at least of her youthful rebelliousness. It was the simplicity of the dress that made it beautiful. Instead of a veil, she wore a tiara embroidered with little pearls, and hand-embroidered gloves that reached to her wrists. It was all in white, except for the buds of the fresh roses in the bouquet she carried. Daniel, her hairdresser, also did her makeup. He outdid himself, employing pink tones which naturally intermingled with the green of her eyes, which shone like two fireflies that night. In her loose hair, she only wore some tiny white florets hidden amongst her coquettish ringlets.

The reception took place at the city's best social club and lasted until dawn. The 150 guests got as much into the swing of things as we two did. All my plans for the event were a splendid success. I was already proving to be an excellent hostess. Even though it was the first formal party I had thrown in my life, the music, food, dancing, and decoration were unsurpassed. Our honeymoon began the following day, when we left on a twenty-one-day trip to French Polynesia. Sebastián had asked me to choose the place, and following the heart of an islander, I thought that the more distant the isles, the more idyllic and romantic they would be. First, we stopped off in Miami for a few days, before taking the plane to Los Angeles and then to Tahiti. Miami re-appeared on my map and I re-activated all those feelings that had made me feel that part of my life would unfold there. This time, I didn't stay in the downtown hotel where I'd been with my mother, but in a luxury apartment on an island near Coconut Grove, with the most beautiful ocean view. We were happy. I soon became the perfect housewife; I wanted to pamper Sebastián as much as I could. We got on very well in bed, and from that virgin he had trained years before, there arose a woman who completely surrendered herself to him. He had his own geisha; he only had to ask for my love, and I yielded it to him in complete submission. Deciding to stay in an apartment was our best move, since there were no housekeepers to bother us and we could wake up and go to sleep making love just as we liked. Sitting on the terrace one night, watching the setting sun and that calm sea whose salty aroma carried on the wind, I told Sebastián about my girlish dream of living in Miami. Now, as a married woman, it seemed to be the ideal place to raise children if we decided to have a family one day.

"I'd like that too. Let's wait and see how things go with the business. Syb, why don't you bring us the other bottle of champagne? It must be chilled by now."

He put on a tape of jazz while I got the ice bucket with the other bottle of Dom Perignon and a silver tray with a perfect arrangement of some smoked salmon rolls filled with cream cheese and chives on warm toast. Our idyll, there on that twelfth-floor balcony, seemed timeless. I never felt closer to the moon and stars. That man – elemental, simple, with the straight-lined mind of an engineer – was now my husband, as ordained by the Catholic Church and Colombian law, in accordance with my wishes. Apart from working and making money, Sebastián did not have many interests. His obsession was to prove himself to Domingo, his father. That also might have been what attracted me. My feminine side was looking for a responsible man, someone who would take charge of building a safe nest for our children's future. He was certainly a good provider; I was never wrong about that.

Her mistake was to think that his excessive fondness for alcohol was simply a matter of upbringing and culture. True, but it was not so simple. Accepting it was part of adjusting to her husband's values and what she now had in her hands was not a game. She had grown used to following a lead – his – and in her eagerness to please him, began to drink when he did, still unaware of that beautiful dance of infinity whereby every action always causes a reaction. They departed for Tahiti on a trip that took fourteen hours. She had always thought that the world was a handkerchief but this journey proved her wrong. She had never spent so much time seated on an airplane. Both of them had high hopes of finding a paradise – and they did. It was certainly one of the most beautiful places on earth and getting to know it might have been a delight – if it had not been for Sybil's inexperience. When choosing the date for the wedding and honeymoon, she had not taken into account that December and January were the rainiest and most humid months in that region. It was the moment to start getting to know what her husband was really like.

It rained so much that Sebastián's apathy soon began to affect Sybil. She felt guilty seeing his bored look and urge to bang his head against the wall. He was not made to enjoy the peace which one breathed in that hypnotic setting. Sitting on the terrace of the Tahara Hotel, a hideaway nestled into the slopes of a volcanic mountain facing Matavai Bay, her husband found relief in all the cans of Heineken he drank while the monotonous rain endlessly fell. Although Sybil did not like those grey days either, she was happy with a good book and the simple pleasure of living amid such beauty alongside the husband with whom she would share the rest of her life. For her, the climate was the least of it.

I would awake in the morning seeing him lying beside me and my soul would burst into a thousand smiles reflected in my tender and radiant gaze. I loved this man so much, there was no way to explain it. To see him so desperate began to upset me. He complained that he had never spent such a boring Christmas and was already thinking about cutting our honeymoon short by a week, even though it would mean losing the money paid for the reservations in other luxury hotels on different Polynesian islands we hadn't visited yet.

They miraculously stuck it out till New Year's Eve. They were in the hotel's restaurant, where a group of Tahitian women were entertaining the guests with a dance to the music of ukuleles. Sebastián, too much under the influence, began to make a spectacle of himself, loudly complaining about the weather and the tediously peaceful and far-from-festive atmosphere, which he blamed on the French tourists not knowing how to have a good time. Embarrassed by his rowdy behavior, noticing the scandalized looks of the other diners as he continued to complain out loud in an arrogant tone, Sybil asked him to lower his voice.

> "Leave me alone! That's how I feel and I'm right. Besides, I don't give a damn about what this bunch of bastards think, who I'll never meet up with again anyway, because as far as I'm concerned, I'll never return to these shitty, expensive islands. You and your stupid ideas, it's your fault for trying to live in a romance novel. Why did you bring me to this graveyard? We could have stayed in Colombia and been happy, celebrating New Year's Eve the proper way."

It was not the first time that Sybil had been alarmed by the aggressiveness and latent violence which alcohol brought out in Sebastián, but it was the last straw—at least while they remained in Tahiti. The next day, January 1, 1988, in the midst of thunder and lightning, they took a Qantas flight from Papeete to Los Angeles, and then flew back to Bogotá by way of Miami. As they crossed the immense Pacific Ocean, she watched the enormous white clouds in the infinite blue sky beyond the window, and, becoming withdrawn, held a conversation with her heart. In a silent panic she could not control, feeling guilty about a thought which reeked of sinfulness, she hurriedly tried to blot out the words that an invisible, diaphanous force kept whispering into her mind:

> "Your marriage will not last forever."

***

Back in their own world, the whole slate was wiped clean, so they could write down that love story which only began now. They lived in a rented apartment on Calle 88, while the house which had been given to them as a wedding present by Domingo, her father-in-law, was being built. It was going to be the most splendid house Sybil could have imagined. Sebastián's father was a generous man who had perfectly guessed what the newlyweds longed for. The day they went to the office of the architects to approve the design and sign the floor plans, Sybil's eyes shone with emotion. She tried to take hold of her husband's hand to show him how happy she was, but he was not given to such public displays of affection. He brusquely pulled it away without her even being able to conceal his disdain from the others. They were going to have to wait a little longer than a year till the finishes were done and then she would do the interior design, which was entirely her responsibility. The first months were spent amid parties and suppers that Sebastián's friends held in their honor. Sybil took her new role as a Mrs. seriously. She quickly acquired a more than professional skill at cooking and the other domestic tasks.

My priority was to please my husband and he always had an active social life, so I soon began to devote myself to organizing gatherings for his friends. In the end, I didn't have many friends of my own in Bogotá. The apartment we were temporarily living in was small, but I set out to decorate it in the same taste I had developed since I was little. My facility for mixing colors and designs, and fabrics and styles, was innate. It had come to me from past lives. With all the ideas that occurred to me, I managed to create a harmonious atmosphere where nothing jarred or was out of place. In my eagerness to fit in, I'd left behind the girlfriends from my childhood, even those from university. Now my friends were the wives of Sebastián's friends, with whom I spent nearly every weekend. We used to leave the city to relax in country retreats in nearby hot-climate villages. I quickly forgot about the people from my recent past who had once meant so much to me. I was so busy learning about my husband's life, I didn't have time for anything else. It was like changing your wardrobe overnight. To show I was like those women, I suddenly wanted to wear their uniform; high society was my world now. In my time in San Andrés, I never imagined that one day I'd be wearing pearls or scarves with English-style hunting or racing designs to go with the suede jackets I now liked so much. My style of dress became traditional, classic, that of an older woman. It was as though I was trying to be the same age as Sebastián. My loosely worn, curly hair also went through a complete transformation. Its color was no longer dark chestnut but had streaks to lighten it, and the hairdryer I straightened it with every day became as important as my toothbrush.

Sybil did all this willingly, but it was a little abrupt. She changed from a happy, laughing, and spontaneous young woman into the señora who now faced her in the mirror—serious, reserved and diplomatic—without knowing how or why. She reinvented herself, inside and out, turning into the wife of Sebastián Obregón and nothing more, because that was all that mattered to her. She completely devoted herself to being a housewife, and it made her feel fully realized. Her days revolved around planning the social gatherings she held. On the Fridays or Saturdays when they did not leave for a warmer climate, she organized suppers that lasted into the early hours of the morning. Books on cooking and decoration now filled her night table and desk. The ones on anthropology were now ornamental, to be placed on the bookshelf beside the fireplace, alongside the photos in the silver frames they had been given as wedding presents. It was as though she had entered a contest to be the best hostess. No detail escaped her. The flowers always matched the tableware and the tableware matched the tablecloth and serviettes. While Sebastián took charge of serving the drinks and putting on the music, she would remain in the kitchen until all the dishes were just right. No matter how late it might be, as soon as the guests left and it was all over, she set out to clean up, clearing away the mess of glasses and cigarette butts, so that Sebastián would find everything to his liking as soon as he woke up.

He seemed to be happy with me. I pleased him in every way. His family and his friends also seemed to like me. Domingo, my father-in-law, and Tomás, my brother-in-law, were very affectionate toward me. I knew it from their looks and the way they hugged me. Sebastián's mother was the only one who never seemed to accept me. She tolerated me but could never digest the fact that a girl from the provinces without the right surname or lineage had become the woman her son had chosen to share the rest of his life. Felicia belonged to an upper-class Bogotá family. Her mentality was traditional, conservative, with a sharp awareness of class differences. I came from San Andrés, where the class to which she belonged simply did not exist.

And what would she have needed to be or do to be considered a member of that class? Been born and grown up in Bogotá, and gone to one of the two or three bilingual schools for the rich. Have one of those surnames associated with the families who had run the country throughout its history or at least some relative who was important in politics or a diplomat. She would have had to be the heiress to some vast hacienda or business concern, and finally, the most important, a member of the Club Mendoza, a badge by which the crème de la crème distinguished the ins from the outs. Without meeting any of those conditions, it was impossible for her to change her past, so she decided to forget about her mother-in-law's opinion of her. She would soon prove to her that she could stand out without having the right family name or exclusive schooling. She would be as good as the rest and blend in, exceeding her expectations. She would even use her mother-in-law as a model to imitate, carefully observing and copying her style of life as the foundation on which to build the family she and Sebastián hoped for.

While I was devoting myself to pleasing all the people who were important to my husband, I reached the end of my university course. I had thought of dropping out several times, but was bound by the promise I'd made to my father before I got married. In fact, when I got all my course credits, I decided to withdraw for a while, since I still didn't know what the subject of my degree thesis would be. I had to undertake a project that would take six months in all, beginning with two of field work. Time flew and flew until an inner voice began to insist on graduating so much that it was no longer a question of pleasing my father. I had spent five years on the degree which had meant everything to me before Sebastián came along, not getting that diploma would mean throwing a big investment of time and money into the garbage. I had to sort out this chapter of my life once and for all. I wasn't the kind of woman to leave things half-done. I would finish what I had started, so I went back to the university without suspecting the new surprise life was readying for me.

It was Christmastime of 1989 when Sybil found out she was pregnant. Yes—pregnant—despite the birth-control pills she religiously took and precisely when she was most determined to finish her studies and it was too late to re-arrange her priorities. What a happy and hopeful Christmas season that was for everyone! Her baby would be the first grandchild on both sides of the family. Sebastián was proud of her. He was sure the baby would carry on the proud male line of the Obregón family. He would take charge of turning the little man into a true macho, successful and worthy of bearing his surname. The whiskey and *aguardiente* flowed like water during the festivities that December, spilling from the table to the floor, and the good news justified such excesses. To deal with her queasiness, Sybil spent the first few months lying down, while her husband began to absent himself more than she wished. Poor thing, she understood it; it was not fair to ask him to stay at home with her when it was she who did not feel well. She put up with it. A couple of nights before, Sebastián had become very annoyed when she called his cell phone after discovering that he had already left the office and still not come home, despite the late hour. It wasn't to control him; in a city so dangerous and unsafe, becoming concerned when someone was later than usual was normal. It also seemed unfair of him not to tell her of the change of plans. The dinner was drying out in the stove and she could not get to sleep. Where was the manual of instructions for recently married housewives! She was getting accustomed to biting her tongue and not asking questions. She did not want to look like an insecure and jealous young bride, who foolishly imagined that her husband was up to no good. Instead, she kept quiet and silently asked herself questions that were never answered out loud. Keeping to her bed, she only had the strength to get up when she had to vomit. Dr. Sanclemente, her gynecologist since she was fifteen, calmed her down, explaining that such symptoms were normal in her state. But when the first ultrasound scan was made, the beautiful surprise that had come a few months before turned into the first great disappointment of her life with Sebastián. There was no fetus at all in Sybil's uterus. Without her realizing it, her pregnancy had ended in a missed miscarriage, which had occurred who knows how long before. She would have to go to a clinic for a curettage to expel the nonexistence that now lay inside her.

Why did it happen to me? What had I done wrong? Hadn't I fed myself well? Might it be that I couldn't have babies? Maybe it was all those birth-control pills that messed up my body? What was Sebastián going to think of me? He would stop loving me. How could I have disappointed him like that? These were the doubts that seized hold of my mind while the Pitocin began to flow through my veins and the nurses waited for my contractions to begin. Lying down in the delivery room of that maternity clinic, my sunken gaze wandered around, noticing three other women who were giving birth while I waited to expel something that did not exist. It was very cruel. I still wonder why they couldn't have put me in another room where I wouldn't have felt like such a useless failure compared to those new moms.

She returned to the recently inaugurated house her father-in-law had given them, emotionally destroyed. All she did was to throw herself onto the same bed where, for twenty weeks, she had been taking care of that child who was now only a figment of her imagination. She went into a deep depression. Day after day, she lay there, drowning in sadness. Cassandra arrived every morning, after Sebastián had left for the office, and helped her to get up and have a shower. Physically, she was all right, and little by little, her body went back to its normal state, but she felt empty inside. She was scourged by destructive thoughts that did not allow her to be at peace. It was a true mourning, for the death of a child who had become real for her, a being of flesh and blood, with a personality.

One night, when Sebastián came home, my disappointment became even worse. A number of weeks had gone by since my loss and seeing that I was still stretched out there and completely listless, he lost control of himself and began to abuse me.

> "Why are you still lying there, pretending you don't know what's happened? I'm sure it was a boy, the boy I wanted, and it may be that you won't even be able to give me any children."

The way he screamed at me was insulting and contemptuous. I didn't answer back but I couldn't hold back the tears that rolled down my pallid cheeks, showing the endless sadness which I still wanted to shield myself with. As though realizing how far his words had gone, he left the bedroom and went to the kitchen for some ice to put into the glass of whiskey he'd just served himself in the study.

He may have felt some remorse for his mercilessness, but it stayed inside him. Sebastián did not know how to ask for forgiveness, to say he was sorry. The next morning, he woke up on the olive-green leather sofa, without remembering exactly why he'd spent the night there instead of their bed alongside Sybil. It was a great advantage for him. He never remembered what he had done or said when he was drunk. It was a perfect excuse, since he did not have to deal with morning-after regrets. Despite their poison, her husband's words the night before had helped her in some way to accept that she could not go on feeling such contempt for herself. The baby was lost and it was time to move on. With a forced determination, she got up and while she showered, it became clear: she would have to start on her thesis. She gave herself a time limit of a year to graduate. Though she was not yet fit to drive a car, it did not matter to her. That afternoon, she went to the university to speak with several professors she was close to, who encouraged her. She would travel to San Andrés as soon possible to do her field work. The next step was to go to her parents' house and get a check for her tuition fees. Her agreement with Dylan not only implied finishing her course, he committed himself to paying for all of it. His daughter's education was his business, and there was no way he would allow another man to be responsible for it. She stayed on the island for two months. It was perfect for her; she needed the space and time to think about things and heal herself, away from Sebastián. Ever since the wedding, she had not done anything else other than mold herself into the Señora de Obregón, a woman seeking the approval of others. She had not done anything but learn to cook, entertain guests, keep her home shiny as a silver platter, and change the candles and flowers so that it would always smell of perfection. Her life was like the photos in glossy magazines, but it was one of appearances. After all the effort she had made, Sebastián's gradual indifference was a strong disappointment. He was still obsessed with expanding his business and the little time they spent together was taken up by dinners and social events where they never had a chance to speak frankly to one another. With each passing day, she grew more and more resigned to the situation, without being able to find relief from the drops of gray rain that pooled in her heart. Her island always awaited her with the same unconditional love with which it had always seen her depart. She had not returned since she got married, because nothing in that islet interested Sebastián, and it was always last on the list when they were thinking about where to spend their vacations.

The Avianca flight landed and as I descended the stairway, I deeply inhaled that sea breeze which revived even the tiniest cell in my lungs. The magic was still there. I felt alive and for the first time since I'd lost the baby, a timid smile spontaneously sprouted on my lips. God, why had I taken so long to return? It was the medicine I'd needed, my native soil which never judged me and always welcomed me unquestioningly. I felt the invisible embrace of the strongest love while I rode in a broken-down taxi to my grandma Ofelia's house, the one she'd moved to after my parents sold the hotel. It was the perfect moment to meet up with my true self again. I felt uncomfortable and sorry, now that I realized I had wanted to forget about my origins ever since I married Sebastián. I had to correct that; I had to feel proud that my roots were in that solid piece of ground. Growing up in San Andrés made me different, yes, but the best of it was that it made me special.

Those two months were decisive. They helped her to rearrange her values and remember what her true priorities should be. The connection with her people made her resonate with life again. It was a reminder of her capacity for unconditional love. She spent hours in the schools of the native districts, researching, sharing with children who, while they did not speak Spanish well and preferred the local patois, found a way to connect their hearts to hers. Her project went full sail ahead. She felt useful, worth something, a feeling that had been absent for a long time. She remembered that she was cut out to be much more than just someone's *wife.* At the end of each day, Ofelia awaited her, in a home that glistened with a simplicity and ease that were sorely missing from the stiff, elegant one she had created alongside Sebastián. There was still a need for candles and kerosene lamps when there were power cuts. She would sit in a rocking chair for hours at a time, watching the flames of the candles enchantingly dance to the breeze that blew through the windows of the sitting room. The evening meals were delightful, and not only because of the meals her grandmother lovingly cooked. There were also all those stories about her ancestors and their feats when they emigrated from Jamaica to San Andrés. This woman was one of the few living witnesses to the exciting events of those years at the end of the nineteenth century. When one is happy, time flies. The two months vanished in a flash, and she soon had to return to Bogotá. She had the material she needed to sit down and write her thesis, and also carried away with her, forever, the final and most beautiful remembrance of her maternal grandmother, who died sometime later.

The day of her graduation, she was radiant. Only three people accompanied her in the auditorium: Dylan, Cassandra and Sebastián. She was one of five hundred graduating students from all the faculties. Dressed in a tailored suit with a dark green skirt, she received her diploma from the hands of the university's president. Her own trembled from nerves, and her smile was so big, it seemed like she was being awarded an Oscar or Nobel Prize. The occasion did not mean much for Sebastián, but he agreed to hold a family celebration in his wife's honor that night. As they were seated around the table, enjoying one of her new recipes—turkey breast with a sauce of champagne and watercress—Sybil broke into the conversation to tell them the big news; she was pregnant again, and this time, everything was going marvelously well. She had not even felt nauseated or had any other upsets and had already seen Dr. Sanclemente, who told her that the scan confirmed that this time the baby inside her was growing with a heart eager for life. During the nine months of her pregnancy, she never wanted to know if the baby was going to be the girl she longed for so much or the boy she had lost the last time (at least, according to her husband's accusations). All that mattered to her was that it would be a healthy baby. This time she took precautions, including giving up alcohol and cigarettes. She felt she had to rid herself of the toxins from the rushed pace and vices of the life she had led till then. This was her second chance and she would do all within her reach to ensure a happy ending.

It was a natural birth, without mishaps. If women from the tribes of Africa and the Amazon I'd studied could give birth to a child so naturally, I didn't see why I couldn't too. I spent nine hours in labor; not bad for a beginner. Luna turned out to be the first granddaughter in my family and Sebastián's. My father couldn't believe it. She was born on his birthday; there couldn't be a better present. We were all happy with that adorable little baby girl with thick dark hair and deep blue eyes.

She slept with her daughter in the clinic that night, and the next day, returned home. Luna was going to have her own room, but during the first few days, she slept beside her mother in a little cot in her parents' bedroom. As soon as they arrived, Sebastián rang all his friends to tell them that a piggy bank had been born to him. The sarcastic nickname hid his disappointment. It was not that he did not love Luna, but in his heart, what he truly he wanted was a son.

I couldn't believe that I was a mother at last. All those games I'd played with dolls as a girl, taking care of and loving them, had now turned into a reality. I finally had a flesh-and-blood doll, the most beautiful of all, with her little feet and hands so tiny and at the same time so perfect. I luxuriated in her tender skin with that smell babies that bring from the beyond. Luna was everything for me now, and it seemed that Sebastián soon forgot that she wasn't a boy. In his own strange and enigmatic way, he loved Luna completely. I knew him well, I knew that my husband was happy, though it might only be evanescently. He was so happy that he had to celebrate, that very night, when we'd just come back from the clinic. There was no peace for the new mother and daughter, just a celebratory jamboree in the best style of the Obregóns.

Luna brought a new aroma to the couple's life. There was

now a reason why they had to get on together and forget any disagreement. Their relationship took on a new meaning, without much communication between them, of course. That did not improve, it simply changed. In any case, it was a positive change. Now they were the father and mother of a child. Their role as spouses and lovers receded into the background, and as though they had made a tacit and secret agreement, each, in his or her way, became responsible for the progress of the new family which they were now creating for Luna.

***

She would wait a couple of years before putting Luna in the care of Mauricia, their trusted nanny. After several months of arguments, she finally convinced Sebastián that she needed to work, albeit half-time. The inner voice that would come out of nowhere from time to time had been telling her that for years now.

"How much longer are you going to put it off?"

He did not understand Sybil's need for work. To him, it was needless. He was selfish and stingy, and had a unique, Machiavellian talent for concealing his motives. At first sight, he seemed exceptionally generous, because, in fact, he was an expert illusionist who manipulated others. He was a good provider who covered all the expenses of their home. They had everything they wanted (or rather, what he *thought* they needed). *Why did his wife insist on working?* He wondered. *Why did Sybil always have to complicate things?* He would always let her know his disagreement. In his zeal to convince her not to work, he reminded her of the promise she had made a few months before their wedding. He had made her promise that he and the family they would create would be her priority. Everything else would be second to that. Now, the condition did not sound like a promise as much as a way to intimidate her. She was not asking for a job that would alter what she had promised.

She only wanted a little space, so that she could feel like something more than a wife and mother. She was handling those roles with great skill, so that there was nothing to reproach her for. The friends who shared his world of appearances had done nothing but congratulate Sebastián, saying how special the home he had formed was. He had a good wife, beautiful and faithful; a daughter who resembled a little angel; the best house; the best life; the best job. It was all enviable. The deal between Sybil and Sebastián took more effort to work out than peace negotiations between warring bands. When he ran out of excuses, he just had to give in. She was going to work a few hours each day in the anthropological institute. Juan Corredor, one of her professors, helped her to get that job as a lab assistant. It was better than nothing. She knew that, despite being so influential, her husband would not lift a finger or pull a string; he wanted to keep her at home. Her new salary did not even cover the groceries but it did not matter to her. Her aim was not money; this was only her first job. She cleaned and classified bone remains from one of the archaeological sites that Professor Corredor and his research team had just excavated in Soacha, on the outskirts of Bogotá.

Surrounded by pre-Columbian mummies as I sat in the cold, dark basement of that hundred-year-old building full of ancient ghosts, I felt the essence of things again, the reawakening of my drive and motivation. Nothing was alive there but I felt a lively emancipation.

My inner voice was silenced, at least momentarily. Now, it was clear that I was no longer putting things off. Juan soon turned into my best friend and confidant. Every day we worked together for the four hours I had at my disposal. The breaks we took over a good cup of coffee and a cigarette brought us closer together as we spoke of our everyday concerns. We both felt the same void in our marriages. I never imagined that a man could feel the same as me. In those years of marriage, I had tried to convince myself that it was a female anxiety, merely a matter of hormones. How different Juan was from Sebastián. I couldn't believe how sensitive he was. He was a man who paid attention to what I said; how well that made me feel. My words meant something to someone. I was used to listening and not being heard; I welcomed that new emotion. We shared so many things. We both loved anthropology, the same books, the same music. My excitement was such that I only listened to the cassettes of Clannad and Enya he had taped for me. At home, even Sebastián listened to them at night, without knowing where I had got them from.

The lab assistant's job soon helped to advance Sybil's career at the university she had graduated from. Juan gave her excellent references, and little by little, she began to be known in the academic world as a disciplined and well-organized worker. Without letting Sebastián find out, she was now holding down two half-time jobs at once. She was happy to be testing herself, to stretching her own limits and timidly advancing beyond them to new challenges. Sebastián continued to control everything at home and even asked her to keep an account of her monthly spending, which wasn't allowed to go beyond a limit he established. She was a dependant, a kept woman. It was horrible to put it that way; the terms disgusted her, but that is how she felt. How could other women put up with it? There were so many of them, living as she did without opening their mouths, in her own circle of girlfriends, in the whole of that *machista* country where she happened to have been born. The place abounded with women who were submissive to the core. The money she now earned was very special for her and as Sebastián never confided his financial affairs to her nor had her name on his bank accounts, she learned to do the same. With her savings, she was able to buy the dinner service and silverware set she had longed for ever since they got married. Sebastián had refused to buy them for her, arguing that he had inherited a number of such sets from his grandmothers. But Sybil, tired of his sick obsession with family traditions, wanted her own things, so she made a present of them to herself.

With all her achievements at work, her world at the university soon became as important to her as the one at home. There, she was appreciated for her own merits and no price could be put on that. Her husband still failed to utter a word to show that he was interested in what she wanted to achieve. There was not so much as murmur to indicate that he was there for her. She felt that she had fought so hard to satisfy and please him.

She was now a successful mother, wife, and professional, and her husband still was not aware of it. The idea struck her with horror. Now that she thought of it, her husband had never told her that he liked, much less loved her, neither when they were fiancés nor now, as a married couple. Never. She began to understand her anxiety. Her quest began to make sense, but it was still difficult to accept what she had just discovered. She was sick, very sick, and the name of her illness was lack of love.

My life continued on its lethargic course. One of my bosses, the academic vice-rector, decided to name me to a post where I would represent the whole university on an international level. It was a big promotion for me, but I didn't tell Sebastián. He hadn't the slightest idea of what was going on in my secret world, the professional one. I didn't need his usual sarcastic smile and indifferent "how nice."

At their first meeting, Vice President Villarraga explained what this new challenge would require of her and accompanied her to the door of his office when it was over. Though she had never brought up the subject of her private life during their long conversation, he was a shrewd old man with a lot of experience of life and after an affectionate good-bye hug in his usual uninhibited manner, he unexpectedly said something personal.

"Your marriage won't last forever."

That was the exact phrase my mind had murmured to me on that flight from Tahiti to Los Angeles, years ago, after my honeymoon. How had it been possible for Villarraga to utter the same words? It couldn't have been a mere coincidence, but instead of the panic and guilt I felt the first time, it was a relief to hear it being said by someone else. I needed hope and by reminding me of what I already knew, Villaraga had just given me that. There was no need to reply. All I could do was to look at my boss and offer him a shy smile of agreement.

The presence of Juan caused Sybil to change the way she had been looking at life in general. He was clearly a catalyst that changed the chemical composition of her physical reality. He helped her to become aware of her human potential. He showed her how intelligent and capable she was. He wakened her from the monotonous nightmare in which she was trapped. In a short time, she managed to become the trusted right-hand of several of the leading administrators of the university where she worked. She felt satisfied and realized that she had reasons to congratulate herself. Her home functioned like clockwork, and at the same time, she continued to enjoy another realm, reserved for her and highly stimulating. Her family life was still governed by the routines that she and Sebastián had established from the beginning. She was happy to see Luna grow up. There was no doubt that being a mother remained one of her greatest achievements. What was new was that, through Juan, life was teaching her to appreciate herself for what was inside, and not around her. That marked a big difference. She had been assessing her own worth in terms of the material image she had created of herself. She had completely forgotten where the essence of her ability to create and recreate herself as she pleased came from. Through Juan, life tried to show her the radiant creature who was inside her, the one she had never been able to see again since she was a girl. It tried to strip off the masks which concealed her inner beauty, a beauty—immaterial beyond time and space—that was not physical but only her true being.

It was a period of much reflection and re-appraisal. I was trying to find out where I was going, while keeping to the same old path, as if by remote control. It was difficult to see clearly; my lenses were completely fogged. Was it really fair to stick to a loveless life full of vice and self-destruction? Sebastián had fully drawn me into his world and I had gone along with him. Drinking was our only pastime. I don't recall a single time that we made love when we were sober. How hard it was for me to accept that reality. We were both trapped in a labyrinth. I had let myself be carried away by my husband's addiction, without his even realizing it was an addiction. For him, his destructive drinking habit was simply a tradition passed on from one generation to the next; first his grandfather, then his father, and now him. It was what he had seen since childhood and he regarded it as a motive for pride. Juan taught me that I could have fun in a natural way, that I could laugh at anything, speak, and think as I liked and be myself, without any need for liquor. When he and I got together, time vanished completely. We had so much to tell each other, so much to hear. He was neither good-looking, rich, nor powerful. He wasn't anything Sebastián was and it was precisely what he was not that attracted me. But that attraction and the affection which grew up between us, day by day, became a dangerous temptation.

What was it she was feeling? She was not in love, because it was not the same thing she felt when she fell madly in love with Sebastián. It must be a passing temptation, one her own dissatisfaction had led her to. It was her fault, always her own fault, and for no motive would she cheat on Sebastián. Her eagerness to win society's approval continued to be much more important than what life was trying to show her through Juan. Perhaps that she had the right to be happy. While Sybil was struggling against her little devils, simultaneously feigning what she felt and honoring her marriage vows, Sebastián continued to live in his own separate world. She did not know what kind or with whom, but he certainly led a parallel one in which she had no part.

I often tried to speak with him, but he always found a way to cut it short by making me feel guilty. He always answered one question with another, said my complaints were presumptuous, and found the same old justifications to shut me up.

> "How can you say I don't treat you right, Sybil? Isn't all that I provide you and Luna with sufficient? Don't you think it's the limit to be always inventing stories like a scandalmonger who has nothing better to do?"

In a matter of seconds, he demolished my arguments. He was extremely clever at manipulating my psyche. He knew me better than I knew myself. Without arguing back, I fell for his version and convinced myself that he was giving me everything and more – when, in fact, the only thing he gave me was the false love that money buys for convenience.

The void in Sybil's soul had nothing to do with what had or had not been given her. Rather, it was what she had failed to be, what she had not found in her marriage. She suffered in silence, not wanting Luna to ever see her crying. She wanted her daughter to have a happy childhood, so she put up with it. Though there were no proofs that her husband had another woman, at every moment, her heart whispered "why not?" It would be so easy for him. He traveled a lot (or so he told Sybil when he was away from home), and with her own eyes, she had already seen that Domingo had a mistress. It happened when her father-in-law had the nerve to take her to a company barbecue, taking advantage of a trip Felicia was on. He clearly did not care that his daughter-in-law and granddaughter were there. If Sebastián's drinking was one family tradition, it was not far-fetched to think that having a mistress was another.

I was a completely submissive woman. I don't know exactly when there arose the fear that I now had of my own husband. I didn't want to confront or upset him. In no way I was going to put my home at risk. Sebastián had given me all that I had asked life for. How could I complain? Also, no one was perfect. In reality, he was a good man. He met all the conditions so many women longed for in a man. It hurt me enormously to think that he'd be unfaithful, but what could I do? I didn't have any solid evidence. I only had a foolish and perhaps mistaken instinct. I became much more afraid when I started to feel Juan's love. I was the guilty one now, playing with fire like that. How could I whine about my husband's supposed unfaithfulness, when I myself was on the point of following in his footsteps? I had to define my position, had to choose between two opposites: security or the uncertainty of an affair. I wasn't ready for what life had placed before me. The social values learned through my mother and education had become deeply incrusted in my subconscious. They won out over love, assuming that Juan could have been the love I didn't have and was still desperately seeking. I never knew what it might have been, because it simply never was. I chose the familiar ground. I couldn't risk it, because losing everything would have been devastating. Luna was my priority. I would have never forgiven myself if she were to discover my unfaithfulness when she grew up. I would have never forgiven myself for setting a bad example for her. In contrast with Sebastián, who was skilled at clandestineness, I was not good at hypocrisy. In some way, my sinfulness would have betrayed me, sooner or later.

Juan went out of her life, leaving the most beautiful imprint on her heart. They say that true love does not bind nor limit; she had to let him go. There was not even the farewell kiss she had often imagined, but she did manage to catch the faint aroma of a man's unconditional love. At least she now knew that it really did exist. How well she and Sebastián matched each other! It was clear that neither knew what love was, but at least she had taken a great leap forward, by acknowledging it to herself. She now understood that what she had in her marriage was a love of convenience, a love based on dependence. She now understood why she had signed a contract with the church and state when she got married. What a fool she had been; if it had been true love, she would not have had to sign anything! How stupid the social impositions she had let herself be conditioned to. It was too late for regrets. She and Sebastián needed each other to keep that contract valid. Good or bad, it was already signed. She was now in the game and had to do the impossible to keep learning from it. Not fully convinced, however, her only justification for carrying on with her marriage was Luna. The game only made sense when she thought of her daughter's future. Children needed a family where they could grow up in peace and feel secure, a nest while they were learning to fly. Luna deserved that nest. She wanted her daughter to fly, much higher than she herself ever could.

***

That Friday, as on every morning, I gave Luna her breakfast, prepared her lunchbox, took her to her kindergarten, near our house in the north of the city, and then headed toward my office, way downtown, near the mountains of Monserrate and Guadalupe. I would stay there until 1:00 or 2:00 in the afternoon, working nonstop so that I could miraculously fit into that time all the different responsibilities I had. I usually didn't have lunch until I returned home, but I did manage to smoke half a pack of Marlboros and drink three or four cups of black coffee, brought straight from the machine by Juanita, the coffee lady. A poor, sweet-natured woman with the longest braids I'd ever seen, she would always give me a few words of encouragement when she saw me sitting in front of the computer, showing the stress of finishing off my pending jobs in time to return home before 3:00, when Luna's school bus left her at the stop a few blocks from my house.

That was the condition Sebastián had imposed: she could have the mornings free—yes, Sebastián thought of his wife's job as a simple pastime, so he referred to them as "free mornings." But once Luna left her kindergarten, Sybil had to completely change her role. She had to devote herself to the girl's swimming and riding classes and then rush home to make the evening meal. Saturday was the only day available for shopping, including food for the dinner party which Sebastián had probably laid on for the weekend. She would then spend a couple of hours at the gym with Billy, her trainer, who was always scolding her for not looking after her health, and go to the beauty salon to touch up the highlights in her hair that her husband liked so much.

It was a little before 7:00 AM. The second-hand Mazda 323 with the color of marble that Sebastián had given her as a wedding present was crawling along in a traffic jam. Without noting the number of the incoming call on her cell phone, she uttered her usual hello while concentrating on the left-hand turn she had to make at the next traffic light.

"Doña Sybil?"

"Yes?"

"Please don't ask me anything, because I just want you to listen. Don Sebastián is having a serious love affair with a woman I work with and I know all about her schemes to make him leave you. I am only ringing to warn you, because I have gone through the same thing myself and it doesn't seem fair that they are making fun of you in such a shameless way. You seem like such a lovely, decent woman. I've seen you at company outings and I know how much you love Don Sebastián and your little girl. That's what gave me the courage to ring you. It doesn't seem right to me. Open your eyes and do something."

The woman brusquely hung up, without giving her time to even ask who she was. She had never heard that voice before. How had that stranger got hold of her cell number? Why should she believe what she had just said? There were no words for what she felt. The call ripped her guts out and left her so dazed she missed the turn for her office and wound up lost in La Perseverancia, a dangerous and unsafe downtown neighborhood, but perhaps never as unsafe as the way she felt right now.

I stopped the car and all I could do was cry. It was ruining my makeup. What would the people at work think? I didn't want indiscreet questions that not even I could answer yet. I breathed deeply several times, closing my eyes, and praying to whatever God there was to give me the strength to confront something I still wasn't ready to assess or make sense of. I dried my tears and touched myself up with eyeliner. I don't know how I arrived on time in the midst of my confusion. I answered some waiting calls, and soon the first meeting of the day began. I had to shelve that mysterious phone call. I didn't have time to think of my personal dramas; all I had time for was to hide from myself once more.

***

That January, we had just got back from vacations. We'd traveled to Florida for two weeks to meet up with all of Sebastián's family. Domingo and Felicia had rented a house near Orlando, where the family and some of our closest friends spent Christmas together. It was the first time Luna had been abroad, and although she was still little, Sebastián and I took her to Disney World for a couple of days so she could see Mickey Mouse and Snow White. She was adorable; she was like a doll who amused everyone because she was the only little girl among so many adults. She looked so much like her father; that was my biggest source of pride.

The resemblance between the girl and her father was very important for Sybil. The reason for it still hurt her. From the time they had met, Sebastián had doubted her chastity. The first time they had sexual relations, she was a virgin. She wanted to surrender herself to the man she had fallen in love with. That is how she had been brought up: to exclusively belong to her future husband. That night, which should have been the most special of her life, Sebastián accused her of being a liar and traitor because she did not bleed when he penetrated her. According to him, blood was the proof of virginity. She still didn't know why she had not bled, but she could never forget such an accusation or the manner in which her future husband got up from the bed, leaving her there, abandoned and despised, like a worn rag, as he dressed again.

I don't want to imagine what might have happened if he had found out about Juan, about the only opportunity when I might have been unfaithful to him and not even then, when I was full of rancor, was I able to. If he questioned my virginity and never wanted to believe me, perhaps he would also question my faithfulness.

While she was continuing to confront her inner void, feeling it without trying to fill it, everything followed its course. It was as though her life were being lived for her, since she was unable to seize hold of it. On her return from that trip to the United States, she visited her gynecologist for a routine check-up and discovered she was pregnant for the second time. Luna was going to have a little brother or sister. She did not want to learn the sex of the baby this time either. She would wait until the birth in October. With so many doubts still unresolved, she was going to be a mother again. She wanted time to stop but it seemed to be playing hide and seek with her. Months had passed since the call from the mysterious and nameless woman who had accused her husband of cheating on her. That big question mark remained in her heart, waiting for her. If she asked Sebastián, it was obvious he would not admit it and might even shout at her for being foolish, as always. She did not know how to deal with that uncertainty. All she knew was that Sebastián continued to schedule more business trips and stayed away from home whenever he liked, while she insisted on creating a perfect home for Luna, one which only existed within her own denial. Now she was pregnant again, she was even more unwilling to ask embarrassing questions or entangle things. There were would soon be two little creatures who deserved the protection of that family. They were her two motives to stay resilient, both now and afterward. Conformity was the only one living happily in Sybil's mind.

Another beautiful and healthy girl was born. Once again, nature deprived Sebastián of the male child he so eagerly wished to infect with his notions of family tradition. Instead, there came Sol, with the golden locks that matched her luminous name. She often asked herself what Sebastián's inner life was like. She knew that he was not happy, but there was zero communication between them. He kept things to himself so much he never bared his heart. He himself joked about it at times, saying that perhaps he did not have one. The only personal thing they spoke about was their daughters. At times, Sybil managed to get him to tell her a little about his work and business deals. He only shed all of his inhibitions when he drank, but not even that allowed him to get rid of his frustrations and blocks. She knew that he had them; he was a human being, after all. Why couldn't he draw close to her and share his sorrows; they could work it out between the two of them. She did not lose hope but he always silenced her with the same scornful phrase that came from the mouth of a man who seemed to be frozen in the nineteenth century.

> "You are a woman Sybil, you'll never understand in any case; it is a tough world out there! You live in a little bubble; you don't know anything thanks to my protection. You don't have to bother yourself as I do!"

***

That Saturday night, they had had a homey dinner. Now that there were two little girls, there were not so many *fiestas.* As often as she could, Sybil tried to arrange romantic candlelit dinners next to the fireplace with her husband's favorite dishes and wines. She had not lost the hope that they would be able to bridge the great gap which divided them and be happy one day. While she put the girls to bed, Sebastián remained in the living room, listening to music as he drank a cognac. When she returned half an hour later, she found him asleep, sprawled on the cold brick floor by the fireplace. He loved to look at the flames and had surely fallen there while doing so. Her heart grew tender, and she was reminded again of the love she had for that man disguised as a warrior who lay, apparently defenseless, before her. She could not leave him. She wanted to wake him so that he could go to bed. It was dangerous to remain there, so close to the still active flames; a flying spark might burn him. She insistently called out his name without any reaction from him. She did not know how much alcohol he had drunk while she was away, but he did not even seem to hear her. She was worried about him and should not have been.

I should have left him there, thrown water on the fire and gone to sleep, letting him wake up on his own, but I had had a few glasses of wine myself. With that liquid courage you get from alcohol, waking that sleeping dragon became a challenge, and a foolish one at that. I never imagined what might emerge from that beast when he came to, when he returned from the pit of darkness. I continued to call him by name, telling him that he might get burnt if he stayed there. Then I dared to shake his shoulder a little, without suspecting that that would be the detonator. All at once, without being able to control himself in a scene that seemed to take on a life of its own, Sebastián got up and he roughly sat me down. He grabbed hold of my long hair as though it were rope, wound it round my neck, and began trying to strangle me with his enormous hands. I still remember having him on top me, as he insulted me and his eyes grew red with anger. He applied such a brute force I couldn't breathe. It was unearthly. I felt I was beginning to die; there was no sound in my screams. Sebastián seemed not to recognize me, and much less did I recognize him. It had to be a dream, a mere nightmare which I wanted to awake from at once. It couldn't be real, I must have been unconscious; that demon couldn't be my own husband. I still ask myself how it happened that, on hearing one of my choked screams, he became terrified. He let go of me, as though something or someone had warned him not to go further. He suddenly nestled down by the side of the fireplace again, sleepy and without strength. I immediately rose, dead with fright. I don't know if I ran or crawled, much less how I reached the nearest telephone.

At that time, there was no emergency line where she could have reported what she had just gone through to the police. Her mother had travelled to San Andrés and the only other person she'd dare to ring at three in the morning was her father. In the midst of her tears, she woke Dylan, without knowing very well what to say.

"Daddy, a terrible thing has happened with Sebastián. I can't say much about it now. I only want someone to be a witness. If I don't wake up tomorrow morning, it was he who killed me."

She quickly gave him a rough account of what happened and begged him not to turn up at her place. Alarmed by the news, he wanted to get dressed and collect his daughter and granddaughters, but Sybil refused. She only wanted someone to be aware of the occurrence in case the situation got worse when Sebastián woke up again. If she let her father into the house after hearing what he had just said, she knew he would try to kill Sebastián. She could not allow that to happen. She would be responsible for fixing things with her husband, if something called the "day after" still existed for her. Their guardian angels looked after Luna and Sol, who peacefully slept through the ordeal. When he woke up the next morning, Sebastián did not remember a single detail of the hair-raising scene. Sybil even showed him how her neck was inflamed and full of bruises from the struggle. As usual, he said she was crazy and in desperation, she screamed and screamed at him, as never before. She would not allow him to question the truth. This time, it did not matter to her if the children heard her arguing with their father. She did not want to think about what might happen if something similar were to happen again. Having to accept that her life was in danger in her own home seemed unreal. But as Sebastián drank his third cup of coffee and absently browsed through the classified ads in the Sunday paper, she realized she was talking to herself. He completely ignored her and was not interested in getting to the bottom of the problem, no matter how grave it might be. Thanks to her submission, it was to be another unresolved chapter of her life. Perhaps her husband was right and it was a storm in a teacup. Perhaps it was the kind of thing a model wife had to put up with.

But from then on, I was terrified, terrified of the man who slept alongside me every night. How little my life was worth. I didn't know what to think of that monster who had awakened before me, showing me all of his destructive power.

As soon as Cassandra returned from her trip, a very worried Dylan told her what had happened a few days before.

> "I'm worried. I'm afraid that Sybil's marriage won't last forever, Cassy."

It was the third time that someone within Sybil's reality would utter that same idea. This time, she did not hear it, because she was not present at the conversation between her parents. It was clear that that affirmation had kept acquiring strength and conviction. Like her boss, Mr. Villarraga, who had said it sometime before, her father was a veteran of the school of hard knocks. This made it easy for him to see that which his daughter's eyes wouldn't want to internalize, even after eight years of married life.

***

For a long time now, Sebastián had been trying to expand the international alliances of the companies he successfully represented in Colombia. In the past few months, he had had to travel to Miami several times for meetings with the directors of some of them. One evening, after getting back early from work, he told Sybil to dress up, because he would be taking her to a restaurant. That was strange; he preferred dining at home on weekdays, but this time he himself ordered Mauricia to feed the girls and let them see a video before going to sleep. He wanted to use the occasion to explain all the details of some plan he had. While they ate, Sybil could not believe what she was hearing. His proposal was that they would live in Miami. His new dealings opened the possibility of obtaining a business visa and taking his family with him. Sebastián told her:

> "It's what you have always wanted. That city has always fascinated you. I also think that it would be great for the girls. Compared to Bogotá, it's a safe, trouble-free city for them to grow up in and they can also learn English at an early age and speak it without an accent. It will be a new start for us, Syb. You're right. Our marriage isn't going very well. With the change, I'm sure we can work things out."

On hearing those words, her heart filled with hope. Without thinking twice, she spontaneously agreed. She would leave behind all of her professional achievements and would not be able to work in the United States because the visa which had been recommended to Sebastián by his lawyers would only allow him to. Once again, she would be a mere housewife, but Luna and Sol deserved to have a full-time mother, at least until they were older. It wasn't a sacrifice. She adored her daughters and enjoyed every moment she spent with them. But even more, she was thrilled by the idea of having a happy home. Her husband's words kept echoing in her mind for days after that. It would be a new start for the two of them. She felt that it was worth the risk. In short, it if did not work out, they could always return to Bogotá. It was not as though they were being forced into exile.

My eyes gleamed with hope again. I felt miserable, but my life couldn't have been so bad, since that kind of opportunity wouldn't have come to me if it had. Seeing that I had so much, it was my fault that I felt so unhappy. How could I have been so dissatisfied? It must have been a loose screw in my head.

Because she had not lived in Boston long before getting married, she had not been able to perfect her English. Her wish to live the famous American dream to the full still lingered. She wanted to learn from her own mistakes and had completely failed to take advantage of the first chance to do so in Boston. She also wanted to realize her childhood dream, and she would not squander her second opportunity. This time, she would not miss out. The future of her marriage was at stake. She wanted to be happy with Sebastián. The move was her last hope. For better or worse, she said yes.

In two months, she arranged it all. She completely dismantled her life. She resigned from her job, sold the furniture, rented the house to a multinational, and packed up the belongings of the four of them. Luna was now six and Sol three. The Three Musketeers, the nickname she used when she wanted to make the girls laugh, were finally on the road to happiness. Sebastián had explained from the beginning, that he would be commuting between Bogotá and Miami while trying to set up a permanent home with them. She understood it perfectly: they could not live without his work. She thus gave everything up and wagered on love, which is what she most wanted and did not have. She had to let go and let life take her along. Such a radical change had to be happening for a reason, although she still did not know what it was.

When she first arrived in the new city, the strong motivation she got from having to organize everything was obvious. She was busy and pleased by the novelty of it. The system was so different from that of her own country. She was not in her comfort zone, but was willing to learn. The girls soon adapted to their school in Coral Gables, and she quickly finished decorating the apartment they had found in Key Biscayne. She devoted all of her time to caring for the girls and her home. Sebastián stayed with them for ten days each month, more or less. Whenever he could, he stretched it to two weeks, but his presence in Bogotá was still indispensable; he had to ensure that the operations he was starting would continue to yield the results he and his partners expected. While the girls were at school, the television became her best English teacher. She had got the foundations from Dylan when she was young, but the chance to speak and practice it had been relatively little. To say that she needed to speak English in Miami was a joke, but she made an effort to practice it whenever she could. She soon had a new group of girlfriends, with whom she lunched now and again. They were the mothers of Luna and Sol's little friends and had similar lifestyles. They all seemed to be cut from the same cloth. She had everything she could wish for. Once again, she lived on the seashore and when she awoke every morning, felt the breeze which reminded her of her childhood. She often walked on the beach with Luna and Sol. She saw that they were happy and at ease in their new environment. Whenever she saw them laugh and run about, she felt that her life made sense.

Time passed and Sebastián never managed to live with them full time. He had another excuse: he was not interested in becoming a resident of the United States because if he changed his status, he would have to pay an unbelievable amount of taxes to the government. Money continued to be his first priority. Not even for his daughters and marriage was he willing to pay a little more. And why all the fuss about saving money? Day by day, his companies prospered. Sybil could not figure it out.

That Sebastián couldn't stay with us all the time was already a fact, so once again, I looked for a way to adapt myself to his changing plans. I wanted to get back to work. Unwilling to accept that I couldn't, I consulted an immigration lawyer with some money I saved out of the household expenses, who confirmed that given the situation of Sebastian's companies, the process of changing our visa to one that would allow me to work would be quick and easy. When I enthusiastically put it to Sebastián on his next visit, however, I got a resounding no. He even told me off for seeking legal advice from a stranger, and again, told me not to be so stupid.

She felt that everyone had their life organized except her. It then occurred to her that it was perfect moment to resume her education. The children were doing very well at school and she would be able to find the time she would need to study again. She had always wanted to get a master's in international relations; her thirst for knowledge was still strong. Sebastián agreed to the idea and to pay for it, even though the course was expensive. She could not believe that he had finally accepted one of her ideas! She spent months doing the paperwork required by the University in Miami and was soon enrolled in the program. Most of the classes were at night; as a postgraduate course designed for working adults, this obviously made it easier for most of the students. She had to find a nanny to look after Luna and Sol for the couple of hours she would be away from home.

Everything collapsed on me like a stack of dominoes. He refused to hire

Eloísa, who already looked after Luna and Sol when we would dine at the home of some friend in Miami. I found it hard to understand the attitude of this man. He had agreed to pay the thousands of dollars it would cost me to study for two years but refused to pay $15 per hour for the nanny I needed. I never found an explanation for those kinds of values.

She felt dispirited again. Miami was not turning out to be the solution to her problems. She had packed them in the suitcase she had taken from Bogotá, and they still remained in her new closet, unresolved.

Her economic situation was paradoxical. What had happened with her master's applied to many other aspects of her life. Sebastián was generous about some things but a terrible miser about others. Every month, he brought her the exact amount of money, in cash, that she needed to live on. For no motive was she to exceed that limit. She did not have a credit card in case she had to buy something else. She lived in an exclusive district of the city, in a new condominium with furniture of the best quality. The private school her daughters attended was also top rate. It was a strange setting for a woman who could not even pay for a gym or some classes in this or that. Sybil seemed to be a kind of slave living in the middle of the twentieth century. Since she was no longer working, her husband assumed that she had time to take over all the responsibilities of the family. She was the driver, cleaner, cook, housekeeper, babysitter, gardener, manager—in short, all that and more, without getting a salary or even a thank-you kiss from time to time.

A couple of years passed like that and whenever she looked back, it was clear that she felt cheated. Sebastián never kept his promises. The husband she had had in Bogotá was replaced by a tourist who visited her ten days each month.

I felt so alone, so abandoned, I didn't even have a job to keep me sane, as I did in Bogotá. Alcohol soon turned into my most loyal friend. In the evenings, after I'd picked up Luna and Sol from school, I would prepare the evening meal while they did their homework. I amused myself by trying out new recipes. During the day, I longed for my date with Pinot Noir or Syrah. At six dollars a bottle, they were the only wines I could afford. It was my only comfort, that nightly ritual before going to sleep in a bed plagued by loneliness.

The wine helped her to escape from reality or least look at it through a less tragic light. Though it had never been her intention, those three years in Miami were crucial for the secret unfolding of her heart. It was a time that allowed her to divorce herself from the person who seemed not to love her; emotionally, that is, so that she no longer loved him in turn. In the end, she spent so much time weeping alone that her tears dried up.

A couple of months before she decided to return to Bogotá, a letter for Sybil arrived in the mail. It did not have a return address, but she could see that it had come from Colombia. At first sight, it seemed like the worst thing that could have happened to her, but she needed the slap on the face. Nothing had worked; maybe this time she would finally react. In the envelope were two photos, nothing more. They showed Sebastián embracing and kissing Madeline at a party for the employees of the company. At last, she could put a face to his secret life: that of Madeline Orozco. She was only to learn her name many years later, but for now, the photos confirmed that there *was* another woman. She never found out who sent that envelope or if it had anything to do with that phone call she'd received several years before. This time, she did not feel that her guts were ripped out. Nothing was impossible for her now; she had become immune to suffering and sorrow, she thought. Why? That was the question she asked herself. Why had her husband behaved like that with her? What did that woman with the face of a high-class whore have that she did not? She felt as though she had become completely invisible. A few days later, on a Friday night, Sebastián arrived in Miami, on the last flight from Bogotá as usual. She decided to serve dinner on the terrace, so that the girls would not hear their conversation. She was afraid, but also had so much to say, so much to unburden herself of.

We dined in silence. I'd decided not to tell him about the photos, only my decision to return to Bogotá. I wanted a divorce, I said, and he began to laugh sarcastically while he chewed over the poisonous words he would speak.

> "You can't leave me. Don't be an idiot. You need me. Who's going to support you, tell me? Or you think it's going to be easy to find another jerk willing to take you, a flabby, middle-aged woman with two kids?"

He served himself more wine from the bottle and continued to mock and insult, without my being able to say a word.

> "Don't you see you can't make a guy stiff anymore? Not even one of those Cuban greasers would want to take you on. Go on, try to find out and you'll see I'm right!"

It was the last thing she heard before opening the sliding door and going to her bedroom, defeated again. She was only thirty-two. Middle aged? Flabby? Who was he talking about? But she believed it with all the rest. She went straight to the mirror in the bathroom to look at herself. She hadn't even realized how old she looked. Maybe her husband was right. What would she do once she was divorced? How was she going to sort things out on her own?

Everyone thought that my life was enchanted, a fairy tale full of love and romance. I'd chosen not tell anyone about my life; I didn't want any consolation from the people around me. There wasn't a single girlfriend of mine who knew the reality of my life. I was so tough on myself. I hated to accept failure. I couldn't get out of this blind alley on my own but couldn't pay for a therapist either. Sebastián hadn't even taken out health insurance for us. What's more, he always made fun of psychologists, saying that they made easy money at the cost of the weak.

Of course, Sebastián did not want Sybil to go back to Bogotá with the girls. He delayed things, ignoring all her pleas. Beating her head against the walls of her dark alley, she continued to drink more and more. She reached the point where it was two bottles each night instead of one.

I felt utterly exhausted that night, so worn out I didn't want to live anymore. I showered thousands of kisses on my daughters. I told them how much I loved them and waited until they fell asleep. I was so proud of them; they were the only thing that made me feel that my life had been worth living. My husband's words during his last visit quickly left their effect on my sick mind and it wasn't long before I convinced myself that, if I was that old and useless, there was nothing left to live for. Their grandmothers and my sister Betrys would take care of them once I was gone. Moreover, although Sebastián was a poor husband, he was a good father and they would be in good hands. It was already late that night when I locked myself in the bathroom, with a small, sharp knife I took from the kitchen. I spent several hours, seated on the cold marble floor, crying as quietly as I could, and playing around with my veins without finding the nerve to sink the knife in. I only managed to make a superficial cut in the skin of my left wrist, which bled a little. The thought of my daughters acted as a lifesaver. They were the angels who protected me in those moments of profound darkness. Their smiling little faces, their kisses, and the way they said, "I love you, Mommy" passed before me, ever more vividly. I couldn't let my demons win this battle. Where was the girl whose desperate wish to live had beaten death some few times in her childhood? Where was my self-respect? I had to find it, to make the effort. The time to return to the other side had not yet come.

The following morning, she pretended as best she could. Although she had not killed herself, she felt physically and emotionally dead. Since she had no one to do the daily chores for her, she got up, showered, and took the girls to school as usual. Then she headed to the bank to get money for the shopping. The door of the elevator she took to the third floor opened, and she got in, downcast and sad. If zombies existed, she was one of them now.

There he was, like a great human statue in the middle of the elevator. He must have been at least six foot six. I had never seen such a perfect specimen of a black man before. The smoothness of his skin and the gleam of his eyes and teeth were not of this world. Impeccably dressed in an elegant white linen suit, he had the bearing of a model. I felt a little intimidated, I didn't deserve the kindly smile he gave me. Remembering that I had tried to end my life the night before, I felt dirty and worthless. I lowered my gaze while I pushed button number three.

She stood with her back to him, looking toward the door. Out of the void, his manly, crystal-clear voice, full of peace, spoke to her from behind.

> "You look sad and unhappy. Have you looked at yourself in the mirror lately, to see your powerful inner light and beauty, without your physical shell getting in the way?"

He paused for a second to let Sybil absorb what he had just asked her and went on:

> "With a beautiful true self like yours, you should be posing for the cover of *Vogue* magazine."

That was all he said. Before leaving the elevator, I turned, timidly smiled and thanked him. I didn't know what else to say.

His image forever remained engraved on her memory. He was an angel, sent from heaven. What else could he have been? He did not even look real. Also, when she thought about it now, she realized that no other button than the one she had pushed had been alight. What did that mean? When she took the elevator down to the car park, she found no trace of him. As soon as she arrived home with the groceries, she put the bags on the floor and rushed to the guest bathroom to scrutinize her face in the mirror. Something had just changed her. That was the last day of her living death. In a matter of seconds, that angel achieved something she had not been able to do in eleven years. She could not continue to destroy herself. She had tried to cut her wrists the night before but she realized that she had been slowly committing suicide for years. She was a permanent victim of mistreatment, starved of love. The angel was right; she had to start looking for her inner beauty. It was not a matter of becoming a model for *Vogue.* She understood the message; what she had to find was her true being. It was still intact; someone had finally confirmed it for her, even though her mental filters were still too distorted and sickly for her to perceive it.

That encounter filled me with faith, and in the paper that Sunday, I found a horoscope that helped me to make the definitive decision. According to the astrologist, everyone under my sign had exactly six months to make a complete change in their lives. I felt it was an ultimatum, at least that is how I interpreted it. With that angel, heaven sent me a sign and for the first time since getting married to Sebastián, I felt a need to pray, to ask for help. I had completely abandoned my spirituality to devote myself to the material world and the addiction to things I mistakenly thought would lead me to the top. Sebastián was an atheist, and even in that, I wanted to imitate him.

What had that man done to dominate even the most distant corners of her conscious and subconscious mind? There was no part of her being he had not passed through, demolishing all like a cruel invader. With a pitiless calculation, he had molded her to his whim, a great sculptor without the fame he deserved. Now Sebastián had a woman made of stone without any self-esteem. She entered the church and felt that light was being re-injected into her. There was no mirror there but she was surely shining like a light bulb. She knelt, humbly surrendering herself and asked God out loud for the strength and wisdom she needed to go forward. She also prayed for forgiveness for having abandoned him during all those years of perdition. God acted quickly. That same afternoon, Adriana, her best friend in Bogotá, rang her to say that she was divorcing Juan Carlos, a childhood friend of Sebastián. They had both got married at nearly the same time. She told her about the woman lawyer who was helping her and Sybil immediately felt that that was the next sign. She listened and without telling her much about her own intention to follow her lead, jotted down the name of that lawyer, who now turned into her last resource.

In the following days, she only thought of one thing: she had to return to Bogotá as soon as possible. She had been wed in a Catholic ceremony and her marriage was also governed by Colombian civil law, so no court or judge in the United States would be able to help her. She had lost her self-esteem, but not her intelligence. She took advantage of Sebastián's absence from Miami to organize the whole plan. This time, she would give him no choice. As soon as the girls finished the school year in June of 1999, the three of them would return. Suddenly everything began to speed up. It was as though a door had opened, showing her a new world full of possibilities. She recovered her hopes again. She felt new ideas reach her mind as if by magic. God have forgiven her and had heard her prayer. She had a goal again and a time limit in which to reach it and knew that she was very disciplined. In the past, she had always achieved what she set out to do. It could not be different now. Her divorce was the only thing she thought about, day and night.

My goal was to obtain the divorce by the end of 1999. I didn't know how I was going to achieve it; I only knew that I would. I didn't understand the consequences or the implications of my decision, only that it was a question of life or death – my life or death.

She was often overwhelmed by doubts. She was scared to death. She did not want to imagine what might happen if Sebastián were to discover that her decision to return was linked to her plan to begin the divorce proceedings as soon as she reached Colombia. She knew how violent he was. He would want to kill her or take her daughters from her or who knows what else. Whatever were to happen, she felt that this was her last chance. She had touched bottom; her life hung by a thread. She was a suicidal addict who needed help and God was offering it to her; she could not disappoint him. Like a puppet being manipulated from behind a screen, she got on that plane with her daughters, without looking back. She had no idea what the future had in store for her but she did know what her past and present were like. Anything had to be better than that.

***

That evening, running on automatic pilot, she turned up at the office of Aminta Bessudo, the same lawyer in charge of her friend Adriana's divorce. When she first caught sight of her, she was overwhelmed. *What a striking woman,* she admiringly thought. *What elegance, what bearing!* Aminta was sixty and the opposite of Sybil. At a glance, you could see she was overflowing with self-esteem and power. A divorced woman who had triumphed, Aminta was in control of her own life and had gained her independence twenty years before, at a time when divorce was a scandalous matter in the country. She exuded confidence through her pores, which is precisely what Sybil needed just then. If Aminta had achieved it, Sybil did not see why she could not as well.

After listening to her story for an hour and half, Aminta gave her a friendly smile and explained that she would only accept her as a client if she was willing to follow all of her instructions down to the last detail. The lawyer wanted the two of them to plan the divorce strategy in secret, without Sebastián finding out. In other words, Sybil would have to pretend to him while Aminta was preparing the whole case, before presenting it to the judge of the family court for a ruling. It was the only way to prevent Sebastián from arming himself to the teeth, like the warrior he was. But Sybil, still innocent and foolish, wanted the divorce to be arranged between the three of them, to do it on good terms, not bad ones. She felt uncomfortable about the trick being proposed to her.

Aminta became cross, and she was completely right. She was the expert, and I was telling her how to do her job. Annoyed, she got up from her desk and said she couldn't represent me.

> "You still don't have what it takes to make this step. Sybil, go home, try to make up with your little husband and someday, when you are really ready, contact me."

I honestly felt insulted. I didn't know what to think of her arrogance. Was this the lawyer who was going to help me get out of the mess?

To feel insulted was a good sign. Her ego had reacted! Her self-esteem began to awaken, that petulance gave her back her spark. She never knew if Aminta's strategy had been intentional, but it was smart of her to have challenged Sybil. Her ego wanted to prove that she would be able to carry it through to the end. The dominating personality of that woman older than herself was doubtless what Sybil needed. The proceedings she would soon start would not be successful if done in a lukewarm way; they had to be conclusive and permanent. This time, the angel that God had sent her was cruel and blunt, the best of its kind. She soon wanted to be like her, inside and out. She wanted to have her confidence, the wisdom she reflected. She wanted to dress like her, live the same way. Aminta was everything Sybil wished to be once she would become fully fledged. She was going to get a divorce and completely reinvent herself. To do that, she needed therapy. Her parents lent her the money she needed to pay the fees of the lawyer and the psychologist.

The moment she returned to Bogotá, she spoke with her parents, and without going into the details, gave a general account of her past few years and her decision to seek a divorce. Both of them gave her their complete support. On hearing what his daughter had to say, Dylan probably said, "I knew it" to himself, recalling his premonition before the wedding and all along Sybil's marriage. Aminta had recommended Mary Cotes, a psychologist who was an expert in marriage counseling. They spoke on the phone before the first appointment; Sybil would have to read several books before beginning the sessions. She could not believe what was in them, there before her eyes. Misogyny was an illness and her husband had a hundred-mile-per-hour case of it. There was not a single symptom that did not fit Sebastián precisely. What a great relief it was to read the testimonies of hundreds of women who had suffered from their misogynist husbands, just as she had. There, at last, was proof that she was not crazy and that, more importantly, she was not alone. She had let twelve years of her life go by before accepting the gravity of what she had experienced. In her first appointment, the question was overpowering and direct.

> "You have two options with this therapy, Sybil. Now that you have found out about the illness you have been living with, I can help you to try to save the marriage and

> to do that Sebastián would have to come with you to the therapy and be willing to undergo a psychiatric treatment. Or I can give you the tools you need to recover your self-esteem, get divorced, and start again. Both options will take time, several years. It is different for each couple, for each individual. You tell me what you want and on the basis of that we will get down to work."

After having devoured those books, which made her familiar with her rival, Mrs. Misogyny, she had no doubt that this was a matter of her own salvation. Twelve years of memories were there, like daggers that made her heart constantly bleed. Her enemy was too strong. She did not have the strength to fight anymore. She waved the white flag and fled from the battlefield. The second option Mary offered her was the one she chose—and without the slightest regret.

***

These were months of hard work. Day and night, she had to pretend, so that Sebastián would not find out about what she and her lawyer were secretly planning. She felt like a criminal; she felt that she was not being fair to him—as though he had ever been to her! It was a state of mental confusion which she would not have been able to overcome without the therapy. She felt completely guilty, yet at the same time knew that she could not turn back the pages of the book. The end of the story was what kept her alive.

It was clear that it was a difficult case for Aminta. Sybil did not know anything about her husband's financial situation. He had never shared that information with her. Apart from the house, which was in both their names, she knew nothing, not even her husband's salary. To work out a way to ensure her client's future, Aminta had to start from scratch. Sybil's inexperience was a problem. She had never made long-term financial plans. All she wanted was to legally remove Sebastián from her life and win custody of their daughters, though she did understand that she would need money to start from zero again. For her, a million pesos was the same as a billion; she had never handled large sums of money before. The budget she had been responsible for only amounted to the household expenses of two adults and two children. Those accounts she handled well enough. The money covered their needs and she paid her monthly bills on time, but her mind was not used to the complex calculations required to secure the long-term future of herself and her daughters. All her life, she had depended economically on others, and it made her feel more helpless than a handicapped person. A multi-million-peso budget was beyond her, but one thing she did know; once and for all, she would no longer be a kept woman. Thus, she was not interested in getting a monthly alimony out of the divorce. Sebastián would manipulate her with that monthly check for the rest of her life, probably holding it back to make her suffer. She had to get rid of her outdated mental schemes, a daily reminder of the supposed helplessness a psychologically sick husband had brainwashed her into believing. She needed to recover her independence. She wanted to prove to herself she could go forward on her own. No matter what the amount she was legally entitled to, she would demand a single payment rather than installments. She wanted to learn what she had never known, a far-from-easy task. Nevertheless, her new life was the guru that would guide her along the road to the end. By the beginning of November, Aminta had everything ready. It was going to be a pretty unpleasant business, and she would have to turn herself into an executioner, but Sybil was still willing to do everything she asked of her. Aminta had just rung her cell phone to give her the green light and the instructions she would have to follow for the next stage.

Sebastián left for the office very early that morning, so I rang him around 10:00 AM *to invite him to lunch at Picazo, my favorite restaurant in the Zona Rosa. I told him it was very important for us to get together and I couldn't wait till that night; I didn't want to do it in front of the girls. He said he had a lot of work but agreed to have lunch with me. It was incredible how much the therapy had helped me. I felt like another person, ready to climb the highest mountain without stopping till I reached the top. Nothing was going to get in my way. Even the tone of my voice had begun to change. If I hadn't felt so emboldened, I would not have been able to say a third of what I said.*

For the first time in the twelve years we'd been together, there were no drinks at lunch. After a couple of lemonades, I began to tell him that I had decided to separate and everything was ready for our divorce. Sebastián was always curt but now he was dumb, so stunned he didn't know what to say to me.

> "Why are you blowing things up like this, Sybil?"
>
> "I'm tired of watching you deny the failure of our marriage all the time. And since you don't want to take me seriously, I had to act on my own."

Then I handed him a business card with Aminta's name and phone number. I explained that she was the lawyer who was representing me and that she would be expecting him in her office the following day at 11:00 AM. *Looking a little sorry, he said that he'd been thinking things over and was willing to find room for me in his business, where I could help him with certain jobs he'd set aside for me. I was right, he added, and he was willing to change, because our family was the most important thing for him. He asked me to forgive him. He asked for a second chance. I replied that it was already too late. I didn't want him anymore. All I wanted was to get divorced. I finished by reminding him of the appointment with my lawyer the next day and this time, I insisted that his presence there was indispensable.*

Her words sounded like a threat to him. Even though he was sober, having drunk nothing more than lemonade, Sebastián lost control. Shouting at her, he made it clear that her foolishness had gone too far. His usual impersonal tone was much more pronounced. With his usual sarcastic smile, he tried to hide his feelings from the familiar faces in the restaurant, which now seemed like a wasp's nest. He got up from the table and gave her a forced good-bye kiss on the cheek while whispering into her ear,

> "Remember that no one gives orders to Sebastián Obregón. I am not going to any appointment and you can tell your little lawyer lady that there won't be a divorce."

I remained there alone, sipping a cappuccino, while waiting for the bill, trying to process what had just occurred. This time his words hadn't frightened me. I felt in control of my power. It was a strange sensation, very new to me.

Now everything was up to him. If he missed the appointment, Aminta would call the judge and instruct him to proceed with the suit. The whole point of his being there was to allow him and Aminta to reach an agreement without needing to go to the law.

I don't know who he believed less in, myself or the name engraved on that elegant business card I'd just given him with the details of my lawyer. In his eyes, we were both women and both equally dumb brutes. If his mind was working in the usual way, he probably wanted to convince himself that it wasn't so serious, and he chose not to believe me. On Thursday afternoon, Aminta lodged the divorce petition before the family court judge who was handling the case. Sebastián never appeared at her office, so, after letting a reasonable time elapse, she called me to say that she had taken the following step. I had just sued my own husband, the father of my daughters. I didn't know what to think. My heart was beating as if it were about to explode. I felt afraid and at the same time liberated.

Sybil was finally liberated after all those hellish months since her return to Bogotá. She had come back to recover almost everything she had thrown aside when she'd bet that Miami would be a happier life. Now she was back, with her house, furniture, club, girlfriends, daughters' school, and everything else that had made her a real person, except for one difference: she no longer loved her husband. It was clear that Miami had not mended her life. It had, in fact, done just the opposite: it had rid her of all the love she had for the man she had promised to live with "until death do us part" with a man whose bed she had to sleep in while all this was happening.

We didn't even touch each other anymore. I only felt indifference and scorn for him. It was difficult for me to understand how that man I had loved so much wound up being a stranger to me. I felt he had done me so much harm. I felt so resentful toward him. I remember how, in the end, I slept with my back to him and as far away as possible from that body which no longer sent me any sign of that false love we had once had.

They continued to live under the same roof as the legal procedures followed their course. Sebastián only learned of the petition on the Friday of the following week, when he had to meet the bi-weekly payroll of the employees of his company. The manager of his bank rang to tell him the bad news: the account was embargoed. His lawyer immediately investigated the matter and learned that the suit originated from a family court. Sebastián did not have to hear any more details; he rang Sybil at once. She cold-bloodedly told him what she had been rehearsing in her mind for the past few days while she waited precisely for this phone call.

> "You didn't want to go to the appointment with my lawyer, Sebastián. None of this would have happened if you had taken me seriously for once."

The lawyer for the Obregón family was Artemio Uricoechea. Dr. Uricoechea made him see that his wife's intentions were serious. Aminta was the best divorce lawyer in Bogotá. There was no way of beating her. She had never lost a case. He advised him to lower his guard and comply with her demands, or rather, Sybil's.

I did not want that much, I only wanted my freedom. How expensive getting it back was proving to be. I remember seeing him there, finally seated in Aminta's office. The fierce and dangerous wolf now turned into a sheep. Seeing him so meek tore my soul apart. I felt full of guilt again, because I hadn't been able to do this in a less traumatic way. I never meant to harm him. I got the custody of my daughters and the house that was in both our names. I would sell it and start with that. My sense of guilt was so great I agreed to split the girls' expenses with him. I don't know why I imagined that the money from the sale of the real estate would last forever. He would be responsible for paying their school fees and health insurance and I would pay for our food, housing, clothing and the rest. Aminta didn't agree with my idea of what being fair was, but I was stupid about money then. I felt like Scrooge McDuck with a vault full of coins and banknotes bigger than that of the central bank. Still manipulating me, Sebastián kept insisting that getting the house meant that his savings were gone, so that sharing what he thought of as my loot with his daughters was the least I could do.

She was focused on her freedom and an easy conscience, something she had only nominally known, because her conscience had never let her be tranquil. She did not want to ask for anything that might cause regrets later on. Dealing with and wiping away the guilt of being the wicked witch who had ruined the fairy tale of the enchanted prince was already more than enough. They signed the divorce settlement in December, just as she had set herself to do—on their wedding anniversary. She felt that ending the twelve-year cycle on the same day it had begun was a good omen. The astrologer in that American newspaper who had given her six months to change her life would have been proud of her. It was the best Christmas present she had ever had and the worst for Sebastián. Now that there was absolutely nothing he could do to avoid the divorce, he had been routed. That woman he had trampled on—the defenseless, submissive one who supposedly was worthless without him—had come up with a perfect strategy, and had followed it through to the end and got her own way.

Once again, the wind blew in her favor. The year 2000 was around the corner. A new year, a new life; those old sayings never went out of fashion. For Sybil, it meant starting the new millennium as a divorced woman. Since it was an event of world importance, it had to mean something very positive for her at last. She was free for the first time in thirty-three years. She realized that she'd always been controlled up to then, first by Cassandra, then by Sebastián. What a painful awakening the acceptance of that had been! She had never controlled anything in her life; others always controlled everything for her and she was fed up with all of them. As soon as she could, now that the house was in her name, she put it up for sale. She decided to pay back the money she had borrowed from her parents and finish paying the fees of the lawyer and psychologist, whose services she did not need anymore. She would buy a small apartment and live off the interest of the rest while she looked for work. She had big plans. She was another woman now, she felt she was the mother she had always wanted to be for Luna and Sol. Now she would finally be able to study for the master's she had not even begun in Miami, the fault of the stupid pretensions of Sebastián and the world he surrounded her with. She would simultaneously study and work at the same university she had to leave when she moved from the country. Her old bosses were there and would give her a friendly welcome again. Villarraga, who had foretold her divorce, was no longer vice-president, but he continued to work there as a titular professor and he helped her to find work. She would attend classes from 7:00 to 10:00 in the morning and work from 10:00 to 6:00 PM. Neither the long hours nor the hard work mattered to her; she was happy. She felt like the explorer girl she had been in her magical and enchanted San Andrés. She was awakening to the most fascinating spring within herself. Perhaps she would be able to fly again and even meet up with the lost guardian angel she was still unable to bring back to reality.

THE GREEN OF THE ABUNDANT NATURE

Just as it had been when she began her life alongside Sebastián, the slate before her was completely blank. This time, chalk in hand, she would write in her own way. She knew that she would make a lot of mistakes, since she did not know what to write very well, but that is what it was about: to learn from your mistakes until you only wrote the best. Her first mistake soon came. She had made a verbal agreement with Sebastián. It was just as well that it was verbal, since she was a beginner at divorce. She needed to experience or rather, to learn from it. Her priority was that the girls would suffer as little as possible, so it had been agreed that their father could visit them three nights a week, when all four would dine together. The idea was to give them a chance to talk about everything that was happening in their girlish world; their school, girlfriends and so forth.

Every two weeks, the girls spent the weekend with him, and on the weekends, when they were with me, we usually lunched at the home of one of the Obregóns. I continued to go there with Luna and Sol. I wanted to maintain friendly links with them. Our families had known each other all their lives; I didn't want to spoil any of that. For the sake of the girls, I insisted on having a cordial relationship with all of them and for that reason, I didn't mind that Sebastián continued to be part of my life. He would be my daughters' father all his life; that much was not negotiable.

Soon the experiment turned into a nightmare. Sebastián kept feeling hurt and defeated because of the divorce, or "Sybil's treachery" as he called it. He still could not believe it. He was living in denial and did not know how to handle his animosity toward her. He began to arrive with a few drinks under his belt on the nights he was invited to dine with the girls. Alcohol continued to alter him. After the third drink, his sick verbal aggressiveness became uncontrollable. He blamed her for everything in front of the children, criticized the way she lived now, the things she spent money on, and her priorities and plans. According to him, everything she did was wrong. Months passed like that and her husband's attitude became even worse. Nothing positive was gained by letting him come so near. She felt married, although she no longer was. The negative energy which Sebastián transmitted was so strong it unbalanced her every time they saw each other.

He kept threatening that he'd never forgive me. He was still terse when he spoke, but he didn't have to say much either. He had been born with the gift of finding the two or three most offensive and insulting words in the dictionary to wound his enemy to death. Now I was his enemy. With the same old cynical laugh, he reminded me of what I never wanted to hear again.

> "You won't be able to survive without me, but I'll lie low and wait. Someday I will see you down on your knees, begging for my help and you'll see how I'll laugh."

The sheep she had seen signing the divorce papers reverted to type—the fierce wolf. When she heard him speak like that, it only served to reconfirm that divorcing herself from that sick human being had clearly been the only option for her and her daughters.

The agreement about the dinners in our apartment lasted a little more than two years. Once again, I'd taken too long to react. The good news was that it took two, rather than twelve years, to wake up to the obvious. Nothing was in writing. One day I called him and said that I didn't want him to enter my apartment again, and when he took the girls out to dinner, he'd now have to pick them up at the porter's lodge.

The period following her divorce was a stage of mixed feelings, of blacks and whites wanting to turn into grays. The inner peace she now had gave her the confidence that she was on the right track. At the same time, without a single key to her future, she felt a great uncertainty. She was afraid of the unknown and this weakened her power. It continually filled her with doubt. It was hard to deal with all those beliefs that she was worth little, which is what her oppressors wanted her to accept as absolute fact during many years of psychological abuse. She was no longer a girl.

It was more of an effort than she'd imagined to learn to use her old mental tools which had grown rusty with disuse, but she had to polish them if she were to create the life she was proposing for herself. Despite the dubious atmosphere, she felt strongly motivated and convinced that she would forge ahead on her own. She wanted to do it for her daughters. She could not disappoint them. She understood her life in another way now. She was proud to be able to give them this new example of freedom and independence. She sensed that some day she would look back and feel satisfied with the path she was taking. When her daughters reached the age when they would make their own decisions, they would avoid the mistakes which she, in her ignorance, had made. They would choose for themselves, not for others.

At a glance, it seemed that everything was running smoothly and the economic agreement with Sebastián was bringing the needed results. She found a dilapidated apartment in an old building in a tranquil district of the city near the girls' school. Using her experience in design and decoration, she completely remodeled it. It was neither as luxurious nor as spacious as her previous home, but each of them had her own room and nothing was lacking. The decor was modern, simple, and harmonious. It was a reflection of the new Sybil, the one she was managing to create, little by little, step by step. Nereida was the woman who helped with the housework while she studied and worked all day. At night, she was so tired when she arrived home that the only thing she wanted to do was to be with Luna and Sol for a while and then go to sleep.

The temptations of being single soon began to stalk her. Her friend Adriana turned out to be too much for her. Both were eager to inaugurate their new civil status. Life could not be just working and studying, Adriana insisted; she deserved a break, to have fun from time to time. They went out to fashionable restaurants. That night life, which was new to her, was like a serpent that beguiled her—only it took her a little longer to realize it than was strictly necessary.

After dinner, we stayed there, drinking martinis and celebrating for a couple of hours more. Terry was the owner of the restaurant we usually went to. He was newly divorced too, and sat down with us when he finished cooking. As three victims infected by the same virus – lack of love – we identified with each other and all wanted to get it out of our system.

Adriana was her sidekick but also her opposite. She didn't work or study. She was irresponsible, a big spender, and lover of the good life, but Sybil felt that her presence in her life was ironically positive. She needed to stop being psycho-rigid now and again. She knew she was too hard on herself at times. After a couple of years, their friendship deteriorated, as might be expected when two women have such different aims. Little by little, they realized they had nothing in common.

I gradually had my fill of those nights of drinking and of the unessential. Adriana began to criticize me for not wanting to go out with the men she introduced me to. I wasn't interested in going out with anyone again, I felt it was still too early. My goal wasn't to replace Sebastián with a man who would soon turn out to be his clone. I wasn't looking for some new boxers, some guy I'd pick up on the street who would take charge of me again. I wanted to be on my own for a time, while I was to getting to know myself. I could only do that by concentrating on myself and not on a new relationship.

The two grew distant from each other at around the same time that Sybil was finishing her degree. Studying political science and international relations had taught her to understand the troubled situation of the country in which she had been born:

a society afflicted by corruption and the loss of values. Her country was a time bomb and all she heard now was its ticking. She wanted to help. Her heart throbbed with an eagerness to make a difference. She wanted to fly high, not to satisfy her ego, but because it was there, at the top, where the great changes she visualized would be accomplished. She wanted to work in the government, without the need of waving a red flag for the liberal party or a blue one for the conservatives. It was her innocence speaking, firmly convinced that it would simply be a matter of displaying her incorruptible honesty and willingness to serve. She would soon be in the big leagues, helping to reform a system in crisis with her own hands. In these two years following her divorce, Sybil had become her own psychologist and therapist. Little by little, her studies and work had enabled her to recover her self-esteem. There was still a long way to go but she already saw the improvement in her mind and spirit, and she looked like another woman, one who had gone through a physical transformation. She was beginning to shine. There was an air of order, peace, and harmony in her home. The girls felt at peace as part of this new feminine trio. They had their girlfriends and had adjusted to their school and new routine. Their father continued to take an interest in them. He now lived in an apartment he had remodeled, wanting—above all—to make Luna and Sol feel comfortable with their bachelor father. He moved there after having lived in another apartment his parents temporarily lent him while he organized his new life.

One day, six months more or less after the divorce, I went to leave him some papers in the porter's lodge of that first apartment, which was his family's. Accidentally, I learned from Abundio, the porter, that Sebastián was living with Madeline. Life follows its own clock, which is clearly different to the human one. I never decided to find out the details of his infidelity, nor did I use it as a reason to separate from him. Now life reconfirmed it for me in the simplest way, without needing to lift a finger. The story told by the photos I received in Miami, photos I wasn't capable of using as evidence in the divorce proceedings – was true after all. Madeline did exist. It seemed that she was the one that mysterious phone call was warning me about. To this day, the caller's identity remained unknown to me. It had been a long time ago but I still remembered her saying that his girlfriend was planning to get us separated. Whether she really planned it or not, Madeline achieved her aim. But the idyll didn't last as long as she might have wanted it to. According to Abundio, she became pregnant a while later, but lost the baby. I didn't know the details, but she wound up without the baby and also without Sebastián. Life continued to teach me its wisdom. I was now divorced and no longer felt like the wife who had been the victim of a dirty trick. I no longer felt hurt or sad, and the story I heard was nothing more to me than a chapter of a mediocre soap opera. I never found out what happened to Madeline in the end. As said by several mutual friends, my husband's hobby now was bedding young and successful professional women, a different one each night of the week I learned that the only time he slept at home were the nights when Luna and Sol stayed with him. Was he a broken-hearted man playing the victim, thanks to me, or the victimizer who continued to harm women whenever he could?

While her savings were producing enough for her to live on, thanks to some courses on economics and finance she had taken for her master's, she gradually came to understand the long-term implications of the property settlement she had signed with her ex-husband. It was completely absurd to think she would achieve much if she continued to live off her salary and a modest interest that yielded less and less every year while her daughters continued to grow and have more needs. It was one thing to say you could support two girls, quite another when you realized they were getting bigger every day and quickly turning into little high-class ladies. While the school fees and health insurance Sebastián paid for them did not rise much, Sybil had to cover the growing costs of their clothes, parties, gifts, and trips, at the same time that the interest she received was falling due to the slowdown in the international economy. There was no way to turn the clock back and change the divorce agreement. There was no way of talking about it with Sebastián, who had predicted a dire future from the start. Hadn't he told her she wouldn't be able to cope and he would see her on her knees, begging forgiveness and asking to be taken back?

All this weighed on her mind from time to time, and she did not come up with any brilliant solution, but she imagined that once she had her master's, she would get a better job than the she had one at the university—and a better salary. She kept in contact with Aminta, her lawyer, and they had lunch together now and then. She asked Aminta to help her join one of the presidential campaigns. She did not mind starting as a volunteer; once she was there, they would learn of her dedication, discipline, and commitment to her country. Aminta was a well-known socialite, with very good connections in the world of politics. If you compared Colombia's young democracy with a traditional European monarchy, Aminta would easily be the equivalent of a princess at least! Her help was quick and effective. Sybil soon had contacts with three of the strongest candidates for the upcoming 2002 elections. Now she had to decide which one she wanted to work with. Among her professors for the master's there were former cabinet ministers, army officers, and ambassadors. Thanks to them, she learned to analyze the reality of the country from the most realistic standpoints: the scientific and the academic ones. She had the tools that would enable her to pick a candidate. She knew how to identify the one who had the ability to change the country into the one she dreamed of. With that one, she would work.

> "Sybil, get ready, tonight you're going out to dinner with Cesar Nazareno Ocampo, the right hand man and best friend of Atanasio Holguín Ruiz."

Aminta spoke with her usual arrogance and air of a conqueror, but it no longer bothered Sybil. She and Aminta were now friends. She had not only been her lawyer, but a teacher who wanted her pupil to triumph, to be an example of self-realization to other women.

Atanasio Holguín was the candidate I threw my lot in with. He wasn't the favorite in the polls, but his development plan was the most complete. If he was elected and faithfully carried out his program, the country would be completely different in four years; I was sure of that. As Aminta called me on the cell phone, the news made me jump with joy. Who could suggest me that this wasn't the gateway to heaven I was looking for? I wanted a job that would allow me to earn just enough, without having to dip into my savings, and at the same time work at what I now regarded as my passion: the neediest people of Colombia. I could devote myself to improving the conditions of their lives. I think that my heart never shed the memories of an adolescent girl from the provinces, just come to the capital and seated in a bus, watching the suffering of those street kids. This was my opportunity to help them. I once identified with them; I once went hungry as they did. No doubt I'd gone far since then. It wasn't as though I hadn't suffered, but life had given me the opportunity to educate and prepare myself. I now felt responsible for those who continued to lack the luck I'd had.

She was still so naïve, still a clumsy beginner. How could she know that the world of politics had nothing to do with helping the underprivileged? How could she understand that a corrupt third-world politician did not have the same interests as an idealistic political scientist like herself, a dreamer, a humanist in the full sense of the word who had previously studied anthropology? How could she imagine that anyone who wanted to join that world had to be willing to put a price tag around their neck?

A cold-blooded and malignant man is what I saw when the door of the car opened. I was invited to get in and sit by his side. The chauffeur took us to a restaurant, where we had dinner in a small private salon he'd reserved for the two of us, so that there would be no witnesses. He had just arrived from Monaco, where he lived, and did not want his return to the country to be public knowledge. I felt afraid when I shook his hand. I had never looked into such dense, dark eyes before, which were skillfully hidden by a wild shock of grey hair. They did not seem to have a connection with any specific soul; they were made of fire. He was well over six feet tall and the khaki safari jacket he wore made his robustness impressive. He spoke quickly and did not listen to what I had to say. He constantly interrupted me. I felt his lack of interest as I naively spoke of the social changes I dreamt of for my country. He focused instead on my body from the neck downwards. He looked at me as though I were an ice-cream cone he wanted to suck and lick the last drop out of. He did not even try to hide what was running through his imagination.

"Well, let's get down to the nitty-gritty. What do you want, Miss? How do you think I can help you?"

"I want to help the candidate with his plans for reform and restructuration, help to research and mount the projects."

"That's easy; it is a done deal. I'll speak with our president tomorrow. Come to the campaign headquarters first thing in the morning and I'll take care of the rest."

She was struck by the way he referred to him as the president without his even having won the elections! Although his physicality put her off, he represented her best chance to work closely with Dr. Holguín. No one in the world of politics knew her. She was an outsider, barely beginning now. She had no other line to the candidate, and according to Aminta, he was his loyal man behind the scenes. She shoved her intuition aside, thinking that she may have exaggerated things and was letting herself be terrified by appearances.

I started going to the campaign headquarters and I soon took part in several of the jobs that had to be done. After the dinner we had that night, I couldn't keep Nazareno out of my apartment. He visited me all the time, always with the excuse of talking about the projects for the campaign. He was a lonely man, with a very bad reputation. He was a multimillionaire lawyer, and powerful in every way. His life was enigmatic. It was full of controversy and mystery, just as he had intended. I remembered now the words of one of my professors, who once compared me to Florence Nightingale. That thirst to help and serve made me think that he was misunderstood, that there was a good man hidden within Cesar Nazareno. I wanted to become his friend besides the fact he was also my direct channel to the candidate. He was helping me and sounded sincere.

In March of that year, Sybil got her master's degree and resigned from her job in the university to work full time for the campaign and for Cesar Nazareno.

I became an elegant executive assistant, overqualified and without a salary, who worked for Atanasio Holguín's closest advisor. I spent hours doing research and drafting small projects that I handed over to Nazareno. I thought that Dr. Holguín was becoming familiar with my work and devotion to the cause, and was sure I'd join his inner circle once he became president. At that time, just like Nazareno, I was certain that Holguín would be elected. His position in the polls was improving day by day, and it looked like the electorate liked him more and more. It was a time of uncertainty. I wasn't stupid; I knew I was dangerously risking my skin by trusting that shadowy and sinister man so much, but Aminta was in favor of him, and that put me at ease.

She began to drink more than ever at night when Luna and Sol went to sleep, although at times she also drank at the lunches she now had to attend to consolidate her position in that new world. It was as though some invisible voices were goading her to try the alcohol, voices she clearly heard. Once she drank the first, nothing could stop her. The second soon came and then the third, until she reached the last, without recalling how she had got there.

I was depressed about this new situation that I myself had created. I didn't know how to control the rhythm of my unhealthy and addictive life. I didn't know how to stop what was causing me harm. The world that surrounded me didn't help either. Sebastián was no longer my husband, but he had bequeathed me the worst of habits. Now, Nazareno was spending most of the day in my small home office, and he drank twice as much as Sebastián. How had I fallen into such company? Did my dream of helping people require my venality? I entered a period of complete perdition. I really felt I was in hell. I'd totally lost my bearings and was adrift. I felt was losing the little I had achieved with my divorce, in circumstances where I was a Mrs. Nobody, again dominated by a dysfunctional masculine keeper. I felt the control of a man who was not my husband, not even my boyfriend. What was I doing wrong? Why did I feel imprisoned again, without the freedom which I'd managed to attain for such a short time?

The presence of Cesar Nazareno in her life turned out to be much more deadly than she imagined. In reality, Sebastián was a baby lamb compared with that man whom she, without wishing to, had now brought into her life—and he was the fiercest of wolves. They became friendly, too much so. In the midst of their drinking bouts, Cesar began to show her what he was able to do with the power of his mind. He was like a grown-up kid, playing at blowing out light bulbs and bending spoons. She had no scientific explanation for what she witnessed every time he showed her a new facet of his psychic powers. She was not sure whether to call him a sorcerer, shaman, mage, or simply a devil.

I began to get worried when he called one morning and told me, in the voice of a pervert, how he had just masturbated while thinking of me. I had just woken up, and the reason was that I felt his body alongside mine in the bed. He wasn't physically there, but his energy was. I felt his vast bulk brushing against me, without being able to do anything to avoid it. I didn't know much about the world of magic in which Nazareno lived. I remember, as a girl, listening to thousands of my grandmother Ofelia's stories about Caribbean witchcraft and voodoo. As an anthropologist, I was also familiar with the scientific explanation for this whole phenomenon, practiced by humanity since man became man, but that was the limit of my knowledge. Now, right in front of me, live and direct, was a worthy representative of all which I still wasn't sure really existed. One night, in one of our many conversations, he told me something that penetrated my very bones.

> "You are a very powerful woman who has lived many lives and we have known each other for centuries. Thanks to your having connected with me in this precise moment, in this reality, I can teach you to recall your power, Sybil. Just let me carry you along; don't resist me. Together, we can be invincible."

She thought he was crazy and drunk when he spoke to her like that. She merely smiled, not knowing how to reply. She had to be honest with herself. Her life now depended on the desires of a sorcerer. The worst of it was that she did not know if he was a good or a bad one! She did not even know what the line between good and evil was anymore. She only knew that he mentally controlled her and she did not know how to stop him, nor how a sorcerer, whether good or bad, would react when he fell in love and that love was not returned. Aminta had confirmed it. Perhaps Cesar had fallen in love with her kindness, or perhaps even with her innocence. That at least is what she chose to believe. She did not want to remind herself of the way he would focus his thoughts on her and eat her up with his eyes. She was in deep waters now. Compared to her past experiences, this was so much worse. There was no doubt that dealing with this man was best left to real witches, experts at revving up their broom when they needed to fly and disappear. How had she landed in such a mess? The laws that had protected her when she had to get a divorce from Sebastián seemed out of date and useless when it came to solving something like this. Where were the laws which regulated the intangible and the invisible? This was real—yet it was not, not real enough to prove anything. For some reason she still could not divine, life was confronting her with the worst adversary of all. She was living in her own flesh clearly a grotesque and distorted version of Beauty and the Beast. The way she drank and the awful depression she felt made it feel as if her life still belonged to someone else. Sybil had stopped being herself. Not even in her worst moments, when she tried to kill herself, had she felt so sick—and she had no physical illness at all. As she had just found out at a medical check-up, she was healthier than ever. It was another kind of seizure she was fighting off, immaterial and much more dangerous. What ironies continued to plague her! Just as science still could not demonstrate that the misogyny of her ex-husband was a real illness, so too did society refuse to punish this type of abuse. And much less did it accept that witchcraft, as a means whereby one person might control another, was provable. So there was no way she could hit back. "What a fragile legal system the world had!" she said to herself. Without proof, the accusation was not valid. She continued to feel that she was a victim of the improbable: a defenseless and unprotected woman in a society designed by men for their own benefit. Why couldn't she yield and adapt herself to the system? Why couldn't she remain submissive? The answer was the deep rebelliousness in her, which not even she was aware of. On the surface, she seemed like a weak and docile woman, but the true Sybil stayed close to boiling point.

***

Although her life continued to seem like a nightmare while she sprawled on that bed, which was too big for her alone, she was finally waking up. On the weekends when Sebastián had the girls, there was no one she had to pretend to. She would enclose herself in her darkness, not wanting to go out, not wanting to do anything. She only wanted to lie there, her gaze vacantly wandering between the television and the four walls, wallowing in her depression like the addict she was, after another night wasted on the stupid vice of alcohol. She had supposedly gained control of her life with the divorce, but she was more out of control than ever. She was in the hands of a sorcerer who had appeared out of nowhere, and she did not know what she had done to deserve the nightmare that was now her reality. This would not have happened if she had stayed with Sebastián. What she had experienced toward the end of their joint life was an extreme, but this was much worse, the extreme of the previous one.

I was wrecked, physically and emotionally. I had completely lost my strength, my appetite for life. This man was doing something to me, and I didn't know what it was. I hadn't felt like that before I met him. All this malaise was caused by his presence. I needed help, but to whom could I turn? How was I going to explain that he was bewitching me? I had headaches all the time, which mysteriously came and went. My depression didn't even let me think clearly. Since the doctors didn't find any cause for it, what was I going to say, that it was the fault of a friend of mine who was a sorcerer? For God's sake, I was an educated person! I had two university degrees. I couldn't say such ignorant things to a doctor. Besides, if that friend was doing whatever he did to me, the doctors were sure to ask why I didn't tell him to go to hell. It was more complicated than I could ever explain.

Her former sidekick helped her. Adriana spent her time seeking out fortune-tellers who would read her future in the cards or other oracles. This was urgent; she rang Adriana and immediately got the name of the best clairvoyant in the city. She was so good that consulting her cost almost as much as a divorce, but it did not matter; she was desperate. She rang and got an appointment with Yesidia the same afternoon. She did not know how she got dressed so fast, but she was soon in her car, heading north to the parlor of the mysterious woman in whom she had now placed all her hopes. She had never visited a clairvoyant before, but there is a first time for everything, she thought, justifying it to herself. The first thing Yesidia did was to read her the tarot. Yesidia was very good at what she did. She did not even ask for details. She only made Sybil sit down in front of her and choose some cards; then she began to describe what she saw in them. Sybil was right—she was in a dangerous situation. The man came out perfectly in the cards. He was "working on her," to use the parlance of the experts. The cards never lied. Nazareno's plans had to be neutralized as soon as possible.

Without doubting, I immediately signed a check to buy the giant altar candles that my new lawyer, of the invisible realm this time, would keep alight, day and night, in her secret sanctuary – the one I never visited, located in a field near the cemeteries in the northern part of the city – until I was freed from the invisible chains which bound me. The money I had to invest in the exorcism was a worry. As a volunteer in the campaign, I wasn't being paid, and I now had these extra expenses. But my whole future was at stake, and the worst was that my future depended on the very obstacle I was trying to clear away. I couldn't break with Nazareno; I would lose my only contact with Holguín. He knew it and took advantage of the situation. I was in a blind alley, knowing that I was completely dependent on the devil himself to achieve my aim. Still unaware of how ignorant I was, I sank even lower. First, it was my mother who controlled me; then I replaced her with a husband who not only did the same job but far exceeded her. And now I was being controlled by an evil-minded male sorcerer and by a female witch who was helping me to neutralize him! It wasn't the kind of life a so-called lettered person was supposed to live. It was as if your degrees didn't bring you true wisdom. I had to believe in someone, and I only had Yesidia, that short, fat woman, a little younger than myself, who had the hair of an angel and the gaze of a devil. What was happening to me might not be that negative; I had heard that the powerful people in the world of politics always had their bedside sorcerer. Well, I had my private one now. Maybe I should get used to her protecting me. There might be thousands of Nazarenos out there.

While Yesidia was realizing her ceremonies, prayers, and incantations to deactivate Nazareno's witchcraft, Sybil had to take daily baths of herbs and floral essences and at the same time still remain Nazareno's friend. Yesidia's aim was to make him fall out of love but keep him close to her so that she could maintain the link with Holguín.

Even so, I had a disturbing intuition. How did I know that Yesidia was really helping me? I was distrustful from the first. The only reference I had for her was Adriana's, and although I liked my friend, her opinion didn't count for much insofar as I was familiar with her irresponsibility and poor judgment.

Election Day finally arrived, and Holguín was, in fact, the winner. The country had a new president, and Sybil was smiling again. At least the prediction of the newly graduated political analyst she was had not been wrong. She felt that it had been worth all the trouble. Before the election, Nazareno had asked her for a short list of the posts she thought suitable for her; they were in the Ministries of Education, Foreign Trade, and Foreign Relations. She did not mind beginning in a middling position. With the projects she had sent him through Nazareno, the president would know how to make the best use of her talents. Holguín had her list and résumé;, it was a question of waiting for his call. He would need some time to organize his cabinet and different work teams. Meanwhile, Sybil began to feel much better, thanks to the help of Yesidia. Her headaches subsided, and her yearning for alcohol drastically declined. She wanted to remain optimistic, but one afternoon, she finally learned why her intuition had not left her in peace during the whole of this murky period of her life. It was a Friday, and she decided to surprise Yesidia with a birthday present. Though her birthday was actually on the following day, Sybil could not see her then. The porter knew her and let her in without announcing her arrival, so she took the elevator to the seventh floor and headed toward the office of her private witch at the end of the corridor. She was about to reach the door when it suddenly opened. Gerardino was leaving with a sealed white package in his hands and effusively pressed Yesidia's hands as he said good-bye.

> "See you later, madam. I'll give the package to the boss with your instructions. Take care."

Gerardino was no less than Cesar Nazareno's chauffeur. It was hard to work out what I was seeing. What was the chauffeur of the sorcerer who was working on me doing there in the consulting room of the clairvoyant I'd hired to help me? My head was spinning. I saw them, and they saw me, and in a flash, I turned around, present in hand, and ran to the stairway as quickly as I could. I left the building, full of anger and disappointment, threw the present into the first trash can I found, and got into my car, drowned in betrayal.

It had all been a farce. Sybil had fallen for the oldest trick in the history of the world. While she drove back home, Yesidia rang her cell phone and left several messages, worried that the goose with the golden eggs had just caught her in the act. In one of them, she said that there was an explanation for what she had just seen and begged her to ring so she could explain.

I don't know why I hadn't paid attention to my intuition before that. God, how obstinate I'd been! I had a radar I could trust in, and I only had to follow it from then on. I never answered or rang her. It was the end of my private witch, but I was really panicked. Now I didn't know what the alliance between these two shady and ill-intentioned people meant; they knew everything about my life. My vulnerability wouldn't leave me in peace. I had never had that sensation of helplessness and isolation before. I felt completely naked and robbed, having paid several million pesos for Yesidia's services in three previous installments. Added to my frustration, there was a horrible unease whenever I asked myself if it was possible that my neurons were misfiring.

It had all been a dirty business. Who knows whether Nazareno had been paying off the witch, or if they joined forces to exploit her, each in his or her own way, seeking to get what they wanted from her: sex for Nazareno and money for Yesidia. She learned another lesson the hard way. It was a low blow that she did not deserve, but at the end of it, one thing became clear to her: she had never been a prostitute and was not going to make an exception now. She would not surrender to Nazareno, a capricious man intrigued by a slippery prey. Once he had her, he would throw her on the garbage dump, along with all the others who fell into his clutches. That was the kind of man he was, the type who used his power to have any woman he fancied. Her job in the government was fully at stake. There was nothing she could do. She would mark time and await Nazareno's reaction, after Gerardino informed him about what Sybil had seen at Yesidia's office. This calm before the storm helped her to think up some other work options, and in a few days, she came up with her plan B. She was not going to let herself be undermined by the recent occurrence. She had to stop being afraid, stop thinking of herself as vulnerable. She made an appointment at the bank where she'd had had an account since the time she was single. Although the money she moved through it was not much, she had been a client for fifteen years and had always managed her account and credit card responsibly, without an overdraft or overdue bill. The manager knew her and her parents well, and he immediately authorized the loan she asked for. She had decided to become independent. She was coming to understand that maybe her best option was to work on her own. It would not matter if she had to work twenty-four hours a day to get her plan going. She felt it was the only safe ground, to be her own boss. She was fed up with the betrayal of others. She was the only one who would not ask favors of herself, much less sexual ones! She would start her own company in a business she was good at: interior design. If she fixed up apartments and old houses, she was sure to do well. She had already done it several times before, and everyone was delighted with her ideas and designs. It sounded great. She would buy properties in a dilapidated condition, fix them up, sell them, and live off the profits. Hence the bank loan. Given her recent setback, she did not know where her enthusiasm bubbled up from, but it convinced the bank manager. Finally, a man believed in her without asking for anything in exchange! You could not put a price on that in the midst of the storm that buffeted her. Hopeful again, she soon assembled a team of real-estate agents, who would find clients for her services in return for a commission or alert her to properties she could buy at a cheap price and then remodel. Part of her work was to go out and look for bargains and opportunities. She looked at buildings all over the city and quickly learned to recognize those with a good potential.

One night, when she was fully immersed in organizing her new business, she got an unexpected phone call from Cesar Nazareno. She had been trying to forget all about that chapter of her life, which still made her ashamed. Saying hello, he let drop that he was ringing from the private office of the president. As always, he spoke so quickly it made her nervous.

> "How's it going, gal? I'm sitting here next to my great friend, the honorable president, and we're going over the résumés of the people who helped us in the campaign, and especially yours, Sybil. He completely agrees that you could be a great help in one of our work teams. What worries me is that you are not willing to give anything in exchange for what I am helping you to get. You and I, we've known each other for months and you show no sign that you're with me, gal. Our president knows about the situation and he's authorized me to personally take care of this matter with you. We're holding the post of vice-minister of foreign trade open for you, but there are three other people under consideration. Think about it and let me know what you've decided first thing tomorrow, by phone."

As usual, he abruptly hung up, without saying good-bye. I was stunned. I sat there at my desk and felt like exploding. The sorcerer turns up out of the blue, pretending to be God, and has the nerve to put me against the wall in front of the president himself! A night to think it over? Well, there was nothing to think about. I felt like a drink, but I stopped myself. I needed a clear head now.

It was not hard to reach a conclusion: she already knew it. As far as her future in the government was concerned, if she joined the dirty game, she would really be Nazareno's puppet forever, and he was not a man she wanted to be associated with. His reputation was so black that even Holguín kept their friendship secret. He never publicly acknowledged his links with Nazareno. There was no way to put a good face on what she had just heard; worst of all, the man she wanted to work for in order to help her country had been a witness to the vulgarity of that indecent proposal. She was not even sure anymore whether she wanted to work for someone with that kind of moral standard. To sum it up, her dreams of helping and serving her country now came down to turning herself into the mistress of that gross black magician who happened to be the right-hand man of the country's leader. At times, the truth was so simple it was absurd, but that did not make it less true.

I went to sleep, and early the next morning, before waking the girls up to get them ready for school, I turned on the computer and began to draft the letter I had wholly written in my mind the previous night. It was a short, cordial one, addressed to the new president. I thanked him for having given me the opportunity to work with him in the campaign, and without going into details, said that I couldn't accept the offer he'd made me the previous night through Cesar Nazareno. I explained that while my commitment to the country was just as firm, I had a much stronger one to my principles and values. I wished him luck with all of his programs and ended with a simple "yours sincerely," along with my initials. I printed out two copies, one for the president and the other for his henchman, proudly signed them with the black Montblanc fountain pen I had bought as a graduation present for myself, put them in a white envelope, and rubber-stamped the word "confidential" on the seal in red letters. I had a shower and was soon ready to head to Nazareno's office, a few blocks from my home. I put it into the hands of Gerardino, his trusted assistant, since his boss had not arrived yet.

She naively thought that the letter tied the final knot. While she still needed a steady income, there was no way she would prostitute herself for a position in the government, not when the idea was to honestly serve her country. In fact, it would have been a contradiction in terms. As soon as she prostituted herself, she would no longer be honest, at least with herself. She would never have been able to forgive herself for that. She continued to think about the example she wanted to set for her two daughters.

Nazareno never rang her again. Holguín was inaugurated and began his term, without her learning more about it. Betrayed as she felt, she decided to forget that chapter of her life. She continued to feel ashamed of herself for having been so ingenuous. She felt disgusted every time she pictured that sorcerer in her mind. If he had wanted her contempt, he'd got it.

I devoted myself full time to the small business I'd just started. I was already renovating one apartment and had my team of workers working full out to finish as soon as possible, so I could sell it. I had put together a small work team with a building foreman, plumber, electrician, and painter, and I was satisfied with the way that my projects were beginning to bring direct and indirect benefits to many people who now worked for or received commissions from my small company. It wasn't what I had in mind when I set out to help my country. I was capable of much more, but, one grain of sand among many, the company was boosting the economy insofar as it created jobs and made use of Colombian products. This new activity completely fulfilled me. I felt useful and independent. With my own eyes, I was seeing what I could create and produce on my own for the first time. My discipline, the things I accomplished, astonished me. I soon had a small office, where I attended to my clients, and within a year I already had a name and a reputation. Although I was not an architect, my work was faultless. I was a perfectionist who didn't rest until I had gotten the right finishes, found the best-quality materials, and came up with designs that were fashionable in the city then, modern and minimalist.

There is nothing more disheartening in life than to fight against a hidden enemy. Her naivety continued to be a weak spot. With the knot she had tied, she thought she could forget about the chapter of her life entitled Nazareno, but she forgot that that was only one side of the story, hers. Nazareno would not give up that easily; she had completely underestimated him. She managed to sell her first renovation, at a small profit. Everything was running smoothly. She paid back the first loan to the bank, and her first deal encouraged her to continue to expand. Two friends had commissioned her to remodel their apartments, and she took out another loan from the bank to continue with the purchase and sale of properties, this time two apartments. Now she could take her first vacation with Luna and Sol. They went to San Andrés for a week, while the work proceeded at a good pace under the supervision of Eustasio, the trusted construction foreman she had known for a long time. Her decision to become professionally independent had turned out to be the right one.

I finished all the projects I'd planned, handed over the apartments I'd done up for my two friends, and the other two were already on the market. María Eugenia Afanador, a good friend of my mother, arrived at my office one morning. She wanted to speak to me for a few minutes. I was happy because she was one of the best real-estate agents in the city. Surely she had a client who was interested in my properties.

> "Sybil, you're going to have to start taking care of yourself. Cesar Nazareno came to my office yesterday to offer a big commission if I stopped showing your apartments and bringing you clients."

I was dumbfounded. My heart found it impossible to believe how evil that character could be. It was lucky that Eugenia was my friend and had come to tell me about it, but who knows how many other real-estate agents had received the same proposal? He was wealthy enough to bribe whomever he liked; he'd admitted it to me when we were friends. Nazareno lived in a world of kickbacks. That was how he made his way and achieved his goals. Everyone had a price, according to him.

With that reprimand, life was sending her a warning. Hard times had now arrived, and suddenly the business was paralyzed. Everyone was fascinated with her work, but they did not hire her, nor did any clients turn up for the two apartments that were ready to be sold. All of her savings were invested in her company, and she also had a big debt with the bank. The months passed at a snail's pace, and there seemed to be no movement in her life.

I wound up broke, without even the money for my daughters' groceries. I was completely illiquid. It was an invisible war. I felt shackled, but Nazareno's persistence was teaching me to be more persevering than I ever imagined possible. I was desperate, and this anxiety made me remember that, sometime before, a neighbor had offered to buy the apartment where I was living with Luna and Sol, so I rang him and asked if he was still interested. He said he was, and in the blink of an eye, I sold my home at a giveaway price in order to pay off my debts and not lose what I had built up with so much effort.

Absorbed in thought, she asked herself why her happiness had lasted such a short time. She was giving her all, and yet every time she found her path, it seemed that something came to block her progress. She often recalled the words of her ex-husband, Sebastián. Was it possible that he would see her down on her knees, begging him to take her back? She would fight to the end to prevent that prophecy from coming true. Now she had a month to pack her things and move to a smaller apartment with her daughters. She did not want them to be shifting so much, but it was the only way to keep afloat and survive while she was trying to sell the two properties that had been on the market for months. She got back from the office tired and sad, silently opening the door. Nereida was speaking on the phone in the kitchen. She thought she had seen and heard it all!

> "Sir, I'll let you know what's happening. I have to hang up now; I think I heard her come in. I'll ring you back as soon as I can."

Sybil went to the kitchen, calm on the surface but with a racing heart barely controlled by something outside of herself. She greeted Nereida and asked her to sit down at the breakfast table.

Her face was red with fright and her hands shook. I took a deep breath and told her that we wouldn't get up from the table until she told me who she'd just been speaking to. She couldn't stop crying.

"Forgive me, Señora Sybil, I only told him about things in a general way. I needed the money."

Money? Nazareno had put his own private detective into my home! He had been bribing my daily help for months, in exchange for information. He wanted to know everything she heard: whether I was going out with anyone, how the business was doing, etc. In short, they spoke to each other daily, and he gave Nereida a monthly check equal to the wage I was paying her. How could he fail to find out everything! When was I going to stop being so stupid? How could I have thought that that man would be content with the letter I wrote him one day, where I firmly turned down his indecent proposal? His silence since then explained everything. That kind of man wasn't going to be stopped by a piece of paper with my signature on it. No one said no to Nazareno.

She had been betrayed again, now by a woman who knew all about her and her daughters. In her soul, she felt more alone than ever. Who else was going to let her down? Her daughters were the only ones left, all that kept her on course in the storm. They were the engine that drove her ship. She now remembered why she had insisted on choosing those unusual names for them. Everything in life had a reason for being. At the time, Sebastián thought they were bizarre, but they had agreed that she would choose the girls' names and he the boys', so he was left out. She had her own moon and her own sun. When her ship was off course, she had only to look at the sky. By night, there was her moon and by day, her sun. The girls were a reminder that whatever might happen, she would always forge ahead without looking back.

THE FIFTH ELEMENT OF LOVE

THE BLUE OF THE CALM AND PEACEFUL SKY

There was a little armoire facing my bed with a small television inside. I looked at the clock on my bedside table. It was 11:10 PM. Luna and Sol had been asleep for a while. I had just turned off the TV and was browsing through a book. Reading a page or two was the best sleeping pill. I was on the point of closing my eyes and falling asleep when I suddenly saw him in front of me. I had to open my eyes and blink several times, trying to clear my sight, to assure myself that what I was seeing was real. I was going crazy now; I was hallucinating. Wishing to clean out my body, I had stopped drinking for some time. I started to think that what I was seeing was surely an effect of my disintoxication – all those years of unhealthy living, of the abuse of cigarettes and alcohol. I hadn't smoked for years, but only now, when my pride had been battered, was I able to admit to myself that my drinking had turned into a serious addiction. But this could not have been a mere hallucination; it was real, completely real.

It was like a slide shown by a projector, only there was no projector. It was a masculine face, full of divinity, the projected image of one, like an enormous hologram that appeared out of nowhere between her bed and the TV armoire. He was so gigantic, she only managed to see his face and part of his neck. Her apartment was on the third floor. It seemed as if the rest of the body of that apparition was passing through the floor between her apartment and the one on the second floor. He was alive, but not of flesh and blood. He immediately woke her up. What she was seeing, what she was feeling, was very beautiful. The loving face radiated a fluid, transparent light. The colors Sybil saw were lustrous, rainbowlike, and in motion. His golden hair fell to his neck in neat curls and seemed to ripple in the wind, even though the window of the room was shut. His eyes were a neon indigo-blue, unlike any human ones. The image seemed to float in the air while he smiled at her with a sweet, loving look.

I was asleep, it must be a dream. There was no other way I could explain it! I sat up in bed, trying to analyze what was happening to me. Two or three minutes passed and then he finally spoke.

> "Sybil, you are facing great dangers. It is time to wake up, wake up, my child. There is no other moment. I will help you. I love you, and I am always by your side, protecting you. Do not forget, wake up and return to me."

As soon as he uttered the final word, he slowly vanished until his image was gone and I was left there, emptier than ever, trying to repeat the words I had just heard to myself again and again, without having a clue about what they meant or what had just happened to me. When my mind registered the perfection in that tone of voice, I knew I would never be the same again. The imprint those words left on my heart was indelible.

She got up the next morning with a strong desire to awaken. But not to wake up physically; she already knew how to do that perfectly. Rather, she wanted to awaken in the sense that the image had asked her to the night before. But in what way, if she did not know how to? And awaken to what? She knew nothing; she was an insignificant human being who was finally realizing how much was beyond her. She wanted to understand what she had witnessed, but who could explain what she had seen? How could she explain what she had seen so that someone else could explain it to her? Following her morning ritual, she showered before waking her daughters. While the warm water ran over her bare skin, she closed her eyes and prayed again, asking God to forgive her for ignoring him. It was the first time she had prayed since that encounter with the angelic black man in the elevator in Miami who had helped her before her divorce. She had not done it again, had not believed in anything more than her own arid and insipid reality. Speaking out loud, she made a heartfelt plea for help again—she wanted to awaken.

I had a meeting in a shopping center that afternoon with Dolores Suárez, one of the real-estate agents who was showing my apartments. The idea was to have a coffee and talk about an offer to buy one of them. I would lose a lot of money if I sold it at that price, but my economic situation was so desperate, I was open to anything. I arrived a bit early, so I strolled around the shopping center to kill time. Though I must have passed it many times before, I had never seen that bookstore before; it was as though it had been invisible to me. Acuarius, it was called. I stopped for a while to look at the shop window filled with magic. The books displayed seemed to be dancing, and I immediately felt an unstoppable desire to go inside. I was more afraid than I'd been when I was about to enter the office of that private witch I had hired some time before, the one who wound up robbing me and allying herself with the person who was now my archenemy. But my curiosity was stronger than my fear. The place smelled of incense, and there was the sound of harp music, which made me continue walking toward some of the shelves at the back of the store. The books were arranged according to subject, ones I hadn't even heard of before, and I was supposed to be so cultured and educated! I looked at the titles, and they seemed to be in an unknown language: alchemy, Kabbalah, occultism, angelology, channeling, Tantrism, masonry, Rosicrucianism, etc. I was overwhelmed by my ignorance, but I had to be there; that's all I knew. Dolores had just rung me on my cell phone. She was half an hour late, and that gave me more time to continue to explore the place, which still caused me to feel a mixture of repulsion and shivering.

She leafed through several books but did not understand a thing. The beautiful melody she was hearing made her less apprehensive, helping her to relax as she slowly felt that it was a safe place. While she was walking around the store, her eyes fell, as if by magic, on a small book placed high on a shelf; it was as though it were calling to her. She asked for a stepladder, climbed up, and took it into her hands. There was only one copy, which seemed to be secondhand. *Prayers to St. Michael the Archangel* was the title. The author was Aura Petrovsky, and it was a translation of the original version in English. She had never heard of St. Michael or Petrovsky. With all those years of religious studies in the nuns' school, she was ashamed to admit that she did not even know the names of the archangels.

There suddenly occurred the most marvelous instance of synchronicity. My eyes were riveted by the picture on the cover. There it was again, the same visage I had seen the night before! The same eyes, the same hair, the same colors; it was the same: archangel! Michael the Archangel had appeared in my room then! I didn't even know what the book was about. I didn't need anything more. I went to the cash register to buy it at once. It was meant for me. It was the conclusive proof that I wasn't going crazy, though it would have to remain a state secret, because no one would believe me. That picture was the only confirmation I had that what I had witnessed was real. At least another human being had seen what I had, the artist who'd done that painting on the cover of the book! By now, I was late. I rushed out of the bookstore with the bag in my hand, toward the café where I was to meet Dolores.

For nights on end, she examined every detail of the cover of that book, which she now kept on her night table. She did not read it, only looked through the pages; she was still too astonished. The book contained a number of prayers that the Archangel Michael had channeled through the author. Her ego, with its rationalism and logic, still would not let her accept that the method of channeling described in the book was possible. Thus, in her disbelief, she did not recite the prayers, but the book was a sign which showed her she *could* wake up, even though she still did not know into what.

A week later, I returned to the bookstore, where I was now more at ease. This time, I gave myself time for a leisurely examination of different subjects. There were no chairs, since it wasn't a library, but even if I had to stand up, I wanted to continue my research. I decided to buy a couple of books, and on the way out, I stood before a notice board where there were announcements of courses and workshops. Synchronicity was still with me. Months before, Mariana, one of my friends from Miami, had sent me an e-mail. When Sebastián and I had been together, we used to criticize her for being too engrossed in these spiritual subjects, so I hadn't paid attention to her message. It was just another bit of nonsense from my crazy friend, I thought, not the sort of thing I was interested in then.

But as soon as I saw that symbol on one of the leaflets on the notice board, I instantly remembered that I had seen the same geometrical drawing on the heading of Mariana's e-mail. It looked like a flower, a circular logo with a perfect design that felt completely familiar to me, though I didn't know why. The e-mail I had ignored contained the same announcement, which I now had before my eyes, an invitation to a workshop in Mérida, Mexico, that would last a little less than a week. When I looked at the photo of Gazardiel, the teacher in charge of the workshop, I felt a deep remembrance, a great attraction toward that paternal figure whose photo seemed to be speaking to me. My rational mind immediately reacted, however, since reacting was how I was trained to think. I couldn't waste money on such a trip. It was a luxury I couldn't afford and would give Sebastián yet another pretext to criticize me. But my curiosity kept me reading. The workshop was to take place in December, which meant that I had five months to arrange things. My heart knew I had to be there. Gazardiel was the next piece of the jigsaw puzzle.

***

She decided to call Sebastián and invite him to her office, first because she wanted him to see the place where she worked, and second because she wanted to tell him about her economic situation, to confront him again and ask for his advice. He might have some ideas that would help her to save her business, and she felt he would be encouraged if he saw that she was trying to include him in her life. She had wanted to remain his friend since the divorce, but it was difficult because, still intransigent, he continued to think he had an absolute monopoly on the truth. The little they saw of each other, because of the girls, only helped her to keep alive the same old Sybil she was trying to replace. Something still was not working. The year 2003 was nearly over, and she felt that she still had a long way to go in re-organizing her life. If it was true that there was still so much to do, how could she survive, given her financial state? At the rate she was running through her money, her future was seriously at risk. She had a few clients who were interested in the apartments. She would have to accept their offers; the places had been empty for too many months. But she wanted to hear her ex-husband's opinion. Chauvinistic as he was, he might be flattered that she was taking advantage of his experience, including him in her affairs. Besides, three years had passed since the divorce, and by now he had surely come to understand the reasons why she had left him, namely, that she needed to recover her own individual space and stop living *his* dreams, so that she could dream her own ones again.

I was wrong again. When we met up in my small office, I began to explain what was happening to me. By God, I became so open, I told him absolutely everything, including my adventures in the world of sorcerers and witches! Why not? I thought that if he was to be my friend, I would have to be open with him, but my honestly proved to be expensive. Once again, I was met by that old sarcastic smile of his, and those eyes filled with poison shooting darts into mine.

> "I told you so, I told you that this would happen but you were too stubborn to pay attention to me."

His voice trembled with a malign joy, as though he were happy that his worst omens had been confirmed. Three years and he still didn't try to understand me. His position had only hardened; flushed with guilt, I asked his forgiveness for the umpteenth time, though I didn't know why I was doing it, perhaps for all the harm I'd done to him or perhaps for the harm we'd done to each other. As happened so many times before, he wasn't willing to accept my apology. Instead, he stood up from his chair while continued to scold me like a little girl.

> "I always told you that working and making money was hard, and you didn't believe me. Now you'll have to sort it out on your own. It's the fault of that little lawyer lady of yours that I had to hand over my savings so you could throw them away. Go find another male to help you now, don't count on me anymore. See you around."

He was as cruel as ever, and his few words still hurt as much. The reformed Sebastián she'd longed for was still lost somewhere in her imagination. She had just humiliated herself before an enchanted prince who had remained a frog. She had even begged for forgiveness, as though *he* were the victim. He must have been overjoyed to hear her confession; it was what he had been waiting for since the divorce. His prediction had come true, to the letter. He had wanted to see her exactly as he had found her. But Sybil had no regrets. While the conversation did not accomplish its ostensible aim, it did reassure her once more that she had made the best decision when she divorced that insensitive and obtuse man. In a subtle and imperceptible way, her heart continued to heal and shed its old skin. With no other guide than her own intuition, she decided to sell the apartments for what she could get. She had wanted to wait for better offers, but she could not jeopardize her credit line or her goodwill. She lived in a city where everything became known in a matter of seconds. She had to be realistic about it: her company was going downhill, and she had not been able to turn it around. It was yet another failure, and she would handle it as discreetly as possible.

First my marriage and now my company. The worst was that I myself was proving Sebastián right. My reasons for explaining why all this was happening to me were based on Sebastián's beliefs. Where were my own beliefs? Acknowledging that was the first step. Now at least I understood that I didn't have any values of my own. How was I going to have a successful company, how was I going to triumph in what I undertook if I was full of doubts and fears about my ability? My ex-husband's cruel wish for me to fail had been repeated for years, so that the echo of his cunning words was always bouncing round the inside of my skull.

The foundation she had built her whole life on was not hers; it was a patchwork quilt made up of pieces borrowed from others. She continued to nourish herself on Sebastián's energy. She still felt married to him; her mind was Sebastián's mind. Who knows in what hidden dungeon hers continued to be imprisoned! Her values were alien to her. To face up to that was the first step forward. She thought she was making progress but stayed on the same rung. The questions she still could not answer pursued her. What did she believe in? What were the values she wished to base her new life on? What did Sybil want: the plain Sybil, the one inside herself and not the one others saw? She had to begin to search for her own mind and not stop until she brought it back.

I became aware of the tip of my iceberg for the first time, and suddenly everything had another meaning. Would it be possible to replace what I now believed in with what I wanted to believe? Was it possible that one day I would know what I wanted to believe? I had spent three years trying to make a career on my own, to prove I-don't-know-what to the world. Three years fitting myself into the mold that television and magazines sold as the ideal model. Three years trying to prove that I was triumphing on my own, that I was the best single mother, the pretty, intelligent and professional woman who would triumph after a lifetime of oppression. In reality, however, everything continued to be self-imposed. I was still living in the world of appearances, seeking the approval of others. Only now did I consider the possibility of living my own life, not someone else's. I thought that the divorce would make me free, that I'd obtained my freedom the way you make a withdrawal from an ATM. I couldn't have been more wrong. The divorce was only the wide-open door. I still had to pass through it to be able to see the landscape outside. Marriage was no longer my cage, it was the bars in my mind that penned me in, and I still didn't know how to get out. I was afraid I would let everyone down, so I'd continued to defraud myself. Legally, I was free, but mentally I was still tied to the past, using lenses and filters which only reproduced more of what should no longer be happening in my reality.

Now that she knew Archangel Michael existed and had offered her help, she felt the urge to go on and not surrender; perhaps he was the proof that there was something more. She continued to visit Acuarius, and the subject matter of the books in her house began to change drastically from the tangible to the still intangible. One led to another through an invisible common thread, which kept her from getting lost and maintained her insatiable thirst to reach her destination. She was fascinated by that mysterious world of the esoteric into which Archangel Michael was initiating her in a very subtle manner. Everything seemed so unreal, like make-believe. She could not stop reading and investigating.

I soon began to feel I was stagnating in my city. In reality, it had never been mine. I'd wound up there because it was a step toward achieving my girlhood dream of living in the United States, where I would reach my goals, but I fell madly in love with Sebastián, and my course thus halted in Bogotá. Now that I was on my own, I wanted to find a new partner, but I had gone on a few dates and nothing had worked. For me, it was very clear that I didn't want to wind up with another Sebastián, yet for some unknown reason, they all seemed to be his twins! I wanted to meet a different sort of man, but I didn't even know what he might be like. Without knowing my own values, how could I attract such a man? All I knew was that even if I couldn't define him to myself, such a specimen was not produced by a city such as Bogotá.

She felt comfortable with her solitude. It was not her style to settle for less, just to prove that she had a man. In that respect, at least, she was not worried about what others would say. Besides, her daughters and her problems completely filled her thoughts. If only she were to work out a way of leaving the country. At times, she had waking dreams of that but could not see a way of achieving it. Once she sold the apartments and received the money, she would liquidate the company. She was not going to continue to risk the little that remained of her savings, not with the two monsters who were stalking her, waiting to inscribe her name on a tombstone. Sebastián Obregón and Cesar Nazareno were too much for her to handle on her own. Her mind still lacked the skills she needed to win the match. She still completely underestimated her power and the power of Archangel Michael.

Although I still wasn't aware of the evolution which my inner being had embarked on, I began to understand that some of my thoughts were manifesting themselves more quickly. Ever since the visitation of the archangel, the events in my life speeded up. In a matter of a week, I sold the apartments, and a client even turned up to buy the office of my liquidated company. They were all bad deals, but selling was my objective. Now I could save the place where I was living, so that my daughters would still have a home. I had some capital again, was free of debt, and recovered a little of my peace of mind.

What next? She had only to ask herself that question, and the answer came almost at once. She never knew the origin of that e-mail. Perhaps her name was in some database at the university where she had done her master's and it circulated through the academic world without her realizing it. The e-mail contained an invitation, personally addressed to her, to apply for a scholarship at one of the best universities in Washington, D.C. She laughed to herself: she wanted to leave the country, and there it was: an invitation that came directly from the dean of the faculty of international relations of that prestigious institution. It was an exclusive executive program for professionals who already had a master's and other academic requirements which, by chance, she completely fulfilled. She was still unaware, still did not understand that she lived in a world of cause and effect, not an accidental one.

I carefully read the information. It would not cost me anything to apply, so I had nothing to lose. I filled it in without raising my hopes. I was sure that they would not accept me, since I was a foreigner and belonged to a minority group. Who knows how many far better-qualified people were applying? Even so, I'd risk it, but without telling anybody, as I didn't want to open myself up to criticism again. So I spent the next few days gathering all the required documents, and once everything was ready, I sent it off by special delivery. I said to myself: what must be, will be.

She felt a new flow of energy coming into her life. She could not explain it; she only felt it was so. Now that she had the money for it, the trip to Mexico increasingly appealed to her. She arranged everything so that Cassandra would look after Luna and Sol during the week of the workshop. It was the first time she would be away from them since the divorce, but she knew she had to attend that course. Being without her for a week would also do them good, she thought. To begin to be independent of her would be a positive thing. She might not be around one day, and it was important for them to learn to survive and become independent. The mystery of that spiritual world she was beginning to discover continued to beckon, although she still did not believe in it much. She regarded those who had long hair or wore tunics to be strange. The words of her mother, Cassandra, came to mind; she had always classified them as hippies and bums, mixed-up people who were probably drug addicts. She was not out to become a convert; she worried what others might say. She only wanted to learn. If she was critical of them, it was because she did not have any idea that the physical appearance and dress of those persons was the result of the way they thought. She still did not know about the direct relationship between the mental and physical world, much less that she had started her own transformation. She had just begun, slowly but surely.

I would go to the workshop, although I would have to overcome all of the reserves that fear had instilled in me when it came to confronting the unknown. I didn't know what to expect, but to be there, no matter how uncomfortable it might make me, was an ultimatum of the same kind that led me to leave Miami and return to Bogotá for my divorce. Where the hell did these famous ultimatums come from!

***

The bus that took me to the retreat center where the workshop was being held suddenly stopped on the outskirts of the city. My friend Mariana cancelled her trip to Mexico at the last moment. Now I was in the place I had been thinking about for months. What kind of crazy situation had I put myself into! It looked like a typical hippie commune, no more, no less. I had let myself be swayed by my heart, but what I now observed was too much for my rational head. I wasn't ready for this clash between different worlds. I felt like a little princess leaving the castle of the fortified city for the first time to explore the forest, with all its enchantments, a completely new world before me. There were a little less than a hundred persons from all corners of the world: Russians, Americans, Indians, Chinese, Latinos, Europeans, Mexicans, etc. In short, a sample of the races and ethnic groups conforming the whole. Some of them exchanged long, loving embraces, while I shyly stood aside. I was open to what might come but still wary. I had never hugged a stranger before; why should I start doing it now? When I arrived at my cabaña, my mind still hadn't found an explanation. I was sharing my dormitory with six other participants. The beds were shoved so close to one another, there was no space to walk between them. I had to store my suitcase under the bed. The bathroom was tiny, had no light, and the door only closed halfway. There was no privacy at all. I had never lived in such uncomfortable conditions before, but something kept me optimistic. I felt that I was where I had to be.

The first night, after listening to a few words of welcome he gave to all of the participants, Sybil met the man who was to be her teacher. She could not believe her eyes. That man—a short Native American with a simple manner and gray hair tied in a ponytail—hugged her with the most unconditional love she had ever felt from another human being. At last she understood what kind-heartedness and compassion meant. She had only heard them spoken of before. She closed her eyes and let herself be enveloped in that wave of calm and disinterested love. From that moment on, she felt at home. She forgot her worries about being uncomfortable. It was all worth it, provided she could hear what this wise and weather-beaten man had to say. She felt herself floating high above her previous definition of the word *liberation.* She would spend a week disconnected from her normal reality, far from a telephone or computer. She was sure that everything was well in Bogotá. She had to begin to let herself be led by her higher self, that abstract concept that her mind still played around with cautiously, as though it were a new neighbor down the road. A true awakening. This was her first big preparatory lesson. Everyone was so full of bliss. They were friendly and respectful beings who practiced a way of life completely different from hers. She could not believe the peace she breathed in there. Everyone was free, thought as they pleased, without fitting themselves into any mold; they were genuine. Her mind continued to open. She soon wanted to embrace others, talk with everyone, be herself, take off her mask. Little by little, she shed her perceptual barriers. There was nothing but real love there. She wanted to learn from it, feel it.

Every day, we got together in a communal hall with a thatched roof and no walls, where we sat on cushions on the floor for hours. Quite simply, my standards of comfort no longer applied. I felt happy, but it was a new kind of happiness. What a sharp contrast with the way I had lived. The food I ate in the modest communal dining room was natural and vegetarian. There were no alcoholic drinks. We worked until late and got up early in order to take in everything Gazardiel had to teach us. I slept among strangers, and I was constantly hugging strangers. I didn't even recognize myself. My ego offered no resistance; I was willing to let myself be led to the end.

In the mornings, she would rise at dawn and meditate before

breakfast in some corner of the unspoiled countryside. Meditate? She suddenly began to meditate with hardly any training, and it came easily to her. She closed her eyes, and it was as though she had accidentally discovered a layer of awareness where only the most loving silence dwelt. At night, after the group dinner, she would go out for a walk and immerse herself again in the beauty of that dark sky of deep blue. She remembered how to look at the stars once more, to let herself be amazed by their light. She was a child again. She danced on her own out of joy, without caring who might see her. How many years had it been since she last stretched out and dirtied herself on the newly mown grass which smelled of damp earth? The stars became part of her again. She felt guilty about having abandoned them until now and without any excuse. Day by day, Gazardiel continued to open her heart in a way she could not understand. He spoke without pause of a spiritual world where all the answers seemed to be. The world in which he lived was too remote for her. She listened to him and knew she was hearing the truth. Her mind resonated with each word of his. For the first time, she did not have to prove anything, analyze anything. She did not understand some of his explanations, but her ego now reclined in a corner of her psyche, like a little tame puppy.

One afternoon, shortly before the end of the workshop, the miracle happened. We had just finished a meditation where we were guided to the sacred space of the heart. I lost all notion of time and space. When I came back to my senses, opening my eyes to return to this reality, I looked up and there he was again, above the others. The Archangel Michael was there, under the thatched roof, as huge and loving as the previous time, only now I could see his whole body. His ethereal figure moved its luminous wings, in slow and quick motion at the same time. His gaze was fixed on my teacher, who was in front of the group. It seemed like they were communicating by telepathy, working together. I felt an urge to close my eyes again, to thank my angel. As soon as I thought of him as my angel, I saw several scenes from my childhood, as if I had pushed the button to make time go backward. Archangel Michael was the angel from whom I had disconnected myself when, on leaving San Andrés, I began to grow up and stopped being a girl. The angel who had been with me since my birth, the one who saved me when I had that kidney condition and when my own father, without meaning to, nearly killed me with his van. It was he who taught me to live in the realm of magic, to understand the glow of the sun and the shade of the moon. How could I have forgotten him? I'd grown up and was now an adult, but he was the same. The passing years had not aged him! I now wanted to fly up and embrace him as hard as I could, completely fuse myself in him. And I was able to fly! My desire was so intense, I went out of my physical body and managed to reach the roof of the hall to embrace my newfound angel. Tears streamed down my cheeks; they were tears of joy. I heard the same voice I'd heard that night in Bogotá, but it was no longer warning me of danger. Now it sweetly calmed me.

> "My beautiful child, all is well. This is the beginning of awakening. You see me because you have finally awakened. Rest. You have heard the call. From now onwards, everything in your life will be different. Many changes will come that you will not be able to demarcate very well. Let go of everything your heart shows you no longer need. Do not hold on to anything. In the end, it will all have been part of the great transmutation you will experience. Your confusion will turn into sharpness. Let yourself be carried away. I have loved and protected you all your life. My love for you is infinite. We are one. Now that you have remembered me, you will be able to

see and hear me every time you feel the need. Think of me or speak my name and I will be there."

I could not stop feeling that emotion which made me want to burst with joy. I could not stop smiling. So many memories came back to me, everything began to make sense. Exactly when had I forgotten to be happy? "Enough, Sybil!" I told myself. It wasn't worth dwelling on what was already done. I felt as if I had risen from the dead; it was as if coming back to life were no longer the exclusive gift of the saints.

The workshop finished, and she had to spend a night in Mexico City before taking the flight back to Colombia. She treated herself to a present; she thought she deserved it. She reserved a room in a five-star hotel, where she arrived exhausted after the journey from Mérida. It was the first time she let herself cater to such a whim. Not even when she had been married to Sebastián did she stay in a luxurious hotel like that one. She walked through the main entrance, feeling like a princess. Archangel Michael escorted her with his enormous wings. The changes were already beginning. For the first time, she felt she was worthy of a night of glory. Never before had she accepted that. She knew that she had never known true love, but never before had she realized that her real illness was not loving herself. For the first time it occurred to her that love was not only hers to give but also to receive, to receive it from her own being. She arrived in Bogotá with another countenance. In Mexico, she discarded her outdated sunglasses, which no longer suited her, and she now wore new ones. With these she finally saw the light she wanted to reach.

I turned on the computer to check my e-mails. How many days without catching up with what was happening in my virtual world! There it was, awaiting me, a message from the university in Washington. Without much enthusiasm, I began to read it, but I had to reread what it said: I had won the scholarship! A scholarship to study at one of the best universities in government and international politics matters of the United States. Why not? My wish to help the people of my country immediately came back to me. Perhaps this new degree is what I needed to achieve that. Yes, this would be the next step. I had spent three years trying to get ahead in Colombia and saw no light at the end of the tunnel. What guarantees did I have of being able to free myself, one day, from the smothering control of my ex-husband and my ex-friend Nazareno? What most worried me were my savings. They had now shrunk to half of the sum I'd had when I got divorced. Maintaining my home and trying to save my business had slowly been eating into my capital.

After their last meeting, she knew that Sebastián was no longer willing to help her, nor was he legally obliged to. Perhaps her future lay in the United States; her compass insistently pointed north. She quickly made the decision. She would risk it and move with Luna and Sol to Washington. It would be a positive change for them; they would make new friends, learn another way of life. They hardly recalled their time in Miami, and it would only be for two years. She would have to rent a small apartment and be responsible for feeding the three of them, but the rest was covered by the scholarship, and by law Sebastián would continue to pay for the girls' schooling and health care. She was worried about risking her capital again but justified it to herself by thinking *nothing ventured, nothing gained,* and she remembered that she now had her angel to protect her again.

I don't know why I chose the worst moment to inform Sebastián of my decision. I couldn't hold it back; I felt so stimulated by that new opportunity. He was spending the Christmas holidays with Luna and Sol and the rest of his family on a farm in Anapoima. It was Christmas Eve, and the girls would be back in a week to spend New Year's Eve with me, so I rang them to say Merry Christmas and share my good news. With all the changes happening in my world, I forgot that I was the one who was mentally evolving, while Sebastián continued to stagnate in the same past I'd left behind. While my voice was bursting with excitement, I rang his cell phone to say hello and then talk with the girls. Who knows how early he'd started to drink that day? Understanding his ways so well, I don't know why I didn't keep it to myself. I told him I had won the scholarship and of my plan to begin the master's in August 2004, taking Luna and Sol with me. We thus had six months to organize, between the two of us, the move and arrange things, I said. I added that he could visit the girls there and we would be returning during the vacations. It would not be for long anyway.

She couldn't process what she had just heard. No oil ran through this man's veins anymore, and his heart had rusted away. At first there was only silence on the other end of the line, and seeing that he didn't answer, Sybil asked if he was still on the phone.

> "Yes, I'm here, but I don't know what to say. How can you even imagine I'm going to allow something so absurd, Sybil? Another master's! What for, if you already have one that's been useless to you? What do you want, to be the perpetual student? You are a selfish woman. You already took away my home, and now you're thinking of stealing my daughters. I'd rather be dead than let you take them away. You won't be able to take them out of the country. Forget about this stupid idea. Your instability has already gone much too far. Grow up. Don't you see the harm you're causing to the girls?"

He continued to rant until she decided to say good-bye and hung up. There was no way she could reason with a drunkard. She decided it would be better to bring it up once he was back in Bogotá, where they might talk in a civilized manner.

The vacations passed, and the new year arrived. Now I had the whole world against me. Sebastián began another campaign to blacken my reputation. Once again, I was the wicked witch of the story who wanted to keep a father from seeing his daughters. I got several phone calls from friends and relatives, urging me to come to my senses. I told them about my economic situation, but nobody wanted to believe me. I explained that this new postgraduate degree would improve my career prospects, but everyone thought that with the money from the divorce, I was set for life. No one ever knew how much Sebastián had agreed to leave under my name after the settlement; they imagined it was much more. Once again I met up with Sebastián and heard what I feared.

> "Do what you like, but I won't let the girls leave the country and much less pay for their school and medical bills in the United States. I'll pay while they are here in Bogotá. If they go, you'll have to pay all of it yourself."

He knew it was impossible for me to assume that additional economic burden. Once more, Sebastián overwhelmingly imposed that great control he exercised over me. I was at a crossroads. I would soon face a difficult and painful decision.

With the meditation she practiced every day, she was learning to see herself through another lens. Although she only achieved it for a few minutes, she was learning to leave the stage she acted on so that she could observe her play from the outside. All those years she had been playing the role of the victim. How well she did it! She had thought herself the poor victim of all those persons who had meant something important in her life. She was convinced that circumstances controlled her life, that life happened by itself without her having any control over what she lived through. Up to then, she had blamed not herself but others for everything that had happened to her. Her marriage to Sebastián was her mother's fault. Her unhappiness and divorce the fault of Sebastián. Not having been able to work for her country the fault of Cesar Nazareno. In short, those were only the guiltiest, among many others. The list of executioners to blame was endless. Whom would she now blame for what was happening to her? Wasn't it the ideal moment to seize the reins and begin to assume responsibility for her own acts and for everything that happened in her life? Her ego was not very convinced of what might come from it; it would miss its comfy victimhood.

I'd soon be thirty-eight. Much of my life had gone on feeling sorry for myself: poor little me, those who heard my story would surely feel sorry for me. As if that would have made any difference, as if some jury would take my side and hand out a favorable sentence. I knew I had to change, yet what others might say still mattered more to me than my own judgment. The workshop in Mexico was a difficult and intense training in self-awareness; I was still trying to assimilate it. The idea that I had never been anyone's victim and had only been creating that reality as a result of my own thoughts, was still too new and painful for me to completely accept. My ego was in a state of denial. How could I be the one who had wanted to destroy myself during all that time? It wasn't possible.

She implored the protection of her angel, so that he would light up her path. Her compass continued to point north. The master's degree was not only her objective, it was her spiritual quest, which now needed to take this great leap forward. The things that surrounded her in Bogotá would not let her jump from the goldfish bowl to observe the water of the aquarium in which she had been living. She had to get out of it for a while. She might even have to go without the girls. Perhaps leaving them with Sebastián would be positive for them. They had never really lived with their father. In Miami, they had always regarded him as a visitor at home, and since the divorce, they had only shared some weekends and vacations with him. Maybe it would be better for all of them if she were to go on her own for two years. She would see them during vacations. It was necessary to continue learning about herself, now that she had her eyes wide open. But Sebastián did not think she would go as far as that and insist on this other plan. He thought that refusing to let her take the girls would be sufficient for her to surrender. He knew nothing of the new Sybil who was slowly emerging, of the inner being within her own self that showed her that the time to be a victim was over and the moment had come to control her life, so that life would no longer control her. Shedding the layers of victimization cost her more work than she ever imagined. There were so many of them, they even felt like the hard shell of a turtle.

I spoke to Luna and Sol and explained what I had in mind. I couldn't imagine my life without them, but it was a sacrifice I had to make for two years. They had grown, and I had never concealed anything in my life from them, nor the economic conditions we were living in after the divorce. Luna had turned into a little woman, and she was the first to encourage me.

"We're going to be fine with Daddy. You must do it for

the three of us, Mommy. We're the Three Musketeers, remember? Besides, if you leave in August, it will only be four months because we'll see each other again in December, for the holidays."

I smiled and felt that they understood perfectly. I hugged both of them, wanting to carry forever in my heart the joy of embracing their little bodies.

Fulfilling her responsibilities was always an obsession for Sybil. She carefully planned the economic arrangements for her daughters before speaking with Sebastián. She wanted to honor the divorce agreement to the letter, even though she would be absent, and make sure that they would lack nothing. Knowing very well how tight-fisted her ex-husband was, Sybil immediately put an ad in the paper for a nanny who would help to look after the girls once they moved to their father's apartment, preferably an older woman who knew how to cook, would keep them company and ensure they had everything they needed once she was gone.

I sold everything and liquidated my assets. I needed all the capital I could get so that my plan would work to perfection. Every peso I had in the bank was budgeted for. Luna and Sol would live with their father, but I would support them. I would continue to pay for their food, clothing, nanny, utilities, and all I had been providing them with till then. I had seventy-nine responses to the newspaper ad, with résumés, including seven from men. I spent a whole week going through them, page by page. I interviewed three women who met all the requirements and decided to hire one called Alma, thinking she'd best fit in with my daughters and above all, my ex-husband. She was an older woman, with the soul of a grandmother and excellent references, who would help me to be a long-distance mom. I still had legal custody of the girls and wasn't going to give Sebastián any chance to undertake a lawsuit against me once I was out of the country. With an ex-husband like mine, I reasoned that I had to have plans A, B, and C, only to discover a little later that life itself had come up with a plan D, which my mind never would have been able to imagine.

During the following two years, Sybil went through the most ironic situation of her life, trying as much as she could to support her two daughters financially while they lived in the home of their millionaire father. It did not matter to her. It was clear to her that the only way to begin liberating herself from the subliminal control of her ex-husband was to go away, although at the same time she felt very guilty about leaving them. She tried to make her departure as untraumatic for them as possible. She re-organized Sebastián's apartment, installing all of her kitchen and household goods. She made a present to him of everything she had been left with after their divorce, so that their daughters would continue to live in comfort. She was left with nothing. It did not matter to her. Up to then, Sebastián had lived a bachelor existence. At most, he had two cups and a coffee maker for his morning cuppa. Now he had a home again. She even left her car behind, so that Alma could take the girls to school and to their friends' homes when the school let out in the afternoon. She organized everything so well that Sebastián did not have to change his daily routine or spend an extra peso.

With these new expenses, I was dipping more and more into my capital. Now I had to maintain two homes, that of my ex-husband and mine, while I was studying and still trying to triumph on my own despite all the dire warnings. Much later, I found out I was even feeding Sebastián with the money I left in the bank for the children's expenses. Alma bought food for everyone, but Sebastián never separated the accounts, nor did he pay anything extra. I confirmed it when Alma returned all the receipts and bills for what she had spent.

Up to the day she got on the plane to Washington, she was completely overwhelmed by doubts. In reality, she did not know if she was doing the right thing in leaving her daughters behind. Her heart was split in half. The girls meant everything to Sybil. It was for their sake that she had arrived where she now was, and for their sake as well she was going to study, so that the three of them might hold on to the same living standards they had. On the one hand, she could not yield to the pressure their stubborn father put on her by not letting them go with her. On the other, she felt that they were still too young to live without her. She was too protective and knew it was a fault, but at the ages of eleven and fourteen, they were not really grown up enough for what they would have to live through. It was one of the most difficult decisions of her life, harder than her divorce.

***

There's no doubt that nature is wise. It was those flowers that made me clearly see what the next step was and ended my doubts. A few weeks before the trip, I got a call from the porter's lodge of my building: someone had sent me some flowers. When I went downstairs to pick them up, I was rendered speechless. It was a funeral wreath made of fresh roses. Then I became so furious, you could almost see the smoke issuing from my ears. I didn't have to be a genius to work out where that eccentric gift had come from. This time, Cesar Nazareno had gone too far. In trying to frighten me, he'd only managed to fill me with bravery and determination. I had to go. I couldn't keep playing such a dangerous game with a hidden character who emerged out of the void to haunt me every now and again. The wreath bore a small envelope with a note composed of letters cut out of a magazine and pasted onto the paper, as in a cheap horror film. It was one line, which read, "You will be sorry if you leave." Nazareno wasn't aware of how rapidly my spirit and mind were evolving. I was off to the only country where his ridiculous control over me would be useless. He couldn't enter the United States. When we had been friends, he confessed he had spent two years in a US jail for possession of drugs. I never wanted to learn the details, much less get to know that sinister man better. All I knew was that he was deported after serving his sentence. Since we no longer had any contact, I didn't know how he managed to keep track of me. This time I didn't care who his new spy was. I wouldn't play a stupid, childish game with that infatuated man anymore. I quickly tore the card to pieces and threw the wreath of flowers into the communal rubbish bin in front of the building.

The following day, she went to the interview at the American Embassy. With the I-20 form that had just arrived from the university, she had all the documents the consulate required for her student visa. Hundreds of persons were waiting since dawn on uncomfortable benches, exposed to the elements, in a sort of shed outside the building. There were spy cameras everywhere, and once the applicant's name was called, he or she had to talk to the consular officials by phone, through a bulletproof window. The security in that place was intimidating. She had to be patient. With the drug cartels and the guerrillas, her country was one of the most dangerous in the world, so perhaps there was a reason for such a deployment: the innocent always pay for the sins of the wicked.

Sitting beside me in the waiting area there was an older woman, as distinguished as she was unpleasant, dressed from head to toe in Louis

Vuitton and Burberry. After a couple of hours there, she broke the ice and we spoke a little. She was from Buga and had a vacation apartment in Miami. She asked me what visa I was applying for, and I blurted out that I had won a scholarship and was hoping for a student's visa. Any other remark would have been more optimistic than the one that came from her bitter mouth.

> "If I were you, I wouldn't get my hopes up. You're young and single, so you meet all the requirements for their denying you a visa. Do you know how many Latina women like you plan to remain in the United States when their visa expires?"

I didn't know how to answer her, but she managed to fill me with that insecurity I hated. I didn't even look her in the eye; I only smiled into the cold wind that was taunting me while I again stuck my head in the book on metaphysics I was reading. At midday, when I was already dying from hunger, I finally got up when they called my name. I was very nervous. When I grabbed the phone to speak to the official, my hand shook uncontrollably. I couldn't have stood there for more than a couple of minutes. He had in his hands the documents I'd previously sent in. He looked directly at me without any expression on his face, and after a brief time, returned them to me through the slot beneath the armored window.

> "Your visa was approved, and your passport will be mailed to your home in a couple of days. Pay the postal costs before you leave. That is all, thank you."

All I could do was smile and timidly express my thanks while I gathered up the documents. I was so moved, I felt like hugging him, but it remained an imaginary hug. As I was leaving, I decided not to look at the place where the woman from Buga who made the wrong prediction sat. I remembered hearing, years before, a saying that Colombia's gravest problem wasn't the guerrillas or the Mafia, but envy. Whoever invented it must have felt exactly what I had just felt.

She now had the visa and plane ticket, and had organized everything so that her two greatest treasures, the most precious thing she had, would be left in the most favorable circumstances. Sebastián had been the worst husband she could have had and continued to be the worst ex-husband, but she had to give him his due: he was a good father. With all of his emotional limitations, Sybil knew that he adored their daughters. He gave them his love in the best way he could, and that was sufficient for her. She wasn't expecting him to turn into a compassionate Gandhi from one day to the next. She only wanted him to take care of them while she was away. It wasn't much to ask. She continued to feel that this period would be beneficial for the three of them. Perhaps life was offering her daughters a unique opportunity to be closer to their father while they were growing up, to erase the distance between them. There were so many ways to interpret this new rung on the ladder of their lives. Despite the social and family pressures and the criticisms hurled at her for making such an unconventional move, she preferred to stick to her optimistic and proactive view.

THE INDIGO OF PURE KNOWLEDGE

I arrived at Washington full of hope and ready for anything. Autumn soon began, and what better season to adapt myself to my new and beautiful city. My apartment in L Street was small but comfortable. I didn't have a car, so I'd chosen a place near the university. The master's offered an intensive program, with night classes, so I studied and did my course projects and papers by day and also on the weekends. It was the hardest challenge I'd faced so far. I was completely out of my comfort zone and aware of my weaknesses. I had to polish my English a lot, and I wasn't sweet sixteen anymore. My new ambit was highly competitive and high-tech. What's more, since most of my fellow students were American, they did not have the language barrier and they also were much younger. But I didn't let that discourage me. I felt I was there for some reason my limited perception didn't understand. I would try to overcome all the obstacles and give the best of myself.

But living without her daughters kept her from being at peace. There were days when she felt miserable without them. They kept in contact by phone and Internet, but it was not enough. At the same time, her mind was now able to accept—at least on the surface—that she was living in the reality she herself had created, that her thoughts manifested themselves as realities. At last, she no longer had victimizers to blame. She finally admitted her responsibility as a creator of her own life. The books and videos on quantum physics she studied began to influence her conscious self.

My mind continued to evolve, even if the change was imperceptible to me. At times, nostalgia for my daughters easily gave way to curiosity and an eagerness to learn more about new things. I was in a modern and cosmopolitan city which had much to teach me. The mecca of contemporary politics was now my home. The Masonic city par excellence; so many mysteries to unravel there. The White House lay a couple of blocks from the place where the sun awakened me every morning. George Bush was my neighbor now! In the evenings, I would go out on the small terrace of my study to watch the sunset. From there, I could catch sight of the obelisk in the distance. I could seize hold of a little of the grandeur of the world that lay before me, the world that was urging me to include it as my own inner landscape.

How fortunate she was. It was a new dream. She felt happy again, or was learning about a new concept of happiness, an inner one that no school or university had been able to teach her. She soon got used to living alone in her small space and developed the discipline to study constantly, day and night. It required her to brainwash herself. She was isolated from everything that pertained to her old world and absorbed by the present, so that her former reality did not exist. Only memories and recollections remained. She went through a transformation of values and principles, expanding a little more day by day. Her mind was opening, while her heart continued to forgive. In inexplicable ways, every new question she asked herself yielded the answer she was best able to grasp. Every day she was capable of more. Little by little, she fell in love with the world she was creating, an alchemist's apprentice fascinated by possibilities that used to be impossible and she was now beginning to understand.

My eagerness to work for the people of my country re-awakened now that I knew more. Two of my professors helped me to design a non-profit organization that would help children affected by the war which Colombia chose to label as "conflict." I now regarded my failed attempt to work for the government while I was living in Bogotá in a completely different light. It was the best thing that could have happened to me. My new courses were teaching me about principles of democracy and transparency – all the conditions for achieving a fairer society that did not exist in my country. I was an innovator, a lover of change, a peaceful revolutionary who wanted to do away with the status quo. I was the antithesis of the prototype of the traditional Colombian politician. Only now did I realize that I could only contribute if worked in the private, not the public sector. Taking advantage of the master's course, I decided to devote my degree project to the creation of a foundation that would provide effective and efficient services for children who had been working in the guerrilla and had no chances for rehabilitation or education. If I managed to get that initiative going, the sacrifice of leaving my daughters would have been worth it. I would be able to help thousands of needy children and adolescents when I returned to my country.

On the inner plane, she continued to meditate every day and put all the teachings of Gazardiel into practice. She saw another person in the mirror; she perceived the mental change in her physical appearance. While her studies required her left brain to be alert twenty-four hours a day, she was also concerned about her right brain. On another level, a higher one, she continued to be guided and she devoted the little free time she had to reading what certain early twentieth-century American mystics and metaphysicians had written about the power of the mind and the ability to heal oneself. She now had vivid dreams full of messages and symbols. It was clear that meditation was awakening her to new realities. The more she understood about what dwelt in her interior, the more information reached her when she least expected it. She could no longer turn back. It was like a new addiction to self-knowledge. She was fascinated by these theories, which were as old as mankind but so new to her. Why wasn't this fabulous esoteric knowledge included in the formal education imparted to the masses in schools and universities? She still could not answer that question, but she experienced a new level of mental freedom such as she had never known before.

Life was unbelievable. As soon as it taught me something new, it would take charge of making me try out each lesson I'd learned. Now I would have to wield my own mental power. Before traveling to Washington, I had gone for a routine gynecological check-up. Since I was going to be living in another country, I wanted a thorough examination, to make sure everything was all right. The results weren't ready before I left, so I had to call the doctor from Washington. The news I got was like a pail of freezing water from the North Pole. Dr. Sanclemente tried not to alarm me. First, he reassured me that if an operation was necessary, I could wait till I returned to Bogotá in December for the Christmas vacations. The early stages of a cancer of the uterus had been detected. Cancer! The word paralyzed my terrified heart. Why me? It wasn't the right moment to become ill! What would happen if my condition got worse and it was already too late when I got back in December? I didn't know what to think, but I decided there was no point to ringing Sanclemente again for a more detailed explanation. I had known him since I was an adolescent, he had said everything he had to say and he wouldn't add another word.

It was a perfect opportunity to put what she had learned into practice. She had nothing to lose and much to gain. She wasn't going to be scared by a disease whose very name caused mass panic, and though she wanted to have a positive attitude, she was affected by the news, or rather concerned. She always forgot that one had to ask for help, but this time she remembered her angel, who immediately began to speak to her in the ear behind her ear.

> "Heal yourself. You yourself can do it."

His loving voice never changed. She recognized the tone and vibration. Even though she was in another country, her angel was still the same. But what was this suggestion he had just made? She did not know how to start healing herself, she thought. Archangel Michael kept on repeating that phrase, day after day, until one morning, in the middle of her meditation, his image came to her and he gave her further instructions.

> "Let yourself go, my child. I will show you how to do it."

My mind stopped putting up resistance, and I began to illuminate the whole area around my pelvis with an intense white light in motion. I found myself being the healer and the observer at the same time. All of my reproductive organs were bathed in that light. I learned how to let myself go. My mind gave Archangel Michael permission to show me how to bring that powerful light to myself. Once I did it for the first time, it became so easy, as simple as remembering what I already knew. I felt the need to do this exercise for a few minutes every day. Something seemed to be happening there, inside me. At times I felt a burning or even a pain in that lower area of my body. I had no way to know; I could only trust in my angel and wait for my appointment with Sanclemente.

That December, she returned to Bogotá. She was dying to hug and kiss her daughters; she had missed them so much. She was happy to see how well they were. Sebastián had fulfilled his role as a bachelor father in a responsible and dedicated way. Though giving Sebastián the chance to get to know his daughters—and they him in return—had not been the conscious purpose of her move, it might have been a subconscious one. Luna and Sol had previously been interpreting reality through the lenses of their mother. She was satisfied to see that they were now becoming familiar with both sides of the story, not only hers. It was clear that Sebastián had as much right as she to sell them his version of his truth, no matter how different it might be.

My visit to the gynecologist was an urgent matter. He got me to turn up first thing in the morning. It was a short procedure, but even so, uncertainty made me nervous. The first part was a biopsy to register the progress of my abnormal condition. Sanclemente's self-confidence was the best tranquilizer. Luckily, my lifelong doctor was perfectly attuned to my way of being. When I stood up from the examination table after they took the samples that were to be sent to the lab, I saw his smile of satisfaction.

"I have to congratulate you. The procedure we just did

is pretty painful. I am impressed by how calm you were. You didn't complain once. It seemed that you didn't feel any pain."

I hadn't felt any, in fact. I meditated while he extracted the tissue samples. That, at least, was a good sign that I was learning fast. I left the clinic to meet up with some girlfriends before Luna and Sol returned from school. Since it was an urgent situation, the results would be ready early the next morning. I vividly recall my doctor's words on the phone.

"Sybil, I don't know how this happened. The meditations you were telling me about seem to work. I analyzed the results several times, and you are completely healthy. I myself extracted the samples, so I have no doubts. There is no need to operate; everything is in order. You can return to Washington with your mind at rest, honey. I'll expect you here next year for a routine check-up."

I didn't go into the details with my doctor, because it would have been impossible to explain what I was living within. Only my angel and I were aware of the healing I had done on my own for three months. Only the alchemy of the mind knew the magic formula.

***

My life flowed like a small stream which ripples around great rocks while it maintains its course toward the mighty ocean. I felt physically healthy because, in emotional terms, my heart had already shed several layers of sorrow and disrespect. From the books I was reading on self-

improvement, I understood that you could not heal yourself from one day to the next. There was so much I had to become aware of, so many outlooks much more advanced than mine that I had to take into consideration. But I was acquiring patience. I was learning to allow myself all the time I needed in order to grow.

She felt realized in Washington. She was like a little girl in a candy store who wants to try all the goodies at once. She did not know it happened, but in some indescribable way, life was restored to her in time to realize her pending tasks. She was returning to the very moment when she had left her early dreams behind in Boston to return to Bogotá and marry the man she had blindly fallen in love with. It seemed like a second chance to walk along the path she had dreamt of. Nobody dies before their time is up; now she understood another aspect of that old saying. Nobody dies before doing everything they have come into this life to do as part of their individual evolution.

But I was still eating up my capital. Despite filling all my agendas with budgets and estimates so that I wouldn't spend a dollar more than I had to, my two daughters were still growing, and Sebastián continued to pocket every peso that came his way. It was not only a material expenditure but an emotional one, insofar as many in my social circle in Bogotá turned against me. I lost several girlfriends who never accepted my leaving Luna and Sol with Sebastián. What I had done was unthinkable for women who still thought of me as a mere housewife who only believed in the ideals of high society. I would soon have to come up with a way to recover my lost capital. If I kept spending at the current rate, my savings would be gone in a couple of years, and that possibility terrified me.

It was in the moments when she connected with her other

reality through meditation that she felt safe again. In some way, her doubts disappeared. In that state of silence and peace, she was certain that someone or something was guiding her through her world while she made her way through the criticisms and judgments of those who surrounded her. Her inner perception was gaining strength. She no longer only saw and heard Archangel Michael but other ascended masters as well, who little by little appeared to her. Each helped with a specific aspect of her life, and each spoke to her in a different tone, some masculine and others feminine. She even came to recognize certain intruders, one or another entity who wanted to deceive her by pretending to be one of them. Her intuition quickly sharpened, and though she felt economically weak, she became inwardly stronger every day. She would go on to the end. Michael made her feel so protected, it was as though she had a battalion of bodyguards behind her.

When I returned to Washington for the start of the next semester, my life continued to fill with new colors and hues. Living outside of the goldfish bowl was helping me to understand so many aspects of myself which I had never thought were mine. My looks kept changing gradually. The expression I now saw in the mirror was full of peace and tranquility. I liked my face, my gaze, my body. I felt satisfied with what I saw. Everything looked new to me. I saw a different beauty reflected in the mirror. A concept of beauty that was no longer physical had emerged from within, and my eyes began to use lenses of unconditional love, of true love.

It was the moment when she recalled the question the angelic black man had put to her in the elevator in Miami several years before. He had asked her whether she knew her true countenance. Only now would she have been able to answer him. Nearly six years had passed, and only now did she understand what that being of light had been trying to make her see. Her stride was confident now; she held her head high. She remembered the bent-over way she had walked when she was the Señora Obregón and felt she was carrying a grand piano on her back. She gazed at the sky again. The stars were now more important as witnesses of her life than the eyes of the inhuman judges who surrounded her. Reminders of her sad past came back to her, more than were needed, but her interpretation of them continued to evolve. What she used to regard as negative was now the best thing that could have happened to her. She was learning to guide herself by the invisible reality, invisible to most, although not to her; to follow the light of the stars which she now even saw in the clear light of day.

That spiritual pilgrimage to Mexico was one of the best investments of my life. That week changed my course from there on. My mind never ceased to expand in ways that not even I could describe or explain rationally. Even Cesar Nazareno was a witness to it. That enamored sorcerer tried to undertake two astral visits to me while I was in D.C., only to find that I wasn't the defenseless and fearful little woman he had known before. I not only felt his presence but saw his invasive figure trying to approach my electromagnetic field, which now served as my protective shield. He could no longer lie in wait for me or get into my bed. He still blew out a few light bulbs to try to catch my attention, but it was now a silly kids' game. I now understood all of his ruses. I knew what I had to do without paying money to a fraudulent witch. I even laughed, as if the experience were the funniest thing.

Studying wasn't everything. Twice a month she treated herself to lunch at her favorite restaurant near Georgetown. Her aim was to save as much as possible, but she also needed to have a little fun. Every Saturday, she went out early and walked around the city, disguised as yet another tourist. She would visit a few museums, lunch over a good book, and return on foot to her study, where dozens of books awaited her, spread along the dining room table she used as a desk, along with her laptop. As soon as he saw her come in, Nathan, the chef of that same café, brought her order: Caprese salad with slices of organic tomato and fresh buffalo mozzarella cheese, a glass of Chardonnay and a decaf cappuccino with the check. She loved to walk along the sidewalks full of snow which, little by little, with the passing days, transformed into sidewalks filled with the flowers that spring brought. She had never experienced the change of seasons before, because they did not exist in Colombia. Wearing an overcoat, gloves, scarf, and slip-proof boots in the winter was a great novelty. How far the shy and self-absorbed girl had come, the one who had grown up amid the ocean and wild places of San Andrés.

That Saturday, as usual, I was walking along M Street, stopping to look in the windows of the art galleries that I liked so much. I looked at a small oil of a sunset over a beach, in bright orange and blue tones, which was like a wakeful dream. When I least expected it, my silence was broken by a voice, which flirtingly whispered behind my loose hair.

"You have very good taste; it is a beautiful landscape."

Caught by surprise, I turned and cautiously smiled without speaking to him. How striking he looked! Like a model in a magazine for teenagers, but he was a stranger, just that. I kept on walking and he followed me.

"With the energy you transmit, you don't look like an

ill-mannered person. Let me invite you to a coffee, only a coffee, and I won't bother you anymore."

He had the right approach. The compliment had been decent and the invitation as well. I stopped and turned to get a better look at him. His English was perfect, and he introduced himself by name and surname when he shook my hand. The people around us kept walking, while we blocked the sidewalk. He insisted on having a coffee again, and I couldn't say no; a Starbucks was in front of our noses. Persistent and irresistible, Carlo Conti filled me with curiosity, and I would never have guessed from his name that he was Colombian. It's a small world, for sure – an accidental meeting between two Colombians on the street of a foreign city. What drew the attention of that man? Man? Now, when he told me his age, I did get alarmed: he was twenty-four!

She was old enough to be his mother, was her first thought, but there was an attraction of energies which neither he nor she could resist. They spent two hours together and still could not stop talking. They had so much in common. He was studying for a master's in international economics, and both wanted to work in Colombia when they graduated. Blessed with psychic powers since he was a boy, he spoke with angels and guides. She was finally able to share her invisible world with someone, without fear of being called crazy or unbalanced. They were so alike, it was frightening. The only difference was one of age. Fourteen years, a big one, but he did not seem to notice. Perhaps Carlo entered Sybil's reality to continue to strengthen her self-esteem. He could have picked any woman of his own age, yet he preferred to be with her. He was very mature. He had so much of what she was looking for in a man, so much that the men she had gone out with in Bogotá lacked. They turned into long-lost soul mates who had met up again. But the post-grad continued to be Sybil's priority. She was sure that what she was doing in Washington was a second chance, and there was no man in the world who would shift her from that this time. What's more, Carlo understood it perfectly. He was not looking for a woman to shift him from his path either. She learned so much from him. She had never imagined that someone so young could have brought so much wisdom to her heart. Her faith in the love between couples was restored, and although both felt that their romance came with an expiration date, it was the best gift Sybil could have had: love when she most needed it. A lover, friend, and confidant who helped to re-awaken her passion and desire for life.

In three months, I rebuilt the idea of love that the twelve years I lived with Sebastián had destroyed. Carlo was the mirror I looked into. I confronted so many defects that my ego fought to survive, distancing me from that which kept on hurting it. I was still inclined toward dependence. My subconscious still sold me the idea that I had to find another man to depend on. Carlos represented the opposite. I needed him to begin to understand the independence which I was paradoxically seeking. I was going through a stage of transition. I was beginning to exchange my old paradigm of beliefs for a new one I still didn't understand. It was like standing on a big stone in the middle of a torrential river, looking back at the bank I'd left without knowing how to reach the other side. With all my insecurity, it was a difficult relationship, but the presence of Carlo made me consider the possibility of taking that big leap.

For the first time, she had met a person who did not want to condition her. Such free love was completely new to her. Carlo was like a wise old man clothed in a youthful body, an old soul who would depart when the right moment arrived, without asking for anything in return. He graduated before Sybil and went to work for a multilateral agency in New York. They loved each other so much in such a short time and with so much respect that neither of the two set out to change the other's course. Her eyes grow moist whenever she recalls the gratitude she still feels toward him. From him she learned that one could live one's life without dramas or attachments.

***

She still had many contacts and friends from the time she lived in Miami as the Señora Obregón, and she spoke to them from time to time. The whole of Florida was now going through an economic boom that seemed unreal. Wanting to find a way to make some extra money, she was still attracted by the idea of real estate, so she made some inquiries and asked for advice from some friends who were lawyers and bankers who invested in real estate. She felt self-confident with the experience of refurbishing properties in Bogotá. The sales had not gone well there, but thanks to her course, she now understood much more about the politics and economy of the world around her. The American market was governed by variables different from the ones in the Colombian market. It seemed to be a safe business. The banks offered loans on very good terms, so she decided to buy a house to do up and sell. While she was living in Washington, she had to travel to Miami now and again to oversee the project. If the first house sold well, it could be the start of a new company that would help her to recover her savings. It could even be a source of the financing she now needed to begin the legal establishment of the foundation for the children who were victims of the war, which was steadily taking on a life of its own in her heart. She had turned into a daring woman. She decided to invest in a haunted house in Miami that looked like it would be blown over in the next hurricane. She was able to buy it cheap and knew that she could completely transform it, so she was not intimidated by the abandoned state it had been left in by its previous owners. Her agenda became filled with budgets and estimates again. Terencio, the Colombian contractor recommended by Manuel Uribe, one of her best friends in Miami, would be responsible for helping her. While Sybil was studying, Terencio commissioned the blueprints and applied for the necessary permits in Coral Gables, so that everything would be ready to begin the job when she arrived in Miami after her graduation. Her calculations were precise. She had enough to pay for the renovation and for twelve monthly loan repayments to the bank. The work would take from four to six months, and once it was finished, it would be impossible not to sell the house within the six months after that, she thought, considering that the market was moving so fast everything was grabbed up. Her friend Manuel was the owner of a real-estate company, and he kept her informed of the ups and downs of the sector. The economic analysts estimated that the boom would last for another couple of years.

It was going to work this time. The timing and circumstances were different now. I was trying to forget about what had happened to me in Bogotá. I was so happy and encouraged that I decided to give Luna and Sol a surprise: we would go on a short visit to New York. It had been our dream ever since they were little girls. We had always imagined the three of us walking along the streets of the Big Apple. It was the perfect moment, because once I began the house project, I would have to cut all of my spending down to the minimum. This time, they would be going to visit me, rather than my going to Colombia. Sebastián agreed to it. I sent him the permission for them to leave the country on their own, issued by the consulate, as well as the plane tickets.

The Three Musketeers in New York! Luna had loved that nickname when she was little. It was another dream that was going to come true. She found a boutique hotel in Soho and spent months reading tourist guides and planning what they would do during those five days. She wanted it to be an unforgettable experience for the girls. She chose the restaurants, the outings they would make, and even set aside some cash to give to the girls so that they could go shopping. She wanted it to be a very special reunion, wanted them to feel that their mother's love was still intact despite the distance between them. She was so proud of her daughters. Despite their young age, their lives had been pretty unconventional. They were kids of divorced parents, they lived with their father, and not, as usually happened, with their mother. She felt guilty. She accepted that the life Luna and Sol led was the result of her own decisions. She often felt regret when she thought of them. Why couldn't she have put up with Sebastián and the life she shared with him so that her daughters would have had a normal existence, like their girlfriends from school? Why did many of her former friends stay married for the sake of their children while they sacrificed their own lives? What kind of mother was she, when she could not sacrifice herself and make do for the sake of her daughters?

Life had another big disillusion in store for me. All of my plans and dreams changed direction when I realized I was getting more and more distant from my past and also, as a result, from what I most loved in my world. Accepting that my daughters were forgetting me was nearly impossible. I was certain that all my life plans revolved around them, that I couldn't live without them, that the point of changing my life was to become a better woman and a better mother. Luna and Sol had been absorbing all the [chauvinistic] energy of Sebastián. Now that I was no longer living with them, they lacked the maternal influence to balance that.

That visit to New York brought her back to earth and made her understand the new reality of her daughters. She could not believe the rancor against her that had built up in Luna. She dreamt of a few days full of happiness so she would tell them of her plans and everything she was achieving in her life. She was so motivated, she imagined that her daughters would understand what she was living through. She still pictured the time when Luna had said good-bye to her, giving her encouragement and approval when she left for Washington. That Luna no longer existed, nor did she support her. Her daughter had turned into a rebellious teenager who only showed hatred toward her mother.

I'd been strict with them when they were little girls. I wanted them to be well-mannered and behave well in society. I was proud of how everyone loved them. I did the best I could at that time. I never took a course to learn how to be a mother. It was a stage of trial and error. I had to raise them as I had been raised, and Sebastián was also strict and disciplined with them. I gave them all my love in a moment when I did not love myself, when I was an unhappy woman who did not have much to offer. I did the best I could, but the result, now before me, left me disconsolate. I never imagined that the consequences of my move to Washington would be what I now saw. I left my daughters with a man who still did not forgive me for having destroyed his family, for having ruined what he thought was the perfect home. The energy in which my daughters' lives were now unfolding had made them completely prejudiced. They now supported Sebastián in his role of the victim. It seemed that the best way to turn the movie into a hit was to make themselves out to be the husband and daughters whom the wicked witch had abandoned and forgotten forever.

In that moment, the world looked like a place that was too harsh and unfriendly. She had to deal not only with a cruel ex-husband but a daughter who was even crueler than her father. Sol was also resentful, but she tried to be neutral. She tried not to judge her mother, whereas Luna did not miss an opportunity to shout at and insult her. The aggressiveness of her daughter was unhealthy; it lit up red warning signals in Sybil's ego.

I needed fresh air to revive my neurons. I left them watching television in the hotel room and went out, walking aimlessly. I didn't want to carry on with that pointless fight. Months had passed since I'd last seen them, and living on my own in Washington had turned me into a tranquil and peaceful person. Luna was now provoking me in ways that made me react in an unrecognizable way. I had been telling them about my project for creating the foundation, the house in Miami, and my plan to return to Colombia after graduation, when Luna suddenly erupted in rage.

> "There you go again with all those illusions of yours. Forget about that stupid foundation. You won't get anywhere. I also don't know why you're thinking of returning to Bogotá when we never want to live with you anymore. Forget about us once and for all. We're always going to live with Daddy."

Her eyes were full of bitterness and disappointment. I wanted to embrace her and ask her forgiveness for everything she was feeling. I wanted her to get it off her chest, but she shunned me. In her obstinacy, she locked herself in the bathroom while Sol embraced me without saying a word as she tried to make me feel better.

She had lost control over the lives of her daughters. To accept that she was losing her daughters was still unthinkable. As she no longer lived with them, she had no idea of what Sebastián's influence on them might be, but whatever it was, it was not very convincing. She felt like she was at a trial where she had just been accused of a crime she did not commit. As she walked through the unknown streets of bohemian Soho, her daughter's words resounded in her mind over and over again, without her being able to assimilate them:

> "I hate you. You're not my mommy anymore. Forget about me living with you when you return. You abandoned us. You were selfish, you didn't mind leaving us behind."

What had she done to make her daughter say she hated her and perceived things in this way? Luna left her position clear during their quarrel. Sol still kept her opinions to herself but gave a silent support to her sister. Sybil searched her mind, trying to recall the origin of all this pain. Luna's childhood had not been easy. She was always a difficult girl, with fixed ideas, who wanted to be more grown up than she was, without her mother yielding to her wishes. But she had also had the most important thing, a mother and father who loved her more than anything, despite their emotional problems and dysfunctional behavior.

I returned to the hotel and immediately rang to reserve a plane ticket. I was going to return to Bogotá with them. What I had just heard frightened me. I had to get together with Sebastián and hear his version, try to understand what my daughters were living through. Since they were minors, I still had legal custody, and I was still paying their monthly expenses at my ex-husband's home. My way of fighting for what I wanted in life had drastically changed, but even so, I still had every right to try to improve whatever was there to be improved. I soon understood that the heart of the monster from whom I'd escaped had been imperceptibly stoking itself with rage and revenge. How could my daughters have escaped such destructive sentiments? The situation was slipping through my hands like endlessly flowing water. Sebastián was still the same emotionally sick man who was now merciless toward the mother of his daughters. He seemed to be happy about what was happening between the girls and me. Trying to take advantage of every minute of my visit to Bogotá, I decided to stay in his apartment for a week. I thought I had to open my heart to the three of them and share their own space. I was willing to completely humble myself if it would help to improve the relationship with my girls. In short, it wasn't a competition I had to win, although at times it seemed that Sebastián was beating me.

She had never been so humiliated. Or perhaps she felt it was so because it was the first time the humiliation came from her daughters. After the trial in New York where her elder daughter declared her guilty, she was now serving her sentence. Alma was on vacation when she arrived, but before leaving, she got a mattress ready for her, in line with Sebastián's instructions. She slept on that mattress, stinking of dirt and long use, covered by two frayed blankets from the attic of her ex-mother-in-law. Lying on the cold floor of that studio, she felt chastised and forgotten, miserable again amid the abundance and wealth of a place where there was no longer a drop of the love she tried so hard to transmit to her daughters.

Sebastián decided there was nothing to talk about. Everything was fine, according to him. The distance between me and Luna was my problem and nothing more. He was very comfortable with the ambit he had created in my absence. The girls' expenses for the following six months and the dates on which the money would be sent – that was important, and there was time to speak about it. My trip had been useless. Luna completely ignored me. Now she followed her father's rules and made her indifference clear to me. My daughters had their world organized in such a way that there was no longer any room for a mother who wanted to be part of it again. I tried to get together with some of my former girlfriends, only to realize that I was not only being put on trial by my relatives but by all those who had known me before, without understanding my life. They all said I had "abandoned" my girls when I had gone off to advance my scholarship. Ill-intentioned voices seemed to gush forth from all the corners of that closed and gossipy society in which my daughters were growing up.

When had they stopped considering as valid her version of events? She wanted an impartial trial when it was already too late to change the verdict. During that week, she came to accept that it might be necessary to take Luna at her word. Apart from her daughters, what else was there in Bogotá to come back to? Dylan, her father, was already retired, and he and Cassandra now spent most of the year in the house in Wales that Anwen had left them. For many years now, her siblings, Betrys and Glyn, had been living with their families in the United States. That was the entire membership of her small family. None of them was in Bogotá. Now, more than ever, she saw Bogotá as a hostile and alien city.

The rationale I'd found for my life changed. It was the first time I considered a life without my daughters. Up to then, all of my efforts had been aimed at achieving a better future for the three of us. I thought that together the three of us formed a family. Now I considered the possibility that perhaps I was completely alone. On the face of it, my spiritual quest was all that was left to me. To say that sounded so bleak, so desolate, and made me sound cruel as well, but I couldn't remain stuck. I had to begin to visualize what might follow from there on.

Luna and Sol felt abandoned by their mother, without knowing that their mother also felt abandoned by them. She returned to Washington discouraged. It was only a short time until her graduation. Those final days in Colombia were clearly a low blow. She still did not detect that her exterior reality was drastically transforming itself as a result of her inner transformation. There were still too many books on physics and metaphysics she needed to read, ones that would have explained the nature of the directly proportional relationship between thoughts and the reality she created and manifested through them. She was on the step where her inner world was still disconnected from her outer world. There were still many layers of cheap indoctrination she would have to scratch away and toss on the ground. Her world was cracking up before her eyes without her mentally recognizing that she herself was responsible for such collapse. Silence gave her time to understand that she was still unaware of the truth and needed much more wisdom and divine aid. She had no idea of how to handle this new situation.

One wearisome night, when I was exhausted from studying, divine help appeared out of the void that I lived within the silence that was now my only friend: Have you worked out what you want to do with your life? Not how much you want, but what and how you want it? So far you have been filling the social mold which you insistently claim to reject. What are you trying to prove? And who are you trying to prove it to? The voice challenged me in a manner which was arrogant and loving at the same time, while I saw a clear image of my new master, dressed in a violet velvet jacket and with his chestnut hair neatly cut. How perfect his hands were as he stood behind me and closed his arms around me in a firm and tender embrace!

"I am Saint Germain, your new guide, my beloved

daughter. New because you only see me now, but I have been part of you for an eternity. You see me because the time has come when you are able to bear my energy. Your mind understands me because it has expanded. You will now hear from me what will often be uncomfortable for you, but it is necessary that I teach you to discern. Look in the Internet and find out who I am. I know that your rational mind still makes you doubt, just as it made you doubt when the archangel revealed himself to you few years ago. It is well. I have all the time and patience there is. Call out my name when you need me and I will be there. I deeply love you. And so it is."

When he finished, he began to laugh out loud at the terrified look on my face. He made me laugh at myself. I loved Saint Germain from his first visitation. He had a strong energy, but it was very luminous and healing. I had to do some research about my guide and find a number of books to reassure myself, once more, that I was still sane.

He was completely right. To fit into the mold continued to be Sybil's priority. The criticism of others continued to be more important than what she thought of herself. She was living in two worlds at the same time: that of others and her own. Sooner or later she would have to move herself to hers forever, with a whole truckload of her belongings. If she really sought to discover herself thoroughly, the only way would be to leave the world of others behind and enter into the realms of her own subconscious. Saint Germain had appeared to discipline her ego's stubbornness and fear.

In recent years, I'd had to make so many painful and drastic decisions in order to follow the call of my heart. I only knew I had to follow it to wherever it led me. After deciding to get a divorce, I had to decide to leave my daughters with their father. Now I had to face another, equally difficult decision. Would I return to Bogotá once I graduated? Should I return to fight for my daughters and try to get them back? I was sure I wouldn't use lawyers to force them to live with me. I no longer believed in the use of force and felt that life was trying to tell me something important through the conduct of my daughters. Whatever it might be, I had to ensure that the decision would be made thinking of me – not of my ex-husband or daughters or the world which surrounded me, but only myself. Saint Germain made me take stock. I felt that it was time to go forward, without looking back. I could no longer go backward. If my daughters formed part of my world, at some stage in life we would be reunited again. Otherwise, I would have to arm myself with courage to follow on my own the path which my heart needed to keep discovering.

She decided she would remain and live in Miami. She wrote an e-mail to Sebastián, informing him of her decision, but this was one of many he only filed without answering. Once again, she risked betting on an uncertainty. She contacted Alicia Conrado, the same lawyer she had consulted years before, when she was still married and learned that, due to Sebastián's negligence, she was not able to work while they lived in Miami during the darkest stage of her life. Though seven years had passed, Alicia remembered Sybil and warned her to be realistic. This time, what she was trying to accomplish would not be so easy. Like her, everyone wanted a work visa, and she no longer had the backing of the businesses and investments of a millionaire husband. She did not allow herself to be intimidated by that but felt that she had to try it and find a job with a company that would be willing to sponsor her visa. It would be difficult but not impossible. She immediately began to send out résumés.

I would soon be forty. The situation with my daughters continued to deteriorate. They were acting just like Sebastían: they no longer answered my calls or e-mails. But all the experiences of loss which I continued to confront made me stronger. Contradictory as it seemed, the negative was turning me into a positive and optimistic person, ready for anything. It was as though adversity were a divine gift. I no longer recognized myself; of that sad and defeated woman, drowning in the vice of alcohol and starved for love, there remained almost nothing.

The wise old men teach that thoughts always manifest themselves in things or situations. She soon found a real-estate company that would sponsor her visa. They would hire her to work in their department of international sales as soon as she finished the master's in May. Her lawyer immediately began to undertake the procedures to obtain her visa. Miami was ideal for her short-term plans. She would work while she was coordinating the renovation of the house and the legal incorporation of the foundation for the war children, which she could handle from Miami if she found a person to help her administer its operations in Bogotá. She would also be closer to Luna and Sol. Perhaps they would change their minds later on and want to live with her. They had liked Miami when they lived there as girls. By March 2006, all the papers for the visa were ready, translated, and sent from her lawyer's office to the immigration services office. The next step was to wait for the appointment to take fingerprints. One Thursday evening, less than a month later, she was about to leave for her night classes when she got a phone call from Alicia, who scolded her.

> "Sybil, what happened to you? Why didn't you go to the appointment you had this morning for the fingerprints?"

She couldn't believe what she was hearing. What appointment? She had no idea of the appointment Alicia referred to. A copy of the notification had just arrived at the office of her lawyer in Miami. The original should have been sent to her apartment in Washington, but it never arrived. It got lost in the mail, as if by magic. She hung up, feeling defeated. To have missed that appointment was the worst thing that could have happened to her, according to her lawyer. In such cases, the immigration office immediately canceled the application, arguing omission, and trying to re-apply was almost impossible. She did not want to think of the number of people who were waiting for an opportunity like the one she had just lost.

As I tried to figure it out, I couldn't keep still. I walked about, sat down, walked again. I was so upset, I decided not to go to class that night. I had to come up with some solution. My attempt to remain in the United States could not end like that; I had already made up my mind. I sat on the floor and began to meditate in order to calm down. The answer soon came to me. I lit up like a light bulb and stood up. I would hire a taxi to drive me to the immigration office where I had to present myself, a three-hour ride from my apartment. Alicia had faxed me a copy of the document I never received. With that piece of paper, I would go there and explain what had happened. They would open at 8 AM and I wanted to be one of the first in line, so I ordered the taxi to pick me up at 4:45 AM. I had no idea what I was doing or why. I was acting by remote control, led by the invisible hand of a benevolent being who had control over me. I don't want to remember what the round trip in the taxi cost, but what had just happened to me was so serious, the money was the least of it. Without the fingerprints, there would be no visa, and without the visa, no life in the United States. Simple.

The Nigerian taxi driver left her in front of the immigration office at 8:00 AM. Sybil was on the point of bursting into tears, she felt so disappointed about the occurrence, though it was not her fault. Now she was full of doubts. Why her? It was 8:02 AM when a tall, thin old man inside the office, dressed in a blue uniform, opened the lock of the glass door, while the ten or twelve people who were waiting organized themselves into a line and were only admitted after showing their notification. She put herself at the end of the line, so she would have more time to think about what she was going to say when it was her turn to show the notification to the guard. It looked like she was about to shed tears when she reached him, knowing it was out of date. She respectfully greeted him and with a desperate look in her eye, began to explain what had happened in her clumsy English. Paying close attention, he heard her out without answering. He only gave her an approving wink as he stamped the notification without even reading it. At the same time, with his right index finger, he pointed to the counter at the end of the office where she had to go and finally let her in with a smile and another affectionate wink. She walked to the far end, where a waiting official took prints of all her fingers and photographed her. In less than five minutes, she met all the requirements and was ready to leave the place. The worries of the previous night, when she'd hardly been able to sleep, were now a thing of the past. She no longer asked herself why such a mishap had occurred to her. She was now wondering whether it had simply been part of a pre-ordained scheme, a test for her. She might not have gone; she might have been sorry for the rest of her days, tormenting herself with the classic "if only I had done such and such ..." and who knows what course her life would have taken? She wanted to say good-bye and thanks to the guard at the door, but he was no longer there when she left. He seemed like a vanished angel. *It was still possible to believe in human kindness,* she thought.

On the way back in the taxi, my mind couldn't stop congratulating itself. I couldn't believe what I had just achieved. I could have given up the night before, but no, I decided to go to my appointment and show my face, without knowing the consequences. My daring ensured that my visa application would go forward. I had to wait patiently, but according to Alicia, there was a good possibility it would be approved, thanks to all of my university degrees, the same ones that had been undervalued by so many people in my life. One country, the United States, gave importance to professionals from other countries with qualifications like mine. The old saying now came to mind once more: definitely no one was a prophet in his own land.

While she was coming to the end of her time in Washington, the permits for the house she had bought as an investment in Miami were taking more time than was necessary. She was already paying Terencio a monthly salary, and they still could not begin the job. The next stage of her life was in doubt; it was like a pregnancy without a birth. She completely devoted herself to her final exams and to finishing the foundation project, hoping to take maximum advantage of the expertise of her professors, who would no longer be close to hand once she moved to Miami. To maintain her standing as a good student was her obsession. She wanted to graduate with an A+ grade-point average, and she did. Her marks reflected all of her effort and dedication. All the knowledge she had obtained in Washington—inside and outside of the university, within and outside of herself—made the world around her much larger. It was now a universe.

It was with nostalgia that I finished my exams, gave up my apartment on L Street, and left for Miami. I didn't want to attend the graduation ceremony. This was a personal victory. I didn't need to celebrate it in public, so I asked the university to mail me the diploma. I did not receive any congratulations from my daughters; I don't think they found out about it. But I felt so satisfied; looking back helped me to realize that it was worth following my path, despite its apparent uncertainty. When I arrived in Miami, I began to work in the real-estate company that was sponsoring my work visa. Latin Americans never stopped investing in the market, and I would be able to offer the company everything I'd learned in DC about the international outlook. I found a small apartment on Brickell Avenue, where I coordinated everything that I was about to do. The project for the foundation, the renovation of the house whose sale would consolidate my small company, the reconciliation with my daughters – they were all pending still.

In the summer, she returned to Bogotá for a week, trying to continue her campaign to win back her daughters. Staying in Sebastián's apartment had been humiliating the last time, but she was willing to repeat the feat in order to close the distance between herself and Luna and Sol. This time, the old mattress was installed in Sol's bedroom, and a couple of sheets had showed up, which improved the appearance of the threadbare blankets that now seemed to have her name written on them. Sol wanted her to sleep in her bedroom, and that filled her with hope. She was no longer in a corner of the study; it was progress. Sebastián had fired Alma and now had a new housekeeper called Silvia. It was curious how her name resembled Sybil's.

I took advantage of my stay in Bogotá to continue developing the foundation project. I had finished the international marketing plan, and all the research was ready. Once I returned to Miami, I would start on its incorporation as a nonprofit organization in the state of Florida. I had the help of a friend who worked in one of the country's most prestigious law firms. A native of Michigan, Patrick O'Neill believed in the project from the start. His soul was linked to Colombia, since he had lived for a few years on its Caribbean coast and was married to a Colombian woman. He was familiar with my country's social problems. His fees were exorbitant, but I had got him to charge less, since it was for a foundation. It was a symbiosis where Patrick knew that I was financing the project on my own with my savings, and I knew that if I did not draft a formal proposal that had legal credibility, it would be difficult to catch the attention of donors who were committed and willing to sponsor the organization and its long-term operations.

The dream was an ambitious one. The objective was to offer a program of rehabilitation and education to children who had served as soldiers in the Colombian guerrilla armies, to rehabilitate and reinsert them into Colombian society. At that time, there were fourteen thousand child soldiers, according to the official statistics, though there might have been many more. Thanks to all the research she had done in Washington, she knew that she needed to renew her links with the Colombian government. She had to familiarize herself with other ongoing projects for demobilization and re-insertion. Having the approval of the government and working in harmony with it would be indispensable. She did not want the foundation to be put on the black list of NGOs working in the country, which were often accused of supporting the subversive forces. Its aim was to offer social help to an unprotected sector of the population while guarding its political neutrality. A couple of years had gone by since she had last seen Cesar Nazareno. She was out of touch with everything that was happening in her country in those higher spheres. She had specialized in studying the functioning and dynamics of the international politics and economy of the world; now she had to integrate herself again into the Colombian context, if the foundation were to have a future. Having no one else to turn to, she thought of him. He was still a key piece, Holguin's right-hand man who worked behind the scenes. This time she would not be asking him for a job or a position. This time she was offering her altruism, through a project that came from her heart. She would work for her country for free. Her initiative, which was a complete innovation, had won the admiration and endorsement of a number of experts in Washington. Nazareno was sure to appreciate that, realizing that there was nothing like it in the country. It might even improve his cloudy and sinister public image. Sybil was not asking for the credit; she would leave that to him.

I rang his private cell phone number. He still had the same one I'd jotted down in my address book when I worked on the presidential campaign. Feeling no rancor, I was happy to hear his voice again. My mind had learned to forgive, to understand the situations I had lived through as lessons that turned me into what I now was and what I now was satisfied me. It was a short conversation, but I arranged to meet him in his office the following day. I would walk there and have a bit of lunch on the way.

It was a long time since she had walked through the city, along the streets that had seen her change from a provincial girl to an urbane woman. She wanted to feel the pulse of the city: its people, disorder, and contamination. Luna and Sol still hadn't gone out for their summer vacations, and they spent almost the whole day at school, so there was no rush to get back until the evening, when they returned. She wanted to be in the apartment to greet them. She reached the building where Nazareno still had the same office; nothing seemed to have changed in her absence. She called his office from the reception area and was ushered in. She began to feel nervous and insecure as the elevator ascended, wanting to go back. What was she doing? How could she possibly turn again to that man who had caused her so many sleepless nights in the past? *No going back,* she thought. *The foundation was worth the effort.* Gerardino, the same man involved in the incident with the witch whom Sybil had hired to protect herself from Nazareno years before, was waiting for her at the door of the office.

> "Madam Sybil, what a pleasure to see you here again. Please come in and sit down. My boss won't be long on the phone and then he'll attend to you."

I sat down on the brown leather sofa and a few minutes later heard him shout behind the closed door.

> "Gerardino, tell my next appointment to come in!"

I stood up and walked toward the door while Gerardino beckoned me to proceed. I softly knocked and opened it at the same time. There he was, sitting behind the same antique desk, giving me a sideways glance above his reading glasses. He didn't even stand up, a discourtesy that made his position clear to me.

> "What's up, gal, sit down."

I did, while he showed me his indifference by continuing to read the document in his hands. I settled into one of the chairs in front of his desk and gave him a friendly greeting at the same time. "How good to see you, Cesar. How have you been?" His answer stunned me, but I kept calm.

> "Well, what's your proposal about? It's kind of late for you to turn up here. Everything that was available is already shared out."

I diplomatically laughed and began to explain the nature of the project and how the government might benefit from it. I spoke with the enthusiasm of someone who believes in her dreams. I was in love with the foundation. So many children would be able to have a future if I was only given an opportunity to implement the program.

She already knew what a poor listener Nazareno was, but it seemed that his rudeness had gotten worse. She hadn't even finished when he interrupted her and came out with the unimaginable.

> "And to think that I only asked to fuck you that time, only that. Can you imagine where you would be today, gal?"

Sybil could not believe it. The sorcerer still had that fixation on what had happened years before, or rather, what had *failed* to happen! She felt insulted and degraded again. It was a lost cause. She got up from her seat as she thanked him for his time, trying not to raise her voice. She felt like screaming at him, like jumping over the desk to hit him, but no, that was not her. With a faint, hypocritical smile that kept her tears back, she stormed out of the office, slamming the door so hard she nearly broke it as she heard Nazareno threatening her.

> "Every door will still be closed to you, Sybil, and only because I say so. Yes, sir!"

Gerardino caught a glimpse of her tear-filled eyes. The world had just caved in for her. Once she reached the sidewalk, still stunned, she aimlessly walked around. She would have to start from zero again. Nazareno still thought of having her as a trophy in his bed. What must she do? Yield to him in the end? It was not as though she had never considered it. She even recalled the time, in the midst of the presidential campaign, when she kissed Nazareno, trying to find out if she might come to like him at least a bit. She didn't feel anything for him then, and much less now, only repulsion.

I felt like an alien from another galaxy. Could you only get things done on this planet through money and sex? I preferred to think it was not so. Turning myself into a prostitute was definitely not one of the ingredients of the recipe for helping others and realizing my dreams.

Seated on the plane back to Miami, she became pensive and melancholic. She could not explain to herself where the force that sustained her wish to go forward came from. Perhaps her ex-husband was right and she was mad. She had spent years fighting for her ideals, and nothing good seemed to have come out of it. She was risking her skin and guts in the attempt to remain in the United States. Now, after a week's visit to the city she used to live in, it seemed that she had no other choice. In Bogotá she only saw stop signs at every turn. For one thing, Luna and Sol continued to reject her, and now it was official: they had decided they would not live with her, either in Bogotá or Miami. In a subliminal way, Sebastián was still selling them his disrespect and scorn for her. For another, Cesar Nazareno had just menaced the future of the foundation in which she believed so much, the one where she might fulfill her mission to serve others. She had not done anything but study and prepare herself to help the people of her country, and she had just felt the slamming of the brakes.

I might have decided that nothing was going right. I might have gotten depressed about everything I saw around me. In reality, my future wasn't very promising. The money I had left continued to slowly disappear through a hole in my pocket. Everything I'd set out to do turned out to be the complete opposite of what I expected, and all of my interactions with the people around me, including my daughters, seemed to affect me negatively. What was it that kept me resilient and strong? At times I felt that my aspirations had a supernatural force. I was alone, completely so; since I did not let anyone control me, it seemed that nobody wanted to help me. But out of those supernatural yearnings there came a call, something that kept telling me I could not yield to my external reality—a passion that made me feel loved and supported in what was now another reality, my inner one.

A new reality was slowly beginning to invade the space of her old life. What a delayed and painful process! She felt the shedding of her skin, the layers continued to fall everywhere, although her eyes were still not able to visualize her newborn skin. Her apartment in Miami was modest, barely furnished but full of the new energy she radiated. One breathed in a different vibration there. Just like the one in Washington, it had a small terrace where she put a little table with two chairs. On the weekends, she devoted herself to reading all the spiritual information and technology that she still had to assimilate, accompanied by the ocean and the breeze, her silent witnesses.

With that view of the sea in front of me once again, I began to practice gratefulness. I had never felt true gratitude in my heart before. I'd spent my whole life without recognizing the abundance that I had mistaken for scarcity. My spiritual awakening continued to show me a path full of promises, despite the appearances; I had so much to be thankful for. One day I even made a list, which I could not finish because of all I had. The moment I stopped thinking about what I did not have, the negativity which had been shaping my life thus far began to feel like an unwelcome intruder. The world I was beginning to create was so full of peace and love, a peace and love redefined in a completely new way. God had clearly begun to relocate within me. Losing my daughters, being alone, my completely uncertain future—it did not seem so terrible, after all. At least nobody that I knew had died from that!

The permits for the house were finally ready. Terencio and a group of five subcontractors immediately got down to work nonstop. For her, it was urgent to finish as soon as possible, so the house could be sold. With all the unforeseen costs that cropped up every day, the money she had set aside for that project was being wasted on the problems that flew out of the Pandora's box she had risked buying. She was also worried by signs that the real-estate market was beginning to slow down. Doubtless the variables of doing business in the United States were completely different from the ones in Colombia, but she preferred to remain optimistic. One night she even had a very vivid dream where a young couple with two small children came to buy the house, though it all happened in Spain. What a strange dream! She had no idea what Spain had to do with it, but it clearly gave her hope.

About two months had gone by since my last trip to Colombia. One night, I arrived at the apartment completely worn out. I had come from the renovation, where I had spent hours cleaning the ceramic tiles recently laid on the kitchen floor with a special acid. In the morning, the plumbers had damaged them when they were fixing some pipes. I was rubbing so hard I had skinned my knees and blistered my hands, but I saved the floor and my sores would get better. The previous day had been a black one. I had to fire Terencio, after finding out that he had stolen money from the renovation budget. I was now short ten thousand dollars, which had slipped into the pockets of my fellow Colombian, and had a squad of Cuban laborers to look after. And as though that weren't enough, I'd had a meeting with Patrick O'Neill, the lawyer helping me with the foundation. A Colombian multi-millionaire, who lived in New York and with whom we had been in contact since my time in Washington, had just sent a letter to us, saying that the donation he had promised to the foundation was no longer available, since he needed the funds for one of his private foundations. Without that money, the project for the rehabilitation of the children was not viable. We needed a million dollars to start operating. I didn't have a spare dollar to keep it afloat. We would have to cancel its incorporation, which meant losing the forty thousand dollars I had invested in my dream thus far.

God squeezes but does not strangle; that night, Sybil was a witness to it. On her way to her apartment, she remembered to check her mailbox in the lobby of the building. There was an envelope with the logo of the Department of Homeland Security on it. Her heart skipped a few beats as she rose in the elevator. She was scared to death. In her hands was the answer that would definitively determine her whole future: the yes or no the letter brought. She entered the apartment, threw her handbag onto the sofa, and frantically began to tear the envelope open while she unstuck the card that was attached to it. She sat down and read it again, because she still did not understand. The letter welcomed her to the United States and stated that her application for permanent residence had been approved. The card bore the photo taken in Washington the day she nearly squandered the opportunity of her life and read in capital letters: "Permanent Resident's Card." She could not believe it.

Was it a joke in bad taste? Had they granted her residence in the United States? It must be a mistake. It was much more than her lawyer had asked for. Incredulous, she scrutinized the front and back of the card. She had to look on the Internet for photos of such government documents. She had never had one in her hands before. Yes, it was definite—they had just granted her permanent residence. Her *green card* had arrived! Miracles still happened in the twenty-first century. She wanted to burst with joy. It was ten at night, too late to ring anyone and tell them the big news. The sores on her hands and knees were still hurting, but she started to jump about, barefoot, like a little girl trying to touch the ceiling. She danced with contentment. She could not believe that life had just sent her such a gift. On the following day, she visited her lawyer to confirm that the card was genuine. Alicia was surprised by the quickness with which her case had been resolved, but now it was official. Sybil had the permission of the American government to legally live in the country where life needed her to experience all that could still not pass through her mind as a new apprentice.

***

The following morning, as usual, I got up early to meditate before having a shower and going to the office. After that I would visit the house, to inspect the work being done. A new guide appeared to me when I was meditating. The Virgin Mary was in front of me, covered in a cloak which emanated the most beautiful light. At last someone appeared that I recognized, and I did not have to do any research! From the time I was a girl, I had seen the Virgin in thousands of religious prints. The nuns at my school had taught me everything about her. I felt a maternal love so special that my recently awakened eyes filled with tears, while I tried to keep them shut so I wouldn't lose that image full of purity. She began to speak through her eyes, not her mouth.

> "I am the Virgin Mary. I have come to comfort you. The time has come for you to experience my energy, my darling girl. You will have to learn to nourish yourself on divine feminine energy from now on. You will have to completely forgive. You will have to completely heal. To do that, you need the energy of the goddess, to which you may now turn. Never give up. As you advance, you will continue to confirm that you are always loved and protected. You must be strong. My love will give you all that you need. You must be willing to lose all to reach the truth and gain all. It is written. The less you resist, the quicker you will arrive there. Trust in your inner God. We are very proud of you, my girl. I am the Virgin, who always accompanies you."

As soon as the image in front of her dematerialized, she opened her eyes and immediately wrote down everything the Virgin had told her, in a notebook she kept on her night table. For Sybil's rational mind, the message was worrying as she drowned in doubt again. What was the Virgin referring to when she spoke of losing all? Wasn't what she had already lost enough? Was it possible to lose more? She did not even want to think about it! She still had some money in reserve to meet the monthly payments she was liable for, but it would not last much longer.

The house was finally ready. I managed to finish the renovation of that property that had been about to fall down and had cost me so much sweat. Once the final inspections were made and everything approved,

I found the best real-estate agent in the whole of Coral Gables, knowing I had to sell the house as soon as possible. There was no doubt Gill was the person. That very day, she took photos and a video of the house, so that she could immediately put it up on her website and advertise it in the local and national papers. Sales were stagnating, and the house had lost a lot of value in a matter of months, but even so, Gill gave me reason to hope. She was an expert and appreciated all the work and money invested in it. It was an attractive proposition. I'd tried to improve all the defects and highlight the virtues of that dodo. I had to sell it as soon possible if I wanted to at least recover the ten thousand dollars Terencio had stolen from me. With the way the market was, it wouldn't do to hope for more than that.

She soon began to earn a decent salary at her job and also received a number of commissions that helped her to support herself in Miami and meanwhile send money to Bogotá for the expenses of Luna and Sol. What a trap the divorce agreement she had signed was turning out to be! Why did she have to support her daughters when they did not even want to live with her anymore? She did not understand, but she wasn't willing to consult another lawyer, who would charge her a load of money she did not have. With the fees she paid to Aminta for the divorce and the ones that had just gone on the establishment of the foundation in Miami, she was quits with the guild of lawyers forever.

Only now, thinking it over, did I realize that half of the money from the sale of the property I'd received from the divorce had been slowly returning to Sebastian's pockets, indirectly, through his daughters. It was too late to complain or remedy the situation; it was done. I still hadn't stopped feeling a victim of Sebastián. It was my responsibility, but I didn't know how to change my feelings toward him. I resented the fact that, being aware of my economic situation, he was still charging me money for the food and other expenses of our daughters. If his position had been worse than mine, I might have understood, but several of his partners I was still friendly with told me his businesses were doing better than ever and he was becoming more of a millionaire every day. I didn't understood how he could be so mean as to continue to charge me. For him, what I was sending was pocket money, whereas for me it was everything. Suddenly the words the Virgin Mary had said to me a few days before made sense. I had to find a way to forgive him and to forgive myself. To see my ex-husband trying to make me fail kept me from healing myself.

Minute by minute, the clock kept running and real-estate prices continued to fall in the whole of South Florida, without Sybil being able to find a buyer for the house, despite lowering the sale price twice. Gill kept her up to date, and the figures were far from promising. Everything was at stake: the house stayed unsold, while the monthly interest on her bank loan suddenly rose. As if that were not enough, the owners of the company where she worked told her they had to lay off staff because of the crisis. She was out of work. The clock stopped ticking. Sybil seemed to enter a dimension of her life where time did not exist. While she walked along the corridors of that empty house smelling of fresh paint and new carpets, she struggled to understand what she was doing wrong, what were the mistaken thoughts that had made her create such a decaying reality. Now that she was beginning to understand metaphysics and the functioning of so many universal laws, she could not explain why she understood them in theory without being able to put them into practice in her life. She was full of worry and anxiety. Not even meditation helped her to calm herself. All she could focus on was her uncertainty, her lack of security. She felt like she was on the edge of a cliff without knowing when or how to leap. She had gone through periods of crisis in her life, but this was the most intense one. The Virgin's message seemed clear: "The less you resist, the quicker you will arrive there," but she was ashamed of herself for failing to know how to apply that rule. It sounded simple, but now that she thought about it, she did not even understand the real meaning of the word *resistance!*

While she was searching for the reasons why her manner of thought was wrong, she had to drastically change her plans and reduce her spending to a minimum if she wanted to survive the storm. She decided to give up her rented apartment and move to the house she was trying to sell. She did not need much to survive: a bed and a reading lamp in one of the rooms would do. She also had to find a way to speak with Sebastián. She could not go on paying the expenses of Luna and Sol in Bogotá. He would be passing through the Miami airport on his way to New York on a business trip the following week, so she rang him to arrange a meeting. She owed him the money for the previous two months, so she would take advantage of the occasion to give it to him and tell him it was the last money he would get from her. Once more, she wanted to trust in her ex-husband and explain what she was going through. Everything would be easier if she could manage to turn herself into his friend. She still believed that Sebastián would change his stubborn position one day. She refused to acknowledge the evil in the heart of the man who had been her mate for so many years.

I tried to look at the positive side of my situation. It was rather ironic, but I had a newly renovated roof over my head despite all. Living there, I was able to assure myself that everything was working as it should, before a possible buyer arrived to inspect it. What's more, since I no longer had a job, the house kept me busy. To save costs, I let the gardeners and pool man go and took personal charge of all the tasks. I thus assumed two contradictory roles at the same time. On the one hand, I was the owner/investor, and on the other, I was simply a caretaker. My values continued to transform themselves. Little by little, I was surrendering and learning how to let go of my resistance. I was no longer taking things so seriously at last and could even laugh at myself. I couldn't observe my own self, but I felt that my ego was starting to cast off its stupid stubbornness.

The day when Sebastián stopped off in Miami soon arrived. She went to the airport with an envelope that contained the last money she would give him: ten thousand dollars in cash, just as he had demanded the week before, when they arranged the meeting. She was shocked to see how haggard he looked. For all the success of his companies, he did not look like a happy man. His wrinkles showed his negativity. He was more hunched when he walked, and his green eyes were now sunk into the bags under his eyes. She tried to be polite and professional, kissing his cheek and shaking his hand. Seeing his forced smile at a distance, she noticed the barrier his energy put up as he strode toward her, so she preferred to approach things with caution. They found a place to sit down. While she handed over the envelope with the cash to him, she explained her situation and her inability to keep sending him money. He did not like what he had just heard. The blood vessels in his eyes turned red as he opened the envelope, and his mouth shot out the venom that his brain had injected into his sparse words in a matter of seconds.

> "But that is the agreement you yourself proposed when you divorced me, Sybil. You have to comply with it, even if you can't or don't want to. The law is clear about

this kind of non-compliance. If I were you, I wouldn't risk it."

By this stage of her life, she had lost all the fear of him. Unconstrained, she yielded to an intuition and answered him without preparing any of it.

"Do whatever you want, Sebastián," I told him. "If you want to set the lawyers on me, do it. My daughters aren't living with me, thanks to your having set out to destroy the relationship between us. The agreement was to support them while they were living with me. They're not living with me now, and I don't have the money to support them, whereas you do and much more, despite the thirst for revenge which has blinded you. You won, Sebastián. You got what you wanted. You managed to strip me of everything: my daughters and the money, which, according to you, I stole from your savings. Well, now you have it all. From here on, I don't have anything more to give you. I hope your trip goes well, and truthfully, I still wish you the best."

Without giving him time to answer, and with sorrow choking her throat, she stood up and began to walk to the parking lot, without turning around. She had just surrendered everything of value in her life to her ex-husband. She had a presentiment that now that she would no longer send money for her daughters, the tenuous thread that had bound them together was sure to snap. Their father would soon tell them about her decision, and to them it would look like she *had* abandoned them. But she did not have any other option. She had never been the kind of person who would do anything for money, like robbing someone or getting into an illegal business. That was not going to change now.

The days following my meeting with Sebastián were very difficult but at the same time liberating. In the depth of my heart, I was learning to feel a new expression of peace. On the outside, everything in my life looked chaotic, but within me, order had just been born. I didn't know how Sebastián would react. He might sue me in Colombia if he still wanted to destroy me, but it no longer mattered to me. It was simple: if he sued me, there was nothing of mine left for him to have! I was no longer afraid; I had finally become immune to the nullifying energy of my ex-husband.

While life was snatching away absolutely everything she had, she was going through an intense spiritual transformation. Whenever she exhaled, her reality disappeared; when she inhaled, she breathed in a new type of air, full of freshness and clarity. She did not understand it but humbly accepted the process. Each day and night she spent in that big old house full of echoes and mystery was like experiencing a lifetime compressed into twenty-four hours. All of it seemed to have a hidden purpose. Her guides seemed to have isolated her even more from the world of appearances so that she would be able to concentrate on the next lessons. The presence of Saint Michael, Saint Germain, and others kept her motivated. They were now all she had. All that was left of her old self was her first and last name. She shape-shifted; her body was different, likewise her mind. In the midst of the drama, her heart was reborn.

Without my daughters, a spouse, money, a job, and a buyer for the house, it was as though my life were unfolding in a sea of deprivation and emptiness. I had to keep my mind sane. I knew that the stage I was passing through was a dangerous one. Many had lost their heads in similar circumstances when they approached the edge. I couldn't give up. I promised myself that through the Virgin. There wasn't a night when I failed to go jogging round the neighborhood, nor a morning when I didn't meditate. All I had left was my health. I couldn't risk the one thing that kept me afloat. A healthy life of daily exercise, raw food, and deep sleep became the staff I leaned on. Without knowing what life had in store for me back then, what I had bought was not merely a house; it was my liberation in the guise of one. All of a sudden, my whole world was disconnected from me. My cell phone was strangely muted. My mother was the only one who rang me, every two weeks, to make sure that I was all right; my parents were worried, but they respected my independence and kept their distance. In the past, they had tried to interfere, giving me advice, with the worst results for them.

The short circuit with my mother still wasn't fixed, since I continued to blame her for holding on to the obsolete and restrictive values of a woman who was dependent, weak, and submissive, the ones she had instilled in me as a girl. I blamed her for my marriage to Sebastián. My guides were helping me to understand that it had all been my responsibility and would continue to be. My life wasn't over yet, that much was clear: there was still so much to forgive, both in others and myself.

The only person who visited her—and then only occasionally—was the woman who was selling the house, Gill. It seemed as though the universe was shielding her from every distraction at the moment when she needed to begin practicing, for herself, all she had learned about that invisible world that was becoming more visible to her every day. The house was a synonym for introspection. She often recalled the words of the Virgin, when she had told her that she must lose all to gain all. That sentence still gave her the shivers, but it was too late to turn back. She had been initiated. In an effort to turn base metal into gold and find a way to hold on a little longer, her next step was to sell the little she had brought with her from Bogotá. She had given away most of her possessions to her daughters during her last visit, thinking that they would appreciate them when they were older. She got a couple of thousand dollars for her luxury watches, wedding ring, and two more pieces of jewelry, and with that she was able to eat and pay the utility bills for a time. Soon the only thing left to her was her car, which was fully paid for. She left it for last, since she needed to get around and Miami was not a city designed for pedestrians. But now she would have to sell it as well. With the money, she would be able to support herself for another three months and pay three more installments of the bank loan. That was the absolute deadline. If she did not sell the house in the following three months, she would have to declare herself bankrupt and hand over the house to the bank.

I was alone, but I felt accompanied. I was defenseless, but I felt protected. There was no man at my side to love me, but I felt fully loved by a battalion of celestial beings. Lacking a car, I had to walk twenty blocks along a road without a sidewalk to the nearest market and return with the two bags I could carry by hand. When Gill had a showing, I left the house and walked around the neighborhood until the clients had gone. My laptop, clothes, and a couple of boxes full of books were my entire material legacy. I was finally understanding that happiness had nothing to do with possessions or people. In a matter of months, I was left with nothing and no one. Nevertheless, I felt more abundant than I ever had.

Sybil spent that Christmas alone in her big old house. She greeted the new year in silence, listening to the sound of the wind in the trees of the garden and the singing of one bird or another who visited her beyond the window. It was the first time she celebrated the beginning of a year in that magical peace that made her feel renewed, a sensation for which there was no word in the dictionary. No one else could have done that for her. There came to her memory all the New Year's Eves she had spent in Colombia in the midst of liquor and perdition. Only now was she able to ask herself how she could have endured that living death for such a long time.

On the seventh day of that year, 2007, Archangel Michael appeared beside me shortly after dawn. He instructed me to burn sage leaves. I had to engage in a ritual of exorcism, my angel explained. I didn't understand what was happening at that moment, but I clearly saw the Virgin Mary, Saint Germain, Jesus, and a number of other ascended beings I didn't recognize forming a circle around me, while my archangel floated in the air, waiting for me to cleanse myself with the smoking sage leaves. You could feel the solemnity of the ritual; it was the calm before the storm. He ordered me to write down what he was about to channel to me. I found the notebook I kept at the side of my bed, and in a second, he seized hold of my hand, without my mind being able to interfere.

> "Liberation, Liberation, Liberation.
>
> From all the darkest and densest alien entities and energies which have lived within and alongside me.
>
> The moment has come to thank them for their role, because it now ends forever.
>
> May Archangel Michael and his legions of light protect and liberate me.
>
> May the Archangel Michael and his legions of light send them home again.

Liberation, Liberation, Liberation."

She had to repeat what she had just written seven times while imagining all her love and forgiveness emanating from the center of her sacred heart. On the fourth repetition, she began to observe two angels emerging from within her back. She saw their wings, but they were another kind of angel. Their aspect was grayish, nearly black. A dark and foul-smelling cloud enveloped them. She felt disgust and an urge to vomit. Archangel Michael immediately placed himself in front of her, covering her with his enormous wings. She was overwhelmed, she was repulsed by herself. She could not believe what was issuing from her own body. It was as though she were giving birth to those horrible creatures. She continued to recite the oration as they rose toward the roof of the house and fled through the apex of a great ethereal pyramid of crystalline white quartz that Archangel Michael had erected beforehand to cover her and the three circles of beings who were helping her in the ritual.

They were much smaller angels, and somewhat deformed: they looked sick. Azael and Azrael, two fallen angels who had entered into my energy, though who knows how, when, or why? Archangel Michael only gave me their names and told me that the only important thing was to heal myself. The ceremony didn't last more than an hour, and when it ended, all the masters in the first circle began to beam the most beautiful and comforting light rays at me, each corresponding to a different color of the spectrum. I felt like I had just had just gone through surgery. The whole of my body began to hurt, especially my back. It was like coming out of the operating room and waking up from the anesthesia. I slept nonstop that whole day and night. I didn't have the strength to walk or eat; I didn't even go to the toilet. I was barely able to open my eyes in the midst of this trance, and only to make sure that I was still alive. A few days later, I was able to go out for some fresh air. What was it that I had just experienced? I preferred to concentrate on my recuperation and continue to believe in my archangel. I had no answer that would have silenced my inquisitive mind.

***

A week after the exorcism, although still in pain, she felt like a new woman. She was lighter, her veins and arteries felt like they were unclogged, and an energy she had never felt before now flowed through her body. In the meantime, Gill called her. Some clients to whom she had shown the house before Christmas wanted another look. It was the first time anyone showed an interest. They would come back the following day. She enthusiastically tidied the house and garden, trying not to miss a detail. She even bought a dozen white roses and a candle with a vanilla fragrance to give the place a cheerful atmosphere. Before going out for a walk that morning, she prayed out loud, asking the aid of whoever might hear her. She needed a miracle, she pleaded, and put herself into the hands of all her protectors. After all, with everything she had seen of late, she no longer doubted their existence.

That very night, Gill rang me again. The cell phone trembled in my hands. The couple wanted to buy the house. They were enchanted with the contemporary design I'd achieved with the renovation. They would finalize the offer as soon as they cleared the financing with the bank. I hung up, and though my hopes were up, I didn't want to celebrate until it was in writing. I don't know how, but I completely let go; I stopped resisting. A few days later, when I had the contract in my hands, I allowed myself a sigh of relief. I was resigned to the price they offered.

With the fall in the real-estate market, I'd be losing absolutely all of the savings I had invested in the house. The sale price would cover the loan from the bank, Gill's commission, and the closing costs. I was left with $11,000 to go back to the drawing board, without a family, job, roof, or car. Not a promising balance for someone who supposedly fit into the social mold of those who had everything.

She had no other choice: she signed the contract and told herself she should be grateful. The latest statistics showed that thousands in Miami and the rest of the country were in the same circumstances as she. The real-estate crisis affected the whole country, and according to economists, was only beginning now. There were stories in the newspaper about thousands of houses being auctioned by banks to recover their unpaid home loans. She continued to be hopeful. She believed that life had a perfect way of manifesting her experiences. A look at the details of the contract confirmed it. The closing date for the house fell a week before the three-month deadline she had set herself when she sold her car, a week before she would have been left without a miserable dollar. It was as though the heavens were playing hide-and-seek with her. A week before she would have become bankrupt, lost her credit history and goodwill, she received the money to pay off her debt, save herself, and come out without a scratch. What a perfect synchrony.

The precision of the universe's clock did not stop there. When I finally met the buyers, I was left speechless. It was the same family with two little kids who had figured in the strange dream I'd had months before, when I had not even finished renovating the house. I had jotted down the dream so I wouldn't forget. It took place in Spain, and that had puzzled me. Now I was finally able to understand. The future owners of the house were Spanish, and they were moving from Madrid to

Miami for reasons of work! How was that possible? Did it mean I had known who the buyers would be well in advance? Was this a proof that confirmed my idea that dreams manifest themselves at some point in our waking life?

She handed over the house in the first week of May. As though it were yesterday, she remembers how she felt when she left the place in a car that a friend lent her so she would not have to call a taxi. She had never been in prison, but she now knew what it feels like when one finishes a sentence. It was there she discovered that physical space in itself is not what limits you. Rather, it is mental stagnation, the failure to control what *is* controllable, that feeling that your life is stuck while the world keeps on spinning. She was lucky: her sentence had just ended. The Virgin had kept her promise. She had lost everything, and now she wondered how the rest of her prophecy would be fulfilled. The "All" in capital letters she was supposed to gain in exchange for the loss of all. That house with a spirit of its own was one of the best teachers she had. It was there that she learned the rhythms of the universe, that she could only control the tip of the iceberg, the part that was visible. Her inner God took charge of controlling the invisible, whose enormous bulk was unimaginable to her because it was submerged.

Where would she go? What would she do with her life? She remembered the sarcastic Colombian saying about those who did not even own a hole to bury themselves in. Now it fit her so well! But she had a new pole star. Sedona would be the next stop on her path through life. When she was studying in Washington, she had seen a documentary about that small town hidden in the middle of the red rock desert of northern Arizona, and ever since then, that oasis never left her heart. The energies of Miami were expelling her. All the motives that had led her to move there no longer existed. She began her journey into the unknown, disappointed and disillusioned with everything that had happened to her. As in many other instances of her recent past, she could not just yet connect the dots to realize that what seemed to be negative was only part of the inevitable positive change of her conscious mind in its eagerness to keep awakening. She wanted to flee from everything that caused her pain, to distance herself even further from Sebastián and her daughters. Luna and Sol did not even answer her phone calls anymore. She did not even want to think about their one-sided view of her. She could not go on begging for love. She had to resign herself to still being the wicked witch. It was impossible for her to defend herself in such circumstances, and perhaps it was even unnecessary.

THE VIOLET
OF THE FINAL TRANSMUTATION

The flight from Miami landed in Phoenix in the afternoon. I hired a compact car, since I still had a drive of two hours to reach Sedona. I'd never imagined what awaited me there. It was like landing on another planet or perhaps another dimension of this same planet. The sun set as I drove along the highway, until a nearly full moon rose on my left. I was trying to concentrate on the road signs when I heard the murmur of voices and drums welcoming me in an unfamiliar language, which my heart nevertheless understood. I didn't know where they came from, but they made me feel cherished as I contemplated the empty path before me, on which I was staking all I had. Paradoxical as it might sound, considering that I had never been there before, I felt like I was coming home.

She was slightly nervous. She got lost on the highway for more than an hour. It was nearly midnight when she reached the hostel where she had reserved a room for forty-five dollars a night. It was nothing fancy, but she had to stretch the eleven thousand dollars she had left from the sale of the house. She also had a limit of nine thousand on the Visa card, which had just been approved thanks to the good credit rating she had maintained after all the juggling to meet the payment dates on her debts in Miami.

I didn't know how to start putting my thoughts in order. With a suitcase full of illusions, I was now there, the same ex-Sybil Vaughan de Obregón. Of that refined woman, who belonged to the best social circles and had the perfect home, as seen from outside, nothing remained now. My faded jeans, worn boots, and unkempt hair had replaced all of that and let me pass for an ordinary gringa. *Sedona was the prize my heart received for overcoming the rational mind for the first time. There was no special reason for me to be there. And I didn't need to have one! It was the most daring and risky move I had made in my life. If I had let logic get in the way, none of this would have made sense. I didn't turn back, because my heart did not have a second's doubt. I continued to feel completely protected. The old proverb says that seeing is believing, but something told me that the person who invented it had died deceived. I chose to believe in order to see.*

At dawn the next day, she had to smile at what she saw outside the window. She felt like she was in the middle of a picture by a surrealist painter. What a bewitching landscape! She could not explain how the place could be real. Her lungs breathed in the purest air, her eyes gazed at the most stunning colors. It was love at first sight. She continued to feel that she had come home. She had breakfast and set out to penetrate those imposing mountains she so wished to walk on. She did not have a map but did not need one. Without her knowing why, everything kept looking completely familiar to her.

As I drove my car through the narrow streets of that enchanted town, I could soon see that I wasn't the only person in love with the place. Hundreds of millionaires had their vacation homes in Sedona. They were a dream, built in a desert architecture I'd only seen in books till then. I could not stop myself from smiling all the time. Their colors harmoniously blended with those of nature; none had a discordant tone. I suddenly found myself in front of a brick-colored mountain in the shape of a bell. It stopped me in my tracks. I had to explore that strange place, which was like something out of a science-fiction movie.

She walked and climbed without stopping until she nearly reached the summit. She sat down to rest when a familiar voice, followed by the rhythmic sound of some drums, erupted out of the silence that embraced her. It was the voice she had heard the day before, when she was driving between Phoenix and Sedona. He welcomed her again and introduced himself: White Feather. She was not surprised; nothing was impossible for her anymore! She watched him with admiration and respect, while feeling the authority of the old chief dressed in white who stood before her. Her extrasensory powers had expanded since the previous night. It seemed like her ears were loudspeakers and her eyes magnifying glasses. Sedona was having a magical effect on her. Her new guide asked her to lie down on the enormous flat rock beside her. She obeyed as she watched the kindly, potbellied old man position himself on her stomach while other Indians formed a circle round him. Another ceremony? Goodness, as if that exorcism Archangel Michael had practiced were not enough! It had been very painful that time; her battered ego still had not recovered from the humiliation of accepting the forces of darkness it had seen fleeing from her interior. But she could not stop what flowed naturally. If there were more blocks in her energy, let them be expelled once and for all. The chief perched right above her solar plexus and began a sacred dance made up of several linked steps while he communicated with her telepathically.

> "It was written that you would return, daughter of mine. It is the time of your reconnection with Mother Earth and Father Sky. At last you are ready to understand the God you bear within. Remember that you are one with God, that God acts through you and not outside you. Welcome, Sedona is your new teacher. She will show you your new level of awareness. She has been waiting for eons for you to be able to return. You have accomplished an exhaustive evolutionary task. We are proud of you."

She does not remember when she fell asleep. She looked at the time on her cell phone when she awoke. A couple of hours had passed since she parked the car on the side of the mountain. As she came to and got a bottle of water out her backpack, she looked around her and saw dozens of butterflies amid the shrubs, tirelessly fluttering and dancing for her. The message was clear: the caterpillar had finally turned into a butterfly. The life force seemed to have exploded in her, but while she was recording what had just happened in her diary, she wondered about the meaning of the chief's words. She did not understand them, but it did not matter. She was already used to the dynamics of such teachings; she only understood the messages of her spiritual guides once their words turned into deeds, when the present was already the past.

I was writing down a description of White Feather when he appeared before me again, it seemed that my thoughts had attracted him once more.

"You will soon remember. You must be patient. These mountains have seen you grow up in another life. They will give you all the information you need. For now, I will leave you with your power animal. He will take care of you. Your eagle will be your compass and will not let any danger threaten you while you are uncovering your divine power in these caves and rocks. I must leave but I will soon return. Walk in beauty."

He disappeared while I, a little frightened, looked at the claws of that small golden eagle which perched on my right shoulder. I didn't know anything about eagles, I had just seen a few photos of condors, but yes, there was my ethereal pet. I stroked it with my left hand while I examined the strange cord which bound it to me. I had to find a name for him; I would call him plain Eagle.

It was still early afternoon, so she decided to take advantage of the remaining daylight. With Eagle on her shoulder, she walked downhill. She now had to work out the logistics of remaining in Sedona. She needed a car and a place to stay. She drove to Cottonwood, the nearest small city, and visited some car dealers to find out what was available, knowing she did not have much money. Everything flowed without obstacles. For a thousand dollars, she bought a desert-colored Jeep that seemed to be waiting for her. They would hand it over to her the following week, as soon as she returned the rental car. Having dealt with the first matter, she now needed a place to live. She was still full of energy, as though the day would never end. Returning from Cottonwood, she decided to stop at an agency for short-term rentals she had noticed before. The lights of the office were still on. Perhaps someone would help her. She went in and saw a woman with a handbag on her shoulder about to close the place, but she decided to introduce herself and quickly explain that she was new in town and needed an apartment. Her luck continued. Hillary put her handbag on her desk and turned on her computer to look at the listings. It was not going to be easy. As they conversed, she learned that Sedona attracted a stream of tourists looking for rentals throughout the year, and it would be difficult to find anything at five hundred dollars a month, which was her limit, she knew. It seemed like another divine intervention succeeded. In a matter of minutes, Hillary was on the phone to the owner of an apartment who was asking 650 dollars. Without many qualms, he agreed to let Sybil have the apartment for six months at a rent of five hundred dollars, if she paid it all in advance. She could not believe how everything in that town seemed to run at a thousand miles per hour! The contract would be ready for her signature the next day. She would check out of the hostel and move into the apartment she had only seen in photos. She prayed that it would be clean and livable.

All this represented a change of major proportions in my life. I had left Miami and my dramas only a couple of days before. I knew that I needed time to decant them, to heal myself. I was so resentful toward the persons who had hurt me. I wanted to forgive them. I had to learn to live with the absence of my daughters from my life. That was going to cost me the biggest effort, but I had to face myself in the mirror and begin to completely focus on achieving my aims. This time I would have to arm myself with courage again, the courage that already felt like an expandable suit that comes in one size. I wasn't going to let anyone or anything get in the way of what I had to achieve. Despite the criticisms and appearances, I would have to do what my heart told me. What was I saying? Not even I knew yet what my goal was. Maybe everyone who criticized me was right. Everything in my life continued to look chaotic. The only one who experienced my inner certainty was I. I had to be honest with myself: this certainty was still disguised as uncertainty.

As soon as they cleaned the apartment, Hillary rang to say she could collect the keys. Anxious to see what she had rented, Sybil parked downstairs and climbed the stairs to the second floor. Her eyes could not believe it: it was a gift sent from heaven. Light entered through all the windows, and without being luxurious, the place was faultless. It even had two bedrooms. She still had not lost the hope that Sebastián would change his mind and at least let her daughters visit her someday.

Everything flowed like magic. Life was teaching me that dreams come true and it was not a process that depended on the bills and coins in your pocket. For so many years, I had been worried about the money from the divorce settlement, only to realize, now that I'd wound up losing it, that I wouldn't die without it, that something much more powerful within myself continued to manifest what I would need to survive. I had gone through all the trials my mind had needed to learn to surrender to that great power. I humbly accepted the process of being emptied out. I had so much garbage inside me, so many false beliefs. Sedona seemed to be the final thrust. Here, once and for all, I would transmute all the grime hidden in the most remote corners of my psyche. From here on, the whole story of my life, all my diplomas and résumés, would rest in peace, because that was no longer what defined me as a person. I was discovering that I was much more than that. I was on the point of finally understanding the reason for my forty-one years of life.

Her new home was modest but full of peace. Her Jeep was ideal for traveling through those mountains, which seemed to act like magnets aimed at her. She was very thankful. She had nothing, and yet nothing was wanting; what an extraordinary contradiction. Her life was simple, detached, and isolated. Her only link with the world she had left behind was her old cell phone and the computer, which she turned on every morning to see if Luna and Sol had sent an e-mail, though they never did. Life itself was her immediate boss. She had been hired to do a new job, without a salary or timetable. The job was playing at being a nobody. She needed to understand what one was when there were no longer any roles to fill. Only by shedding all the social masks would she be able to know herself. She had still not been able to answer the million-dollar question: who am I?

Hours, days, months passed by, before I was able to understand the gift life had given me by guiding me to this place where I was reborn, despite being grown up. Every day I got up thinking I was already cured. However, there was always another piece of dirt I had to free myself of. Where did all that garbage come from? I didn't have a psychologist or psychiatrist, but invisibility took charge of this intensive therapy. If I felt like crying, I cried alone. If I felt like speaking, I spoke to myself. I was completely uninhibited, while I gained more and more strength. I was learning to be happy without focusing on my external circumstances. I began to develop that supernatural and inalterable peace that I had seen in many of my spiritual masters. I don't know how I did it, but I was finally deserving of that state. My awareness became purer day by day. Now I understood the usefulness of the stubbornness which had turned into my persistence. I would not rest until I had removed the last stain of dirt on me.

While her inner peace was growing, Sebastián made sure to write an e-mail from time to time, to let her know that her madness had touched bottom and her instability was notorious.

Her main activity was now walking and climbing mountains. By the standards of her past life, that was the same as being a vagabond, a deadbeat who deserved no respect. But the levels of happiness she reached did not allow either her ego or that of Sebastián to sabotage that special awakening she was going through. She found herself in the middle of that desert for reasons not even she could explain, but she would not question them just because others wanted her to justify herself.

I soon became familiar with many of the canyons, caves, and trails Sedona could offer me. I would leave early with my backpack, cell phone, and climbing boots to play at being the explorer I had dreamed of as a teenager. Four months had passed. I still didn't want to stop; I was so at home that I dreamed of living there forever. One night, there was a full moon, and I already knew the terrain well enough to walk in the dark. Something told me I had to undertake the next feat, and I couldn't resist. This time, I was going to climb the mountain known as Chimney Rock and try to get as high as possible to observe the moon and the stars. With everything I needed at hand, I also took a blanket. The temperature abruptly fell at night in autumn. Seated on that rock on the edge of the precipice without needing to be someone, I knew what it was to have the world in my hands. I'd heard people talk about invincibility. At last I was invincible, as I turned into a tiny brush stroke in that picture painted by nature for me alone. I had come out of the nothingness and had to return to the same nothingness to remind myself of the perfection of everything. The words did not reach my mind, because they were no longer needed. I was in ecstasy. Could it be that I had gone to heaven and still did not realize it?

She never saw a moon more yellow and majestic. It seemed to be only a few miles above her, so close did it appear. She could almost touch it. The night was flooded with stars. It was like being in a great planetarium, where she had the only ticket and sat in the front row. The most hallucinatory silence surrounded her. Those who believed that silence did not have music were fooling themselves. She did not want to move; she was still, in a time that ceased to exist, observing the now without a before or after.

Suddenly I fell in love with that "all" and that "nothing," and I felt an urge to sleep there. Could I do it? Of course I could! I had eaten in my apartment before going out and could use any bush as a toilet. I remembered Eagle, and in fact he was still there, perched on my right shoulder. Eagle would protect me and warn me of any danger. I had to be careful about the native snakes, tarantulas, and scorpions. Behind me I found the overhang of a rock that my body fit into perfectly. It would not rain tonight; everything was conspiring to make it easy for me to stay there. Covering myself with the blanket up to my neck, I watched the moon rise in the sky before me, becoming smaller and whiter as it moved away from the Earth. I don't remember having closed my eyes, but I soon began to feel strange when I saw how the rocks around me were beginning to move and twist themselves, changing their size and shape. It was like being in a hall of distorting mirrors. It couldn't be a dream because I felt I was awake. Could it be that I was in a state between sleep and wakefulness? I wasn't drinking anything apart from the bottle of spring water I had in my backpack. As I looked at the rocks, feeling dizzy, I heard him walking toward me in the distance, but I still did not envisage him. I kept still, my gaze unflinching, lying among the rocks that embraced me, and waited for what approached with curiosity but no fear. The footsteps were slow and clearly heard. He seemed to be stepping on water, but I only saw the dry soil of the desert. He slowly materialized until I could hear his voice and see his outline against the beautiful clarity of the night. It was a thin old man with long silver hair falling in soft waves that luminously shone. He wore a white tunic with long sleeves. I didn't manage to see his face very well, but when he greeted me, he told me not to focus on his image but the message he brought me. I saw him open his arms like the statue of Christ at Corcovado, but he couldn't have been Jesus because he was older. He asked me to close my eyes so that his external appearance wouldn't distract me and I could thus completely open my heart to connect with his. As soon as I obeyed, his heart began to emanate a column of pink and fuchsia light. The two colors continued to flow from heart to heart in the form of a spiral. His voice did not issue from his mouth. Rather, his pineal gland and mine activated themselves in unison. They looked like cobalt-blue light bulbs that were turned on while the old man beamed his thoughts at me.

"How beloved you are.

You have become worthy of the truth.

Not your perception of the truth, that is the truth which is socially learned and imposed, it is the false truth.

I refer to the truth of the infinite multiverse.

That which liberates the treasure seekers like yourself, from the world of forms which you thought real up to now.

Nothing which surrounds you is real, my child.

Can you not see how I have made the rocks twist themselves so that you may understand that everything is an illusion?

You feel like you are playing at being an explorer, and you are right, life is a game which everyone plays until they are ready to discover what the game has been about.

The rules of this game are not known before you start playing, only afterwards.

And just as the path you took to prepare yourself has been painful and arduous, so too do you begin to be rewarded well.

Few know the truth.

Nothing has been accidental, everything has been causality.

From the time you were born, you have been preparing yourself to arrive at this encounter with me.

To facilitate your human understanding, I will divide the truth into three pillars that you must use as the foundation of the new life you will begin tomorrow, when the new day arises.

First, time is not linear but simultaneous.

Thus, the past, present and future happen in a parallel way.

Second, space does not exist, so your reality is an illusion formed by moving particles of light which create the material world.

The third and final pillar includes the two previous ones and it is the one you will have to focus your attention on.

Your physical body is an antenna that is a receptor of God.

It is the vehicle used so that God may know himself, so

that God may experience life through you.

The life of God and your life are one, they are the same.

Only when you subjugate your ego and all your human arrogance, you are ready to understand that you are God.

For that reason, it was so important that you experienced all that you have thought was humiliating.

Pain and sorrow are great teachers. Thanks to them you vanquished your ego.

Without ego, all that remains is essence, the essence of God.

You and God are one.

You bear the name Sybil in this life, but you are not only Sybil, and you do not only have this life.

Tomorrow, when your mind doubts my words, you will go to the Bible and confirm them in John 10:34 and also in Psalm 82:6.

Tomorrow, when your mind begins to ask for logical explanations, you will have to remind yourself of the great ocean and all the billions of drops that make it up.

The drops are without doubt, much smaller than the great ocean, but each drop contains absolutely each and every one of the characteristics of the great ocean.

You might imagine the drops separated from the ocean and also separated from each other.

In reality, they are always connected, forming part of the

great ocean in an infinite manner, without beginning or end.

Once this physical life ends, one continues being part of God forever, in the following level of evolution.

Once it passes through certain proofs, the drop is ready to accept that it is the drop and the great ocean simultaneously.

It will take a little time to assimilate the truth.

Your mind will find it difficult to believe, but your heart will dominate the process.

From now on your responsibility is much bigger.

On becoming God you turn into love alone.

Opposites and the dual world end, when there is no need to use them in your new lessons.

Sybil, darling Sybil,

Your true mission has been to come to discover the truth, not yours, not that of others.

You have arrived at the truth of all the multiverses, of all that is.

That is the finality the Archangel Michael and your guides: the alchemist Saint Germain, the Virgin Mary, and the Indian White Feather, were always leading you to.

What you are experiencing tonight is your awakening, a true graduation.

Go to sleep peacefully now, everything will be well.

I will devote myself to recalibrating and updating your DNA so that you integrate yourself completely into God.

It will dawn and you will be God playing at being Sybil.

We continue to be proud of you, beloved.

Your work has never been in vain, we know what you have gone through.

They have been lives upon lives.

In some, you have not been able to fulfill yourself.

Nevertheless, you have never surrendered to the dark forces.

Your light becomes purified as you expand yourself.

The laws of the universe are wise, all has been a game.

Think of it in that way, from the beginning to the end, so that you may understand the objective of everything and everyone who has passed through your life.

Without everything and everyone, you would not be God.

You must be completely grateful.

From here onwards your path will be that of love and forgiveness.

A person very important for your evolution will soon reach you, both of you arranged this encounter before you were born.

You must be open to teach what you now know.

You must speak your truth, that which is the same truth of God.

You will have to accept the results of this encounter, whatever they may be, remember that nothing is good or bad anymore.

Now, only what is, will be.

This encounter will be the final proof.

Your divinity will have to overcome your humanity.

I am God, you are God.

The two of us are one with God.

You are love and light forever and I love you eternally."

She heard the birds and crows welcoming the dawn. Where was she? They were not the sounds she usually heard at daybreak. Little by little, she remembered that she had slept out in the open the whole night, but she did not want to open her eyes. She was afraid that the rocks would still be writhing about. The glare of daylight forced her to wake up. Everything around her was normal. She put away the diary and pencil she had used to write down the message from that mysterious and nameless old man. She did not even remember when she got the diary out of her backpack. It did not look like her handwriting, but she remembered what she had experienced, and it coincided with what she read. What a night! Who would believe it? She had to collect her things rapidly and descend the mountain before the tourists and the cameras invaded the place. Back in her apartment, she had a bath and gave thanks for what had just happened to her. She still did not understand the new responsibilities she had acquired upon learning that truth. It was as if life had promoted her to a more important post, with a broader scope. Just as the old man foresaw, her skeptical mind began to question everything. She had a lot to think about. She felt confused and completely divided. She would try to follow his instructions and keep focused on the path her heart pointed toward; it was difficult but not impossible. Silencing her mind was the next challenge.

When she reached for the Bible, trying to still her unease, it was confirmed. John 10:34 read: "Jesus answered them: Is it not written in your Law: I have said you are gods?" and verse 6 of Psalm 82 also declared: "I said, 'You are gods,' sons of the Most High, all of you."

***

It was time to get back to earth and deal with my reality. My lease had nearly run out and likewise the money I had when I came to Sedona. I wanted to stay there forever, but I had to stop dreaming the impossible. I'd been born into a democratic, post-modern era, where dollar bills provided me with food, not in some remote past where I could have lived off hunting and gathering. Apart from hotels and restaurants, there wasn't much to the place's economy. Everything revolved around tourism, and I had already left job applications in several hotels, in case a vacancy came up, even if it was as a housekeeper or waitress, but they all turned me down. The world was still full of irony. I had studied so hard to be a success on my own, and now I couldn't even get a job at the minimum wage because I was overqualified.

The next day, she decided to visit Hillary, her friend from the rental agency, and tell her that she could not renew the contract or remain in Sedona any longer, because her money was running out. Her path was curious: as she advanced spiritually, her material world seemed to keep shrinking into a dead end. She was still questioning herself. Looking back, she did not understand; she had given absolutely all to know God. Now she not only knew God but also that he lived in her and *was*her! And what did that amount to? Now she was God, but if she was God, how it was it possible for her material world to still be so full of limitations and hardships? Life became strange and confusing at that point. Ever since she had met her some months before, Hillary had a special connection with Sybil. In fact, without her, Sybil would never have found the apartment where she was living, given the high cost of living in Sedona and the kind of tourists who went there. She must have been paying the lowest rent in the whole town. This time, Hillary wanted to help her again. She told her she would mention her problem to a client who had placed several residential and commercial properties with her agency. Maybe he would be able to give her a job or some ideas. He was a very wealthy man from Southern California, and Hillary emphasized how kind and generous he was. She had nothing to lose. She would wait for news from Hillary and meanwhile get the maximum enjoyment out of her last weeks in that world's hideaway that had healed and positively transformed her. Despite outward appearances, she still felt happy and fulfilled, without even knowing why. There was now another way to interpret everything in her world. She had finally stopped being a victim of circumstances. She finally understood that her past was the best thing that could have happened to her. Without all those personages she had regarded as her victimizers, she would never have been able to arrive so far. Thanks to the whole path she had taken, to all she had lived through and the choices she had made, she now had God within her. What more could one ask for? Happiness was not outside her now. She was the source of that very happiness.

Happy, but I still couldn't free my thoughts of uncertainty. I would soon be without a roof and food again. I was human, after all; those concerns would worry the saintliest of saints. What was the lesson for me this time? How could I learn to live like that, to feel safe without any possessions, without something to hold on to? If I looked around me, almost nothing was under my control; people's lives continued to go on nonstop. Nature never stopped evolving, nor left off its expansive movement. Why not let God take control this time, without hindering his job with my ignorant doubts? All I achieved with that insecurity was to disconnect myself from him and delay the manifestation of my next step. The lesson for me was to remain consciously aware of my divinity for as long as possible; that would speed up everything. One Thursday, while I was walking in the mountains, my cell phone rang. It was a local call. Surely it was a mistake, since I didn't know anyone in Sedona who might call me. It was him. He politely introduced himself and explained that Hillary had given him my number. His name was Ed Watkins, and he was calling me in person because he was interested in meeting me, so that we could talk more calmly. I agreed, of course I agreed and enthusiastically accepted his invitation to dinner that night.

It must have been her inner God acting on her behalf and putting her in touch with the new personality types who were required in her new world. She felt so comfortable in the presence of that man. He reminded her of Dylan, her father. He was a native of New Zealand but had lived for a long time in the United States, where he owned several corporations based in California and Texas. The perfection of the universe was now before her. Ed needed a human resources manager for one of his companies on the Fortune 500 list. She had never worked in the American corporate world, but the offer did re-awaken an old ambition, dating back to her student days in Washington, when she had dreamt of joining that sphere. She now recalled how she had shelved it in order to develop her philanthropic project, which in turn led her to look toward Colombia, where it seemed she had only encountered desolation and failure. She was stunned. The God who now dwelt in, and not outside her, had not missed a detail. He was responsible for manifesting every one of the wishes still lurking in her subconscious, even the ones she no longer remembered.

He must have read the résumé I'd sent him by e-mail before our dinner date. We were drinking coffee and he'd asked for the check when I heard him say something in his warm, reassuring way.

> "You deserve an opportunity, Sybil. Life still hasn't rewarded you for your efforts. With all my years of experience, I recognize a courageous woman when I see one, and I've known a few like yourself, women who have had the door shut in their face by the masculine and then withdraw from it all. I know you don't trust me, but I'd like to be the one who gives you the opportunity you need in order to trust in life again. You may have been taught by guides from other dimensions, but you now need a flesh-and-blood one."

He was right. I didn't trust him or anyone else, but my inner God did trust him, and I had no other choice but to accept his offer. I agreed without thinking about it. If God had brought this into my life, it was for some very important reason. I could at least find out where this new adventure might lead me.

The thousands and thousands of dollars they would pay her for the job were unbelievable to her mind. With the new salary, she would be able to completely re-organize her life. It was more than she had ever dreamt of. She was to start in December, after a short period of training, and relocate to the Galleria area of Houston, another drastic change, of course. She would have to discard her hiking boots full of the red mud of those magical mesetas and put on the tailored suits and high heels of the professional woman, a refined, elegant look she had not used since her postgraduate days. Instead of talking to the birds and hugging the trees that transmitted so much love to her, she would go back to interacting with members of her own species, the vile and worldly humans she so distrusted. How could she now deny that the God she bore within was creating the whole of this new reality? All of it was a miracle she would not have been able to create on her own. She had controlled absolutely nothing this time. The last thing she remembered was completely giving up and surrendering her life to God. She felt nostalgic, because she did not want to leave her simple life in the desert, but it seemed that she needed the madding crowd. The purified energy she now radiated would provide the necessary balance to the denseness of the big city.

Another move; she did not even want to think about the remarks of those who lived in the dimension that was now her past. She would have to try to distance herself from their wagging tongues. Worrying about what others would say would not be a positive contribution at a time when God was teaching her to fly with her own wings. Now that she had a steady income, she decided to visit her daughters in Colombia and her parents in Wales. She needed to see all of them. She needed all of them to see the new Sybil, who, despite all the prognostications, was better than ever. She needed to heal and forgive in the company of her biological family for the last time. After she started her new job in December, she would not have a vacation for a long time, and she did not want to let her new boss down. Ed needed a stalwart person to whom he could delegate a number of confidential matters that were still unresolved in the company. She could not fail him; the friendly stranger was taking a chance on her without having any guarantees that it would work out. She felt his paternal concern, which led him to keep believing in her as each day passed and he got to know her better.

***

Seeing them served to measure my progress. I felt transformed within; my soul felt fresh and rejuvenated, as if it had just had a long, warm shower. I first went to Bogotá, and while the circumstances in Sebastián's house were the still the same, I *wasn't. There was no change, because Sebastián's mind was stuck in the nineteenth century. Eight years had passed since our divorce, and my ex-husband still saw me as the traitor and the guilty one who only deserved scorn. My daughters continued to absorb the same resentment and still couldn't understand the reasons for my decisions. But now that I was able to understand what they could not, I was able to put myself in their shoes, though they couldn't put themselves in mine. Sedona taught me about true forgiveness. The purpose of my visit to Colombia was to ask for it, not only from Luna and Sol but also from Sebastián. I was ready for that step. Since I was God, I could understand the suffering I had caused. It wasn't repentance; it was understanding – acceptance without remorse. Though I asked for forgiveness, I did not get it from them, but I had also learned to live without expectations. I did not expect anything in return. I had done my part. I opened my heart to the three, but none of them appreciated the lesson in humbleness I offered them. Now time would take care of my daughters' growth and awakening to God, just as I had awoken when my time came. From Bogotá, I went to Wales, leaving the doors open for my daughters to visit me; they were equally welcome to live with me in Houston, now that my economic situation allowed me to support them again. But our living together was a remote possibility. The three were still singing the same old song. Their version was that I had to sacrifice my life and my dreams again, returning to the mold I had left behind, which was now too tight and suffocating for me. They couldn't think of any other solution. The world was as they visualized it. For them, I was still the unstable and irresponsible Sybil their eyes saw. None of the three felt that their wish to cut my wings was selfish. The egoist was myself, only now I accepted that without sorrow, supported by a healthy pride. Twelve years of self-sacrifice and delay had been enough, and now all I could offer was unconditional love, the opposite of the self-interested love, full of demands, which they wanted me to accustom myself to again. I could no longer sacrifice my evolution. Now that God was lodged in me, I couldn't turn back. What was happening could only be understood by someone who had gone through a similar transformation. Sebastián certainly wasn't and never would be that someone.*

When she reached her parents' home in Wales, she did the same as she had done with her daughters and ex-husband. She set out to forgive and heal, to find the flimsy patches she had tried to place on her tender heart when she had been a girl and an adolescent She had spent too many years blaming her mother for forcing her into the conservative, provincial mold Cassandra regarded as ideal. Only now did she understand the role of her mother. Only now did she realize that, with her mental limitations, Cassandra had only acted in accordance with her own values. Out of love, her mother had sent her along the same path she had traveled, and it proved to be a favor. She did not know any better, so she was not able to show her daughter a side track. Her mother had wanted Sybil to be a clone of those in her social world, but Sybil now proudly focused on the persistence and courage that had prevented her from being cloned. As with her daughters and Sebastián, she was able to put herself into the shoes of others and understand her mother without expecting the same in return.

These re-encounters were very meaningful to me. It was the first time I dared to go back to the past as the present that I was now, being God, without being afraid to return to that unhealthy past that I needed to experience again for a few days in order to get rid of the garbage I'd left behind, which was starting to fester. For the first time, I understood that the past and the present existed simultaneously. By transporting myself to the past while fully loving what I now was in present, I lost a few pounds of the invisible toxic waste I'd accumulated over many years. Once I left my false pride behind and asked everyone to forgive me for everything, I became a witness to my divine power, even though my ego still did not feel guilty of anything and continued to resist God. The effect was immediate, and I received the benefits myself. There was no better drug on the market. You didn't need a prescription, and it was free to the public. Why did so many people stay sick, filling the doctors' waiting rooms, simply for failing to buy some bottles of forgiveness?

The following step in her life was not the one her conscious mind had visualized as her next creation. She still did not understand why the freedom of Sedona gave way to a kind of regression when she returned to the square-angled world of the masses. But the rules of the divine game were now clear to her: to let herself go and accept that she was not at the helm. She did not understand but was willing to experience it unquestioningly. She accepted that life had times and spaces completely different from her own. By natural law, there was a reason for what was happening in her reality. It had to be the effect of a cause and would, in turn, soon turn into the cause of another effect, just as God enjoyed it: a process beyond the human mind with no logic or label. She would go on to the end; yes, she would.

***

Post Oak Boulevard, December 2007

Her inner God leapt ahead, suddenly turning back to watch her physical body sitting in front of the computer. Her green eyes were fixed on the screen while her fingers hurriedly skipped over the keyboard. She liked the melody, it sounded like a musical instrument which strangely communicated with keyboards that other hands stroked in the distance. She was enclosed in a 80 sq.ft. cubicle made up of head-high panels lined with a gray woolen weave. She heard voices in a non-native language which, she had already incorporated. In the cubicle behind, someone was turning over the pages of a manual full of technicality, while hurried and stressed footsteps were heard going here and there. She got up to collect a document she had just printed on the office copier while smilingly watched all those godless faces and silhouettes, who nevertheless had sharp and worried minds.

With one or another diploma, that was what gave them value. It smelled like cold air, like the air conditioning scent whose chill sometimes gave her goose bumps. It was a whole human ecosystem. The windows were so far from her cubicle there was no way to feel the joy spring would bring in a few months. There was only inertia and inertia did not inspire even the most decrepit and miserable mosquito.

How the hell had I agreed to be here? It was the question I asked myself that first day on the job.

> "You created it, my beloved child, at a time when you still had not learned to consciously direct your thoughts, at a time when you still did not believe in your true creative nature."

It was Saint Germain, who had returned to accompany her while she adapted to a new but once again dense environment.

> "Did you not want to work in the US corporate world with a fat six-digit salary? To make use of your master's from that elegant university near the White House when you were George Bush's neighbor? Make an effort to remember your wishes from that recent time, Sybil. They have become a reality, even though you forgot about them in Sedona. There is an unfinished bit of the story you have to live through, my child."

But why live it now, if I no longer like it? It is what so many long for, spend a whole lifetime preparing themselves for. It's rigid and harsh. All these faces and silhouettes wouldn't even understand why I feel that this ambit is so alien to me; they don't even question it. They've reached their goal. The goal is to get a job to pay all their debts and pension plans, without any enthusiasm or conviction. They only care about holding on to their jobs so that they can keep re-creating more of the stuff that society demands, even when they can sense the itching emptiness produced by the knowing that one has not identified God within just yet. To give it all up would be to give up what they wrongly think of as the realization of their dreams. The tiny ego does not allow them to be aware of anything else; it blocks the remembrance of the meaning of the world of mages, and of the flight of imagination leading to the truth.

> "They have forgotten how to be children again, Sybil. They are asleep, that's all. Everything is backwards for them. When they sleep, they think they are awake, and when they are awake, they think they are sleeping. Now you can see it for yourself. Before, you were one of them."

The words of her guide illuminated her with wisdom. A few months before, she had just remembered her divinity, thanks to that magical night when she had slept out in the mountains. A short time before, she had understood each and every one of the realities she had created during her forty-two years of life. Because of her ignorance and subconscious intentions, God had brought her absolutely everything she had asked for. Whether good or bad, her life had been the exact manifestation of what she had wanted to live and feel. Only God knows how many years—or perhaps lives—it took her to feel that she deserved to bear him inside her. Or was God a she? For thirty-three of those years, the process of indoctrination and conditioning was severe, but without it, she would not have been able to spend the next nine erasing the tracks from the path she had walked and reach the marvelous state she was now in. In Sedona, she was able to remember that she was God. Now she had to put on the disguise worn by millions of beings on this planet, who turn mere survival into their idol—a survival that lacked any sense of the quest for self-knowledge for which she had been born. With her new disguise, she needed once more to experience the chronic illness of those who inhabit a realm where there is no room for the divine. She needed that contrast to complete the final stage of her learning process.

While I was adapting to my new reality, that week I had to have a check-up so I could join the company's health plan. It was routine; they simply wanted to make sure that their new acquisition was healthy and free of contagious diseases. It was my first Friday in my new city, and I decided to spend the whole day at the medical center, where the doctors would carry out the exams. I took a book, so I wouldn't get bored in the waiting rooms. It was the first time I had visited a hospital in the United States. I'd been lucky that way. I understood that my good physical health was the result of ridding myself, in the past few years, of all the toxins that had built up in me. My inner state was reflected in my outward one. Up to then, I hadn't had any health insurance, and God had taken care of my needs in that respect. I was calm. I was only going to the appointments because it was required of any employee; at least that is what I thought!

She put on the hospital slippers and gown, left her clothing in a locker, and went to the waiting room they indicated. In her usual self-absorbed way, book in hand, she walked to the far end of the corridor, but something made her notice a doctor who was going the other way while they exchanged a glance for a few seconds. She shyly smiled at him, feeling ridiculous in the green pastel gown she was wearing. His expression was serious as he rushed by, dictating notes into his cell phone from a clipboard he carried, and he merely nodded at her. Then, after a few paces, he closed the cell phone, turned around, and caught up with Sybil, who was still slowly walking—as if he wanted to get a better look at her.

> "Excuse me, madam, don't we know each other?"

She stared at him, wondering what to say, but did not react at first. Something about his gaze was familiar; she had seen those eyes before. But where? Then, all at once, he switched from English to Spanish and spoke her name.

> "Sybil? Is it you, the Sybil I used to know in San Andrés?"

She was struggling to remember those eyes when he came to her aid.

> "Don't you remember me? I'm Santiago Avellaneda. We lived in San Andrés when we were kids. You must be Sybil. I'd never forget those eyes."

Santiago? Her Santiago? The one she had loved so much when she was only a girl? No, it was impossible. She couldn't believe it: the same hair, the same eyes, the same voice, only now it was more mature. She had to pinch herself to make sure she was awake. In the middle of a check-up, just arrived in Houston, she had run into her first love, the man whom her heart had never forgotten, even though her mind had given him up as a lost cause without even trying to find him.

I couldn't help a fit of nervous giggling when I found myself in that corridor, standing before a doctor whom I now recognized as my old love, and wearing a short gown that barely covered my naked body. God certainly had a funny way of arranging my meetings with the people who were significant in my life. We couldn't stop talking. He accompanied me to my next exam, while he explained that he was a specialist in obstetrics and gynecology and finishing fellowship training at the hospital. Thirty years had passed, and I'd lost any hope of finding him again. We had no mutual friends or any other link that might have caused us to meet up since then. It was love at first sight – for the second time and with the same man. The last time I'd seen him was in the airport of San Andrés, when he left for Miami, and I couldn't even remember how old I was at the time – no more than eleven or twelve. Though he was a little taller, a little older, the doctor dressed in white was the same old Santiago. At that moment, we became two children again, playing at doctor and patient.

> "What are you doing tonight? I'm not on call until Monday. If you like, we could go out for dinner and I could also show you the city this weekend."

My eyes, full of hope and joy, said yes as they shone with that special light love gives. I still couldn't get over my astonishment at all the new things that had reached my life in only a few days. It didn't seem possible: a native of New Zealand turns up in Sedona and sends me to Houston, where I run into the very man I needed to wind up the unfinished business of my life! It was like a fairy tale. There was no explanation for it, so I didn't even bother to look for one.

***

That weekend, Sybil became the star of a love story that has never been shown on the screen. There would be no way to stage such an idyll. They had spent thirty years waiting for each other, for this opportunity which, now that they were living it, seemed farfetched and unreal. They could not get over their astonishment, nor did they want to. They were so full of joy, nothing else mattered.

> "My sweet Sybil, you have come back to me. I longed for you so much. Now that you are here, I'll never let you go. This time you'll stay with me forever."

She could not believe how tender this man was. The plan to drive around the city was shelved for now. They only wanted to be together, to continue to lie there and discover each other, touching, loving, as they had dreamt when they were children. Santiago confessed that he had never had the courage to go and tell her that he loved her. He was so timid and insecure, he thought that she would never pay any attention to him. And she, at the same time, had felt just the same! They could not stop laughing at themselves while they ecstatically embraced one another.

Sybil's life continued to change drastically, even more now that she shared it with Santiago. Although she had a luxurious apartment near her office, which the company was paying for, she preferred to spend weekends with her love in the modest apartment he lived in on the outskirts of Houston. She was radiant. She felt that she had finally found the man of her life. They had so many things in common and were so compatible. He didn't have any interest in spiritual matters, but it did not matter to her. She tried not to speak of her inner world, since she saw that he would not understand. She realized she could not have everything, so she decided to concentrate on the things that Santiago did have. She chose to see what it suited her to see and forget about what did not. She blindly loved her doctor, but Santiago's life was a little murky. It was chaotic and disorderly, quite different from the peace and harmony of the one Sybil led. He was always short of money. He had told her he was separated from the woman with whom he had lived for fifteen years in Florida before moving to Houston. She had two children from her first marriage whom he had adopted. They now lived in Orlando, and he still supported them. He was a silent and reserved man, even bad-tempered at times. She felt his wounds, knew that he had suffered, but could not find a way to get to those depths. He always preferred to evade such issues. She respected his rhythm and thought that, little by little, he would open his world up to her. But her God continued to make her feel that something was not right, something she chose to ignore. Even her boss, Ed, had warned her about that when he met Santiago at a company event Sybil invited him to.

> "I don't trust a man who cannot look me straight in the eye without flinching. You better be careful with him, Sybil. I don't think he is right for you."

They say that when you don't do your job, life does it for you. Santiago's summer vacations came up, and although we had spoken of returning to San Andrés together for a few days, we decided to put it off. It was important for him to visit his adopted children, whom he had not seen for a year. So that week he left for Orlando, and I stayed here in Houston and concentrated on carrying out several projects that the company's board of directors had just approved. My career continued to prosper in a magical way, and Ed remained the flesh-and-blood guardian whom life had sent me, so I could realize the potential that so many people had made fun of and doubted in the past. It was clear that this was my best moment. Though the longing for my daughters still tore my heart, I had so much to be thankful for. The lessons labeled with the name reward *were the best ones.*

She took advantage of the free time Santiago's trip left her in those days to visit her gynecologist. The irregularity of her periods, which had started in Sedona, continued to bother her, and she wanted to have a hormone count. She had not had one for many years, and given her age, perhaps it would be advisable to get ready for her menopause.

I woke up that morning in this same room, from where I watched the sun rise among the skyscrapers of this big city. While I lay in bed for a few minutes before having a shower, I remembered that the results of my exams were ready. I was going to ring the doctor's secretary around eleven to find out.

At her office, she rang the doctor's office while she was waiting to begin a phone conference with two managers from the home office in California. The doctor spoke to her in person, and she could not believe what he said. She had to go outside for some fresh air. She got her cell phone from her desk, rushed to the elevator, descended, and made for the lake in front of the building, where she sat down on a bench, trying to regulate her breathing and calm herself. Now more than ever, she needed to remind herself of her divine nature, recover her self-control. According to the exams, she was pregnant. Her irregular periods had ended in a pregnancy. She did not know what to make of the news. At first she felt happy, but then she began to get realistic. *Please!* She told herself. She would soon be forty-three. Who would take care of the baby while she was working all day? Also, Santiago did not know anything about it. Santiago! How could she have forgotten him? She had not spoken to him since he had gone to Orlando. She had to call and tell him the news.

Breathing deeply again, I returned to the office and decided to call Santiago at lunchtime. How endless the hours were that day! I called, and there was no answer, so I tried twice more later on, with the same result. That night, I decided to write him an e-mail, thinking that he might feel uncomfortable speaking on the phone with his children around. I didn't even know whether they knew about me. The e-mail told the truth. I calmed him down, explaining that I felt responsible for everything in my life and was only asking for his support: a phone call, a friendly hand. I felt so alone in those moments. Who better than he to encourage me a little? It was the time to make decisions, and I wanted to take into account what Santiago felt. After all, the pregnancy was our shared creation, and likewise, deciding whether to have the baby should be a shared decision, I thought then.

Santiago never appeared again. He never answered the mail, never rang her back, not even to say good-bye. Her heart shattered into a thousand pieces. All she asked him for was a word of support, and he had not even been capable of that. She never understood the contradiction: he was a doctor, and to round it off, the kind who brought babies into the world.

I'd thought that doctors were generous persons, concerned about others. I'd just met up, for the first time, with one who couldn't even respond to a simple human wish for a phone call asking how I was. He probably treated the janitor at the hospital where he worked better than the woman who was bearing what might become his child. What was left of my broken heart was in deep silence now that I'd surrendered all my love to this man, who only seemed like a mirage, the one who'd told me he'd never let me go. I'd waited for a man for thirty years, and now that he had arrived, he'd left me emptier than ever. He not only abandoned me but our potential joint creation. I didn't understand, though I assumed all of the responsibility. We were both creators of that life. How could he have vanished without saying a final word? Anything, like "I'll support you with the abortion" or "I won't support you or be part of your life anymore." Whatever it was, it would have been sufficient for me. With the spiritual world that now existed within me, Santiago already had my complete forgiveness, though I didn't understand his cowardice, his lack of integrity, and much less, his inability to finish our story.

It would not remain unfinished for long. In the depths of her soul, Sybil knew that nothing depended on her ego anymore but on the God she had become. She would not let what she was going through slow down her march to the land of the beyond. She felt so exhausted, she had to close her eyes and breathe deeply several times in order to enter into her divinity and ask for help, the help which immediately arrived:

> "You are only a step away from leaping towards the Promised Land, my dearly beloved child. What you are living through now is simply the last moment of choice. This embryo which you carry within will make you choose whether to live in the third dimension awhile longer, if you allow it to be born and grow. That was the reason why Santiago came into your life: to give you this last opportunity to choose. This has been a great gift of love, even though you now feel it as lack of love. That is why he has gone from your reality. His mission is over. Perhaps you wanted it to end in another way, perhaps

you wanted it to last longer, but believe me, though it does not seem so, this outcome helps you more. Now you must choose between this dimension and the following one corresponding to your next level of expansion, that new dimension you have been preparing yourself for during eons and for which you are now ready. Whatever you choose will be equally beneficial, my child. You must choose like the God you are. There have been no errors or failures in your life, nor will there be any. All continues to be perfect, by law. I say it is so, and I am Michael, your archangel of the great blue ray who never abandons you, either in the light or the darkness. The only thing you must take into account when deciding is the following: if you choose an abortion, you must end your pregnancy before the forty-ninth day of gestation, when the soul which has chosen this new being has still not placed itself in that little body. Rest and sleep now. Tomorrow will be another day, and the light will help you in your decision. I will be watching over you and supporting you, no matter which of the two scenarios you choose, so that you may continue to play the great game of illusions and realities. I am the Archangel Michael."

Santiago had been a shooting star I needed to round off the whole of my past story, to close the circle from girl to woman and from woman to girl. If he had not appeared, I would not have been able to go on to the next stage of my evolution. I, in turn, had likewise appeared in his life to give him the opportunity to choose. I wasn't aware of his choices at that time, but I no longer needed to be. I had to focus on mine; only those were real. It was decided. Once again my God made sure I would act quickly. There was no time to lose in that state of non-time where I now lived myself. I couldn't go beyond the forty-nine-day limit

Archangel Michael had warned me of. Giving birth to a child without being able to offer the abundance of love which that new being deserved was not one of the experiences I wanted in my future. I wanted to transcend, not go back.

She was five weeks pregnant. She would have the abortion in the next couple of days. The clinic she chose was a well-run and legally recognized medical center, not one of those places she imagined in that corner of her mind where there was a minimal remnant of her religious indoctrination, impregnated with guilt and sin. She was aware of the obsolete nature of the beliefs she had been freeing herself from. Perhaps this was the last on the list. She had never had to decide an induced abortion before. She remembered the loss of her first baby, the one she had conceived with her ex-husband Sebastián. She had longed for it, like the two daughters she did give birth to and still loved so much. This was different; this was not a complete baby, only half of one. No, this being definitely did not deserve to be born without having what she now knew was needed to feel oneself loved in life, that foundation of love she herself had not had. The surgery cost her a thousand dollars. Fortunately, money was no longer a problem. She would ask for a day off and go back to work on the following one. Doctor Yancovitz had assured her it would be a simple, ambulatory procedure without major complications, and no one would find out. His instructions were clear: someone had to accompany her, and she could not drive when it was over. All she could think of was to order a taxi to drive her back to the apartment and ask Archangel Michael to accompany her, though only she would see him. When she entered the clinic, the nurse asked if someone was with her.

> "Oh, yes, he's certainly right beside me, but you can't see him. He is the most beautiful angel you can imagine."

She said these words, confident and sure of herself, while the nurse doubtfully smiled. Only she was a witness to that loving presence. Archangel Michael never left her and remained behind her when they got her to lie down on an examining table that made her tremble with cold and sadness. She felt the wings of that beautiful and ethereal holographic being who embraced her again, full of compassion and tenderness. Without his love, she would not have been able to endure it. Now, in solidarity, she felt the loss that millions of women on this planet had felt somewhere along their paths; it was a collective sorrow. She was soon completely sedated by the shots that another nurse had just given her. With her physical body anesthetized, she listened to the unpleasant sound of the aspirator, which now emptied her uterus of what no longer had potential. She was still calm about her decision. She was tired of this dimension and its denseness. Now that she had awakened to a new truth, she no longer wanted to create more of the same chaos. It was time to climb the following rung. She still did not know how that would work, how that ascent from one dimension to another would take place in her reality, but she trusted the words of her angel and all the guides and teachers who, in the previous nine years, had patiently taught her how to heal herself and reach the lightness she would need to continue her journey. That was all she needed to know in this moment when she was liberating herself from the last traces of human sorrow and pain that still remained in one or another corner of her heart. She was nearly there; all that was left would be her fully-exposed divinity. She would finally cease to uphold those false values and principles she had fought so hard to overthrow. God had lovingly invaded her whole human nature, and this was the last step in that appropriation she had so longed for.

I don't remember how I got up from the table or how I got dressed. The same nurse who had given me a skeptical look when I'd told her that Archangel Michael was accompanying me was now pushing my wheelchair to the waiting taxi.

> "Thank you for restoring Archangel Michael to my heart, Sybil. I caught a sight of his wings fluttering behind you in the operating room while everything was going on. Yes, I saw them; they were enormous and very beautiful, and I'm not crazy. I'm a nurse! Thank you so much for helping me to remember how believing is seeing."

She whispered this into my ear as she said good-bye with a long and affectionate hug. Overwhelmed by that special farewell and nearly asleep from the after-effects of so many drugs, I climbed into the taxi. I don't know how I remembered the address of my apartment when the driver asked me. God guided me by remote control. As soon as I got home, I put on my white silk pajamas. I was happy that I'd bought, the day before, the dozen white roses that stood in my favorite vase on the night table. I lay down without wanting to analyze or digest what had happened.

Now it was done. The end of that love story which had begun when she was a girl was now officially over after more than thirty years. It was the conclusion that opened the doors to the start of her experience of the next dimension. Night had not yet fallen and, feeling completely drained, she fell asleep, quietly weeping so that the very silence would not hear her. It was her way of liberating herself from the final traces of an expired past that would never be a possibility again.

THE WHITE OF THE RETURN TO INNOCENCE

There were no big changes in Sybil's life over the following months. She soon recovered from her minor surgery, and everything was normal again, at least on the surface. She threw herself into her job and the projects she was restructuring and expanding. Ed knew about Santiago's disappearance and was happy for her. He constantly tried to encourage her. He had never liked him, and it was only now that he could reveal that he had always suspected such an outcome but had been too discreet to say it aloud. He was a wise old man. He knew that you had to let others learn such lessons on their own.

At the end of December, I magically got into contact with Maya again, my childhood friend who had grown up with me in San Andrés. It was my best Christmas present. We hadn't seen each other since we were teenagers. She stayed with me for a week, here in Houston. She lived in Holland and only came to see me. Her visit was very important for this moment I was living. With its orderly synchronicity, life united me for the final time with all the people I needed to see in order to disconnect myself. First I had traveled to Colombia and Wales to say good-bye to my biological family: my daughters and their father, and my parents. I then lived the unspeakable with Santiago, and finally Maya turned up. We had created so many dreams together when we were girls. Now that we were adults, I needed her at the moment of my final judgment. I would be her jury and she mine. It was a time to celebrate. We had walked a long road, and our feet were witnesses. There wasn't enough time to tell each other all our stories; we stayed awake the whole of several nights trying to, and I didn't mind arriving at the office without having slept a wink. What a marvelous life we had both been able to experience! We had both wanted to defy the world with our particular style. We broke the molds our families tried to fit us into and decided to be the opposite of conventional. Now we laughed at our delicate rebelliousness and reserved daringness. Among all the presents Maya brought me, one was very special. Without intending to, she gave me the missing piece of my relationship with Santiago, the one I needed to close that chapter of my life. Though I had healed my heart and forgiven him, I still wanted to make sure he was all right. I couldn't help wondering whether he had had some kind of accident when he went out of my life without leaving a trace. Maya ended my doubts. Some girlfriends of hers knew him and also his wife. It had all been a farce. Just as I had always sensed beneath my stubborn belief in him, Santiago was a mirage. He had never left his wife. He went back to Florida with her and their children and now worked in a hospital in Orlando. That explained everything. I had graduated with honors from the course in untruthfulness the world taught me and didn't need to learn a bit more.

Maya had already returned to Holland when Sybil suddenly

fell into that strange physical condition. She spent the whole of January consulting a number of specialists who tried to find out what she had: cardiologists, neurologists, the list was endless, in short. Though the city housed some of the country's most advanced and sophisticated medical centers, no one gave her the slightest clue about her condition. All of the exams came out normal, indicating that she was completely healthy. There was nothing that might explain why the whole of her body was progressively losing mobility, while her brain and heart functioned perfectly. Ed, her boss and mentor, was very worried. He could not help her and felt powerless. Money was not a problem for him, and he brought in several doctors from California for a second opinion. His darling Sybil rapidly deteriorated without anyone being able to explain it. The machines that charted her vital functions were not designed to detect the cellular transformation she was going through. From the outside, her physical body seemed to be immobile, while within, it was only beginning to function in a different way. It was complicated for science to prove that the butterfly no longer needed its many caterpillar legs. A brave and strong butterfly that was about to emerge from its chrysalis and be ready to fly: that is what life had turned her into. She gracefully accepted her new condition. The process was not painful. Though she could not explain it, it was just the opposite; she felt happy. She never gave up. Within a short time, she converted her room into a home office. She got a new telephone with several lines and a new computer, which allowed her to work in bed, lying down. She still did not realize that all the symptoms of what seemed like a strange and unknown illness were only part of her natural process of ascension. How could she have known, since she had never ascended before? She was a beginner at it and medical science as well. Ed visited her every day. He wanted her to feel that she was not alone and keep her up to date with everything that was happening at the office. He hired a day nurse to help her, now that she could only move around the apartment in a wheelchair. She could not bathe herself on her own and wanted to continue to go out on the terrace every day to meditate in the morning sunlight. She could no longer make any physical exertion; her hands were all she was able to move. While they were a little slower now, they faithfully served her as she answered her last phone calls and e-mails. My role as her scribe was very important to her. It was what kept her motivated and radiant in her final weeks. When she said all that she had to say, she let me know. In a subliminal way, I felt in my heart the moment when the wings of the butterfly were finally ready to fly.

EPILOGUE

Hidalgo Street, March 2009

That year, it was as though winter had decided to be shorter and the sun to change its warmth. One breathed a new beginning, an early spring. The flowers gaily began to show their buds, even though my heart had not gotten over its loss.

When I arrived that morning, she was not there. I opened the door with the keys she had given me months before. The first thing I did when I came in was to call out her name several times, while I sought her in every corner, wishing that she was only playing hide-and-seek and would magically appear behind one of the pieces of furniture in that very beautiful space she called her home. As soon as I entered the bedroom where she and I had shared so many moments, I began to realize that I was waiting in vain. It was there, in that room, that we had so lovingly created every page of the story to be published, her true story. She had lingered in this plane only long enough for me to know all the details that would allow me to fulfill my promise to write her book once she was no longer with us.

I felt a profound abyss when I saw her immaculately made bed, with its marble-white duvet and decorative pillows. The still-fresh roses perfumed the air, the rays of the sun filtered through the window, although the lamp on the night table was still on. It was if she had left during the night.

I had to sit in the same armchair where I used to sit to hear her stories while I typed and recorded the raw, unedited material. My mind began to summon memories from the recent past, all the roars of laughter, all the tears that had made us so close. I was there now, breathing deeply through my ears as I tried to hear her sweet voice, tried to bring back her presence to my reality again. I couldn't resist my tears. I felt tears of joy blend in a strange dance with my sadness. I was happy for her because she had reached the next consciousness level. That is what she wanted, and it had been her aim in this life. I was sad knowing that I wouldn't be able to embrace her again and would never see her in the flesh anymore. Sybil had taught me so much in such a short time that I felt lost and adrift now. I felt very grateful. Thanks to her, I had understood life in a different and more meaningful way. My perception of the world was no longer the same. How could I carry on without my friend and teacher? I felt empty; nothing made sense. I was full of questions. Why hadn't she said good-bye to me? Why hadn't she thought of me when she vanished like that? Now I did not have a single clue about the kind of thoughts I had to begin to imagine.

I wasn't really ready for her departure, though I knew it was going to happen sooner or later. A week before, she had been speaking to me of that new dimension in which she had already begun to create her new life. Meanwhile, she was simultaneously dematerializing from this one where I now sat in the same place, where I had observed her inner beauty so many times, radiating through the words and remembrances she offered me so freely. She intentionally created her final years in order to make peace with everything and everyone, to make peace with herself by asking forgiveness for what she had and had not been, closing chapters and trying to leave none of them unresolved. She called that other dimension the New Earth, as if this one were out of date and obsolete. I have to admit that I agreed with her, even though it made me feel antiquated and obsolete at times! I went there. I was a witness to her new reality, and she wanted me to speak of it. Everything was so perfect in that place without time or space, a completely uncontaminated and crystalline dimension. There was neither darkness nor night, only light. There, the planet was very like this one, but everything shone. Everything felt lighter, without denseness. The trees seemed to be animated, and the flowers twinkled with the colors of the rainbow. After that night when she took me in a lucid dream to her New Earth, I was never able to think in the old way again. There I learned to breathe love. Could you really breathe love? There I had inhaled and exhaled it. I had even tasted it; it was like savoring the flavor of heaven.

I got up from the armchair and began to walk through the whole of her apartment again. My mind needed to get back to earth, to begin taking care of the details. Sybil had thought of every detail. When I opened the drawer of her night table, I found several folders, carefully labeled, with all the instructions about every subject she wanted me to follow, now that she was no longer here. God, how could I explain what happened to my friend? She hadn't left a single trace behind that could help to track her down. I opened her elegant leather portfolio. There were two small, sealed envelopes inside, one for her daughter Luna and the other for her daughter Sol. The third envelope was open and addressed to Sebastián. I had to read it; maybe she had intentionally left it open. In her beautiful but now shaky handwriting, she had written:

> "My dear husband: without you, I would never have been able to remember the wings which would bring me back home. I will always be grateful to you. With all my love, Syb."

She also left a list with all her bank accounts and credit cards, Internet passwords and user names, and everything that she wanted me to check. It was merely a matter of verifying that all was in order, things she had seen to herself a few days before. She did not owe a penny. I did not have to erase a single fingerprint; she had already wiped out all of them. And now I could not help thinking, once more, how absurd this situation was. It was true that I had witnessed her whole spiritual life through all her accounts, but I couldn't believe that I wouldn't even be able to hold a funeral in her honor. That there was no body to bury or cremate! Exhausted, I sat down in the armchair again. It was morning, and I was already worn out. I closed my eyes and tried to rest. For a few minutes, I returned to the lucid dream she and I had shared, where I was able to visit her new dimension. I returned to that place to watch her for the last time. Sybil had a very beautiful home, not so much because of its luxuries as for its peace and the bright light that nearly burned my retinas.

There, she shared her new world with a gentle man, feminine and full of tenderness. Antoine spoke little, and from his accent, did not seem to be of our Earth. He preferred to look at Sybil, his eyes shining with love, while his smile said more than words. Both lived in the purest unity and were completely happy.

I opened my eyes, knowing I would never see her again. I had been able to return to that lucid dream for a moment; it had been her way of saying good-bye. Now all I had were my memories of her. It was up to me to keep them alive or let them rest in peace within these pages I had written. But what a stupid thing to say! I would still have her magical gaze whenever I remembered her daydreaming, her favorite fragrance when I'd smell the white roses that I would now buy in her honor, her preferred flavor when I'd drink the vanilla soy chai that I used to bring in the mornings before starting to work, her warm touch when she'd take my hand to thank me for believing in her. More than anything, I would have all that Sybil taught me. Thanks to her, I was now able to turn my world into whatever I wished. She had left me the most beautiful gift of love. She had shown me the invisible path along which one comes to be the God she now was.

67085470R00186

Made in the USA
Lexington, KY
01 September 2017